YOUR RIGHTS

to healthcare

**Helping older people
get the best from the NHS**
Lorna Easterbrook

AGE
Concern

First published in 2005 by Age Concern Books

This revised second edition published 2007 by Age Concern Books

1268 London Road, London SW16 4ER, United Kingdom

ISBN: 978 0 86242 422 0

A catalogue record for this book is available from the British Library.

Whilst every effort has been made to ensure that all the information contained in this book is true and accurate at the time of going to press, neither Age Concern nor the author can accept any legal responsibility or liability for any errors or omissions, or changes to any procedure or law that occur after publication. Reference to any agencies, products or services in this book does not constitute a recommendation by Age Concern.

Edited by Gillian Clarke

Cover design by Red Stone

Text design by Keith Hawkins

Typeset by Intertype, London

Printed and bound in Great Britain by Bell & Bain, Glasgow

Contents

About the author viii

Acknowledgements ix

Introduction x
  Where you live in the United Kingdom x
  Keeping up to date xi
  How to use this book... xi

1 'I Know My Rights'..1
  How does the NHS work?...1
  Where are our rights set out? 3
  Other entitlements...12
  Our rights to the NHS 17
  Rights for older people..19
  The NHS's rights...20

2 Asking For and Getting Help..23
  NHS Direct England 24
  NHS Direct Online...25
  NHS Direct Interactive 27
  GP surgeries and out-of-hours services..27
  NHS walk-in centres 27
  Pharmacists 27
  Hospital Accident and Emergency (A&E)...28
  999 calls and emergency services 29
  Minor Injuries Units..30
  Keeping healthy 31

3 GPs and Primary Care Services 33
  GP services..33
  NHS services you can be charged for 41
  Out-of-hours services...42
  Community nursing services..43
  Private doctors 45

4   Dentistry..47
Finding an NHS dentist..47
Emergency NHS dental care...50
Home visits for NHS patients..50
NHS dental treatments..51
Oral health..52
Dental professionals...53
Paying for NHS dental care..53
How much does NHS dentistry cost?............................54
Private dentistry...55
Dentistry in hospital...56
Anaesthetics...57
Public health...57

5   Eye Services...59
Sight problems...59
Sight tests..61
Getting glasses or contact lenses..................................64
Loss of or repairs to glasses or contact lenses..............64
Other support...65
Screening for people with diabetes...............................67
Hospital eye services..68
Other private treatments...68

6   Hearing Services.......................................69
Introduction..69
Losing hearing...70
Diagnosis...70
Audiology tests..71
NHS hearing aids...71
Private hearing tests and aids.......................................72
Tinnitus..73
Hearing dogs..74
British Sign Language..75
Cochlear implants..76

7   Therapies, and Other Support....................77
Types of therapy..77
Occupational therapists (OTs)......................................79
Art, music and drama therapy.......................................82
Speech and language therapists....................................82
Physiotherapy..83

Dietitians 84
Complementary therapies 84
Falls Services 87
Intermediate care 89
Stroke services 90
Complaints 91
Other support 91
Help with NHS charges 93
Joint Equipment Stores 99

8   Mental Health 103
Mental ill-health 103
Depression 104
Dementia 110
Schizophrenia 115
Mental health legislation 118
Consent and decision-making 122
Other issues 130

9   Chiropody and Foot Care 131
Chiropodists and podiatrists 131
Why is foot care important? 133
Finding a chiropodist 134
Chiropody from the NHS 134
Nail cutting 136
Private chiropodists 138

10   Pharmacy 141
NHS prescriptions 141
Taking medication 143
Private prescriptions 145
Who can prescribe? 145
Repeat prescriptions 146
Side effects 148
When you are away from the UK 148
Pharmacists 149

11   Going to Hospital 151
Being admitted to hospital 152
NHS healthcare given overseas 156
Private healthcare 157
Consenting to treatment 157
Other factors in hospital 160

Day surgery 166
Out-patient clinics 167
Moving between hospitals 167
Leaving hospital 168

12 Coming Out of Hospital..169
Planning ahead for discharge 169
Being discharged..173
Refusing to leave hospital 175
Private patients...177

13 NHS Care Where You Live 179
People who live in a care home or sheltered housing 179
People living in nursing homes..181
Continuing NHS healthcare 184
Illnesses and accidents when you are away 189
UK citizens who live abroad..191
Non-UK citizens who live in the UK..194

14 Organ and Blood Donation 197
Blood donors...197
Tissue and organ donation 198
Refusing transplants and blood transfusions...202
Donating your body to medical science...203

15 Death and Dying..205
Diagnosis...205
Palliative care..206
Hospices and other services 207
End-of-life issues 207
Withholding or withdrawing treatment..210
When someone dies 213
Other issues..219

16 Making Complaints 223
Complaining about the NHS 223
Making a complaint 224
Making complaints about individual professionals 235
Claiming compensation from the NHS...240
Complaints about private healthcare services..241
Other investigations 242

17 Information and Communication..245
If English is not your first language...246
Information before making decisions 247

Access to your health records 248
Applying to see the records of someone who has died 251
Agreeing for others to see your records 251
If you cannot consent 253

18 Getting Involved in the NHS **255**
Patient and Public Involvement Forums 255
Expert Patients Programme 257
NHS Patient Surveys 258
Clinical trials 258
Other involvement 259
Campaigning 260

19 Keeping Up to Date with Change **261**

20 Keeping Healthy **263**
Check-ups and preventative measures 263
Physical exercise 264
A good diet 267
Stopping smoking, drinking or drug-taking 268
Looking after your sexual health 269
Emotional health 269

Appendix **271**

About Age Concern **287**

Index **289**

About the author

Lorna Easterbrook began working with and for older people as a theatre stage manager taking productions into older people's care homes, long-stay hospital wards and other community settings. She then spent ten years working in the voluntary sector: for a Care and Repair Home Improvement Agency; Age Concern England; and the King's Fund, where she was Fellow in Community Care.

Since 2000 she has worked as an independent consultant, specialising in health, housing and social care services for older people. Lorna is currently a Visiting Senior Research Fellow at the Centre for Research on Ageing, University of Southampton.

As well as training in stage management at the Royal Welsh College of Music and Drama, Lorna has a degree in Archaeology and Prehistory from the University of Sheffield and also in Creative Writing and Personal Development (University of Sussex) and Social Policy and Planning (London School of Economics).

Acknowledgements

A number of people have been involved in the production of this book, whether with layout, editing, comments or general support. Thanks go to all staff at Age Concern England who good-naturedly kept everyone on track and to time, and particularly to Sheelagh Donovan from the Information Department who provided helpful comments on draft versions of this book.

Acknowledgements can be an odd thing. They can sound overly gushing and contrived ('finally, I must also thank the postman, for delivering the manuscript'), consist of slightly bizarre entries ('thanks also to Binky and Tiny, for tea, biscuits and tail wagging') or just list the many people to whom the author has probably forgotten to send a birthday card in the past year. That aside, this book was helped hugely by the editorial skills, kindness and patience of Gillian Clarke.

Introduction

This book provides information about the main entitlements to healthcare for older people, in particular NHS services in England. All of the information applies to people aged 60 and over but much of the detail also applies to younger adults.

Your Rights to Healthcare covers all types of healthcare and health needs, from chiropody and toenail cutting to dentistry, major operations, mental health services and long-term care. Although many of the subjects covered are complicated, this book aims to explain them in as clear and straightforward a way as possible. It cannot cover all situations and circumstances, so each chapter indicates how to find out more information, including details of local and national sources of help.

Much of the treatment you receive as an individual depends on the precise nature of your illness or disability. So this book cannot diagnose what might be wrong with you or tell you whether you are receiving the right type of medication; but it can tell you about getting a diagnosis and what to do if you are worried about your medicines. It also explains your rights if you find that you need healthcare.

WHERE YOU LIVE IN THE UNITED KINGDOM

All the information applies to people living in England (although some will also be relevant throughout the UK). For further information specifically about healthcare in Scotland, Wales or Northern Ireland, contact Age Concern Scotland, Age Concern Cymru or Age Concern Northern Ireland. Their addresses are on page 287. You can also go to the National Health Service website (www.nhs.uk), and choose the name of the country in the UK where you live, to find out more about NHS services there.

Your Rights to Healthcare also includes some information for people who used to live in England but now live abroad, outlining their entitlement to healthcare from the NHS on their visits back to England.

KEEPING UP TO DATE

This book is based on information available in April 2007. Arrangements for healthcare services, however, can and do change. For example, in the 1980s older people lost their right to free eyesight tests from the NHS, only for this right to be reinstated in 1999. Some rights have existed for only a few years whereas others have been in place for over 50 years. Chapter 1 explains some of the ways these changes happen, and a number of possible future changes are mentioned throughout the book.

Chapter 19 gives you some ideas on keeping up to date with change. If you need information on the latest position on these issues, or you have questions about particular points, please write to Age Concern at the address given on page 287. You might also like to contact NHS Direct (details on page 282).

HOW TO USE THIS BOOK

One of the aims of this book is to provide a jargon-free explanation of your rights to healthcare. But we have deliberately included some terms and phrases because you are likely to come across them at some point as they are commonly used in the NHS. Below are some examples.

- **Carers** In this book 'carer' means someone who provides support to another person (whether through practical help or personal care or with emotional support) but isn't paid to do so. This might be a member of your family, a friend or a neighbour ... or you. Sometimes, carers are also called 'family carers', 'informal carers' or even 'unpaid carers'.

■ **Integrated services** These are provided together (jointly) by social services departments and the NHS. Examples include Falls Services (to help reduce the numbers of falls by older people) and Joint Equipment Stores. Social services and the NHS are being expected to work together more and more.

■ **Local council or local authority** This is the system of local government where you live – the London or Metropolitan Borough, County Council or Unitary Authority. Social services and housing departments are part of the local authority/local council.

■ **Multi-disciplinary** This term describes a group of different professionals who may work together to support your health needs – for example, the doctor, physiotherapist, social worker and nurse.

■ **Private organisations** There are many different private health clinics and hospitals, some of which may have a contract with the NHS to provide care for NHS patients. Some health professionals have private patients as well as working in the NHS.

■ **Social services** This is part of your local council. In some areas, social services departments are being renamed – examples include 'Social Care Services' and 'Social and Community Services'.

■ **Voluntary organisations** These include charities and not-for-profit organisations such as housing associations. Voluntary organisations can consist of paid staff as well as volunteers.

Different types of healthcare and healthcare services are described in separate chapters. You can dip in and out of this book or read it as a whole. If you want to know where and how your rights to the NHS are set out, you could start with Chapter 1. But if you want to know only about getting NHS eyesight services (for example), you could just read about this in Chapter 5. The index should also help you to find the relevant information.

Contact details of all the organisations mentioned in this book are given in the Appendix.

'I Know My Rights'

Most of us know that we have rights and entitlements, but we may not always know what they are in practice. This chapter explores the rights we have to NHS services in England. To begin with, though, it may be helpful to set out briefly how the NHS works.

HOW DOES THE NHS WORK?

The NHS is quite complicated. It consists of lots of different organisations, all with their own role and responsibilities. In broad terms the NHS consists of:

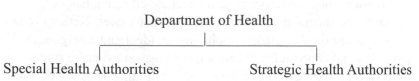

Department of Health

Special Health Authorities   Strategic Health Authorities

Department of Health (DH)

Civil servants at the Department of Health work with the Secretary of State for Health and others to draw up and issue laws, regulations, guidance and targets.

Special Health Authorities (SHAs)

These bodies provide NHS services across the country. Some cover the whole of the UK, such as UK Transplant; others, such as the Health Protection Agency, cover England and Wales. Other examples of Special Health Authorities include NHS Direct, the National Institute for Health and Clinical Excellence (NICE) and the National Blood Service.

Strategic Health Authorities (StHAs)

There are ten Strategic Health Authorities in England. They develop plans for improving health services in their areas and monitor the performance of local health services. They support Primary Care Trusts and NHS Trusts in putting national policies into practice, and are a key link between the Department of Health and local NHS bodies.

Primary Care Trusts (PCTs) England is subdivided into 152 local areas, with a Primary Care Trust responsible for managing NHS services in each area. Primary Care Trusts provide community services such as district nursing, and they contract (or commission) other services that they must ensure are available from the NHS in their area. Over all, PCTs hold 80% of the NHS's total budget.

The services they are responsible for include GPs, dentists, optometrists, mental health services, hospital services, NHS walk-in centres, transport for patients (including accident and emergency), screening and pharmacies. Primary Care Trusts must make sure there are enough health services in their area – including planning for the future. They also have to ensure that the local health and social care systems are working together to improve things for patients. Since April 2005, GP practices have been able to choose to commission (purchase) some NHS services for their patients (see Chapter 3).

NHS Trusts manage a range of NHS services; each organisation is managed by a separate NHS Trust. Some NHS Trusts are regional or national centres for more specialised care. Others work with particular universities to help train health professionals. The most commonly known Trusts are those running 'acute' services (the medical treatment of people with short-term illnesses or injuries or people recovering from surgery) in local NHS hospitals. Trusts can also provide services in the community; for example, through health centres or clinics.

Other important organisations are:

- *Foundation Trusts* These are a more recent type of NHS hospital/ organisation, run by local managers, staff and members of the public. At the time of writing, there are 52 Foundation Trusts in England.

- *Mental Health Trusts* These provide specialist NHS mental health services, such as hospital places and community support for people with severe mental health problems. They may also offer some therapy and specialist medical help.

- *Ambulance Trusts* There are 12 of these in England, providing emergency access to healthcare. They may also provide non-emergency transport if they have a contract with the local Primary Care Trust to do so.

- *Care Trusts* These provide both health and social care. There are only a few of them at present, and they tend to provide specific services such as mental health or care for older people.

WHERE ARE OUR RIGHTS SET OUT?

People who believe they have a particular right to something often think that this must be set out in law. Yet there is no 'Magna Carta' for the NHS. In other words, there's no single document or Act of Parliament that sets out every individual's entitlement to all NHS services. Instead, our rights to healthcare come from many different sources, many of which have changed over time (and keep changing). These include:

- Acts of Parliament (also called statutes).

3

- Case law – when individuals have challenged the NHS by taking a legal case to the High Court and established a new understanding of what the NHS must do.

- Directions, Regulations and Guidance. These are issued by governments to describe the detail of how particular sections (or clauses) in Acts of Parliament should be put into practice.

- Best practice – there are three general types of best practice. The first is what is generally accepted at the time by healthcare professionals and health organisations as the best way of providing treatment or care. The second type is how government uses examples to support a particular approach, such as services that help reduce the numbers of older people who fall. The third is 'evidence-based' best practice – for example, the National Institute for Health and Clinical Excellence (NICE) looks at all the available clinical evidence on particular drugs, operations or other treatments, before telling the NHS what it should (and should not) be offering to patients.

- Standards of services – which can cover the buildings where services are provided as well as the behaviour of staff and the treatment received.

- Government policy decisions. This is when the government of the day decides it will introduce a change to the NHS that doesn't require a new law to be passed.

Acts of Parliament

Although some people may believe that our rights to the NHS are all described in great detail in Acts of Parliament, this is not the case. But Acts of Parliament do play a crucial role. The NHS itself would not exist, for example, without the original National Health Service Act of 1946 (much of which has since been replaced by later Acts).

Acts of Parliament relating to health tend to set out the key or major ways in which health services and organisations are to be provided, funded and run in this country. They are sometimes called 'primary legislation'. Regulations are then issued by Parliament to explain more of the detail of the law – these are sometimes called 'secondary legislation' (see page 9); the Secretary of State for Health also issues Directions and Guidance, which often go into further detail about applying the law in practice.

The most important right that we all share, and which *is* set out in Acts of Parliament, is that the Secretary of State for Health (whoever she or he is at the time) has a duty to make sure that the NHS provides what is judged to be needed for the whole population, within available resources. The most recent Act setting this out is the National Health Services Act 2006.

However, providing sufficient services across the population isn't the same as every single person having the right *no matter what* to receive a particular treatment. We don't all have this right, partly because we are unlikely all to need the same treatment. Another reason is that the NHS doesn't provide every possible treatment – some cosmetic surgery, for example, is not available on the NHS.

An example of something the NHS *does* provide is treatment for cancer. Because we will not all develop cancer (although many will and do), it would make no sense for all of us to have an individual right to receive treatment for cancer, because this would mean that people without cancer would be just as entitled to demand – and get – treatment they didn't need.

Nevertheless, the Secretary of State has a duty to make sure that *enough* cancer treatment is provided for everyone in the population who *does* get this disease *at the time it develops in their life.* This means that, if at any stage in my life I develop cancer, I have a right to expect that the NHS will provide the treatment that NHS doctors say I need, in line with NHS guidance. I have this right because the NHS must provide the services that the Secretary of State for Health says are needed across the population, of whom I am one person, and which include cancer care. So my right to NHS care comes when I actually need the sort of treatment that the NHS has been told should be available to help me.

The Secretary of State doesn't reach a judgement about the services that are needed on his or her own. It is only that he or she has the legal duty to make sure the NHS provides enough treatment within available resources. This is important in terms of the amount of funding received by the NHS as well as how the funding is spent.

Box 1. 'Enough treatment'

You may be surprised at the idea of 'enough treatment', especially if you (or someone you know) feel you have not received 'enough' treatment from the NHS, needed because of a particular illness, disease or disability. But this is where your 'rights' to healthcare are also closely linked with the clinical judgement of the health professionals treating you and with the priorities for treatments set for the NHS. They play a very important role in deciding what sorts of treatment or support you should receive, for how long, and why.

Which means that this book cannot tell everyone who has a stroke (for example) exactly what medication they will be given, or exactly how long they might stay in hospital, or whether the NHS will definitely fund their longer-term care. These are matters of clinical judgement that will vary according to each person's circumstances. But it does explain the overall rights to healthcare shared by everyone who has a stroke, no matter what their individual circumstances.

Sometimes, a Primary Care Trust says it will not fund a particular treatment – even when doctors say this is needed and NICE has recommended it. But these funding decisions can be challenged – see Chapter 16.

Most Acts tend to set out how the NHS and other providers of health services should be structured, regulated and inspected, and how healthcare professionals should be registered and patients protected.

In recent years there has been a lot of new legislation that affects how healthcare is funded, regulated and provided. If you are interested in finding out more about relevant Acts of Parliament, you can:

- see if there are copies you can read in the Reference section of your local library;

- search on the Internet – for example, on the website for the House of Commons (www.parliament.uk/commons), or The Stationery Office, which publishes Acts of Parliament and other official documents (www.tso.gov.uk);

- ask your MP for information about recent Acts;

- find books that look at these aspects in more detail, such as the annual *Welfare Rights Handbook* published by the Child Poverty Action Group (CPAG; contact details on page 274). Your local library may have a copy of this book.

A number of charities also provide information about the NHS, including explaining what the law says should happen. Some charities, such as Age Concern England and Help the Aged, have details for any older person. Others, such as the Alzheimer's Society, the Parkinson's Disease Society and Arthritis Care, have information aimed at people with those particular health conditions and their families and friends. Details of these charities and other useful organisations are given in the Appendix.

Case law

Case law describes the ruling when an individual takes a case to the High Court (or to a higher court, such as the Court of Appeal). This involves the person testing some aspect of the law, to see how it applies in his or her circumstances. Often, they bring a case to court because they feel they have grounds to challenge a decision that the NHS has made about their care.

There are lots of challenges and case law that are quite well known. They include:

- *The case involving Tony Bland* Mr Bland was left in a 'persistent vegetative state' (PVS) after being involved in the disaster at Hillsborough football ground, Sheffield, in 1989. His parents sought the court's help to decide whether or not doctors could

7

lawfully withdraw the artificially provided food and fluid he was receiving.

- **The case of Diane Blood** Mrs Blood's husband died very unexpectedly and quickly. At her request, and in line with what he had previously told her he would want to happen in these circumstances, his sperm was taken and frozen by health professionals after his death. But because her husband's views were not written down, Mrs Blood had to go to court to get permission to try to conceive the children she and her husband had planned.

- **The case of Diane Pretty** Mrs Pretty had motor neurone disease (MND), a gradual disease for which there is no cure at present. The effect of the disease meant that as she reached the end of her life it was very unlikely she would be able to commit suicide unaided. She wanted to know that, if it was her clear wish that her husband assist her, he would not be prosecuted afterwards if he had helped.

- **The case of 'Miss B'** Miss B was a social worker who was profoundly injured in an accident. She went to court to prove she was mentally capable of deciding not to continue with artificial support, in the full knowledge that this would hasten her death.

- **The case of 'Child B'** Child B's father went to the courts on behalf of his daughter, who was terminally ill with cancer. He challenged the decision of the NHS doctors and hospital that were responsible for her care not to try any further treatment once a certain stage had been reached. The doctors felt it was not in her interests to continue with treatment that could not prolong her life but that, in their view, might cause her further distress.

- **The case of Pamela Coughlan** Ms Coughlan's injuries from a road traffic accident were so severe that she lived in a specialist NHS unit; when she had moved there she had been told that it would be her home for life. When the relevant NHS health authority decided to change the sort of service offered by this unit, it said she could not remain in the unit but would have to move to a nursing home and pay towards the cost of this care. She challenged the health authority's decision that it was no longer responsible for funding or providing her care.

If someone (or an organisation) is ruled against, the judge's decision can be challenged; ultimately, the Law Lords (some of the most senior members of the judiciary, who sit in the House of Lords) hear the highest court challenges.

There are many examples of case law apart from those listed above. Doctors, patients, lawyers and others use case law to work out what is lawful according to the current understanding of the law. Many case law rulings, though, are quite specific to the detail of the particular individual who brought the case. This can mean that, later on, another person will bring a case that is similar (but not identical) to a case that has already been heard, because some further clarification is needed.

Case law is often reported in broadsheet newspapers, such as The Times. Major cases often feature in the news on TV and radio.

Directions, Regulations and Guidance

Regulations (also called Statutory Instruments) are issued by Parliament. They explain more of the detail of particular Acts of Parliament. *Directions* and *Guidance* are issued by the Secretary of State for Health and go into more detail about putting these Acts into practice. Unlike Acts of Parliament, Directions, Regulations and Guidance can be changed fairly easily and quickly – provided that whatever is issued stays within the current legal understanding of what the Act says. Recent examples of Directions, Guidance and Regulations include:

- The NHS's contribution to the costs of registered nursing care in care homes (see Chapter 13).

- NHS responsibilities to provide continuing healthcare for older people and others (see Chapter 13).

■ Access to NHS healthcare for overseas visitors to the UK (see Chapter 13).

Another example is the arrangements for the services provided by general practitioners (see Chapter 3 for more details about GPs).

Best practice and standards of service

Lots of different organisations look at various aspects of best practice and standards of service. They may also regulate services according to nationally set standards. They include:

■ *The National Institute for Health and Clinical Excellence (NICE)* NICE makes recommendations to the NHS across England and Wales about the treatments (including medicines and technology) and care it should provide. It does this by considering the best available evidence. You have the right to expect the NHS to provide the 'treatments' that NICE recommends.

■ *The Healthcare Commission* This inspects NHS services in England such as Primary Care Trusts, hospitals and clinics, and publishes annual 'health checks' for each, outlining quality of care and use of resources. It also regulates and inspects private and voluntary healthcare services in England, under the Care Standards Act 2000. And it plays an important role in the NHS complaints system (see Chapter 16). It aims to help improve the quality of these services. You have the right to expect that services inspected or regulated by the Healthcare Commission meet certain minimum standards.

■ *The National Patient Safety Agency (NPSA)* The NPSA is responsible for how errors and incidents within the NHS are reported. It aims to improve the safety of NHS patients, including issues such as clinical errors, and food and cleanliness in hospital. One example of the NPSA's work is the issuing of guidance to NHS staff on keeping their hands clean. You have the right to bring any errors and other incidents to the attention of the NPSA.

■ *The Health Protection Agency (HPA)* The HPA works to protect the health of the UK's population – for example, infectious diseases – and preventing harm when hazards involving chemicals, poison or radiation are involved. They are also responsible for helping to prepare to deal with potential health threats to the UK, such as avian flu ('bird' flu).

In the summer of 2004 the Government published *Standards for Better Health;* this was updated in 2006. It sets out all the targets that the NHS must either meet now or work towards for the future (see also page 18).

It also describes a series of core standards that all NHS services in England must meet. This includes services that the NHS buys on behalf of patients from private health clinics or voluntary organisations. The Healthcare Commission reviews all the NHS's services against these core standards. It will also look at each organisation's progress towards a series of developmental standards.

There is more about these standards on pages 18 and 19.

Government policy decisions

What the NHS provides is affected by the policies of the government of the day. One example of a government policy decision is NHS eyesight tests. People over the age of 60 used not to have to pay for eyesight tests from the NHS. At the end of the 1980s, however, the government of the day decided to withdraw free eyesight tests for older people. It did this by making an announcement and withdrawing the scheme. No new Act of Parliament was required because there was no Act that said that everyone over the age of 60 was entitled to a free eyesight test.

In 1999, a different government decided it would re-introduce this entitlement. It also announced the change, put in place the necessary arrangements to reimburse optometrists who carried out the tests and made sure that any government leaflets about having eyesight tests included this information. Again, this change didn't need a new Act of Parliament or even a new Regulation.

Many rights such as the entitlement to free eyesight tests are not necessarily permanent, or set in stone. Our rights may change depending on the government of the day and current views about how different healthcare matters should be pursued.

Targets

Another very good example of government policy creating 'rights' is by its setting targets for how quickly you should be able to see your GP or how soon after being referred you should have an operation or other hospital treatment. There is more about the targets for different types of NHS care in the relevant chapters in this book.

Targets are not universally popular, and in 2004 the number of targets the NHS has to meet were reduced. But while they exist, they give all of us, as NHS patients, a clearer idea of what we have the right to expect. See also page 18.

OTHER ENTITLEMENTS

Other rights (or entitlements) are universal – we all have them. They are partly set out in the law, partly established by case law, and form part of government policy. They include:

- the right to receive primary care from a GP (see Chapter 3);
- the right to NHS dentistry (see Chapter 4);
- the right to complain about services (see Chapter 16).

We also can expect certain things, such as:

- to have our human rights respected, as set out in the Human Rights Act 1998 (under the European Convention on Human Rights);
- not to be unfairly discriminated against because of our age;
- to receive the NHS treatment we need, regardless of how much (or how little) money we have.

Some of these rights are fundamental to the whole NHS. They are the principles or the starting point for the running of all NHS services.

Many have been in place since the NHS began, in 1948. More recently, they have been repeated in documents such as *The NHS Plan* and the various National Service Frameworks (NSFs).

The NHS Plan and National Service Frameworks

In 2000 the Government published *The NHS Plan*. This set out ten core principles of the NHS (Box 2).

Box 2. The ten principles of the NHS

The NHS will:

Provide a universal service for all, based on clinical need, not ability to pay.

Provide a comprehensive range of services.

Shape its services around the needs and preferences of individual patients, their families and carers.

Respond to the different needs of different populations.

Work continuously to improve quality services and to minimise errors.

Support and value its staff.

Devote public funds for healthcare solely to NHS patients.

Work together with others to ensure a seamless service for patients.

Keep people healthy and work to reduce health inequalities.

Respect the confidentiality of individual patients and provide open access to information about services, treatment and performance.

National Service Frameworks (NSFs) set national standards for particular services (for example, cancer care or renal services) or a particular part of the population (such as older people), as part of an overall drive to improve services. Each National Service Framework sets out the dates by which any changes should be in place. National

Service Frameworks are being published one at a time over a period of some years, beginning in 2001.

For anyone aged 65 or over, the most important one is the National Service Framework for Older People. This sets out eight standards to be met by the NHS (Box 3), together with local authority (local council) social services departments where this is appropriate.

Although there is a specific National Service Framework for Older People, most of the other National Service Frameworks also apply to older people. The exception is the National Service Framework for Mental Health, which is written for adults up to the age of 65 – although, even here, there are some overlaps for the small number of older people whose severe mental health problems began when they were under the age of 65 or who are already 65 but develop a severe psychotic illness. (See also Chapter 8.)

Box 3. The eight standards of the National Service Framework for Older People

Rooting out age discrimination You should not be discriminated against (treated unfairly) by the NHS or social services because of your age. NHS services should be provided on the basis of your clinical need – regardless of how old you are. Social services must not use age in their eligibility criteria to restrict people's access to services.

Person-centred care You should be treated as an individual, and be able to make choices about your care. The NHS and social services should make this possible by using the Single Assessment Process (SAP) to assess older people's needs for care and support. The NHS and social services should together run community equipment services and continence services (sometimes this type of service is called a 'joint' or 'integrated' service).

Intermediate care The NHS and social services should provide increasing amounts of intermediate care services to help older people stay at home for as long as possible and to reduce the number of unnecessary hospital admissions (see Chapter 7).

General hospital care All NHS hospitals that provide care for older patients must have a specialist old-age multi-disciplinary team, and have an agreement about how older patients' health needs will be looked after across different hospital wards, clinics and departments. It will be clear to patients who in the hospital has the overall responsibility for the nursing care of its older patients (eg a matron or other senior nursing staff).

Stroke All NHS general hospitals that provide care for people who have had a stroke (including younger adults), must have a specialised stroke service. All GPs work to a local agreement for identifying and referring their patients who are at risk of stroke.

Falls All local health providers (including independent organisations) must have procedures in place to help reduce the risk of older people falling. There should be an integrated falls service (see page 87) in each area from April 2005 at the latest.

Mental health The NHS and social services should use the same set of rules to manage older people's mental health. GPs should use a locally agreed procedure to diagnose, refer and treat any patient who has depression or dementia.

The promotion of health and active age in older life Local plans drawn up by the NHS, social services and others should include programmes that promote good mental health, and make sure that people know about flu vaccinations and other measures.

A second phase for the NSF for Older People began in 2006. This set out three key priorities:

- dignity in care
- joined-up care
- healthy ageing.

There are also National Service Frameworks for:

- coronary heart disease (CHD)
- diabetes

- renal services
- cancer.

A further National Service Framework for people with neurological and other long-term conditions was published in 2005. This looks at NHS care for people with epilepsy, multiple sclerosis (MS), Parkinson's disease, motor neurone disease (MND), and brain and spinal injuries. It also looks at issues that apply to people with other long-term conditions and disabilities, such as information about services, rehabilitation, and care and support at home.

Under the NSF for Coronary Heart Disease, some of the things you can expect include:

- help to stop smoking;
- advice and treatment if you are identified by your GP as being at significant risk of cardiovascular disease;
- professional assessment if you are thought to be having a heart attack and aspirin given, if indicated, within 60 minutes of asking for professional help from the NHS;
- appropriate advice and treatment if you are admitted to hospital with a heart attack;
- symptoms of angina or suspected angina to be investigated and treatment given to relieve pain and reduce the risk of this becoming more serious;
- referral to a cardiologist as a matter of urgency if your angina becomes more frequent or more severe;
- suspected heart failure to be confirmed (or ruled out) and the reasons identified;
- to be invited to take part in a programme designed to reduce your risk of later problems from coronary heart disease.

Under the NSF for Cancer (often called The Cancer Plan), you can expect:

- to be *invited* for breast cancer screening every five years, if you are a woman aged between 50 and 70 (women over the age of 70 have the right to *ask* for – and receive – breast screening but will not receive an invitation to do so);

- to wait no more than one month from diagnosis to treatment for all cancers;

- to wait no more than two months from your GP making an urgent referral to your being treated by a cancer specialist.

The NSF for Diabetes is in two parts. The first part covers aspects such as:

- receiving good-quality care throughout your lifetime, including support to control your blood glucose and blood pressure;

- being encouraged to take part in decisions about your treatment and care, and supported to lead a healthy life;

- to have your diabetes managed effectively during a stay in hospital for whatever reason.

The second part of the diabetes NSF looks at issues such as primary care and end-of-life care.

Our rights to the NHS

We all share the same basic rights. These include:

- respect for confidentiality (see Chapter 17);
- respect for our privacy, dignity, and religious and cultural beliefs;
- clean and safe hospitals and clinics;
- free care from our GP, nursing and therapeutic staff (see Chapters 3 and 7);
- free hospital consultant care (see Chapter 11);
- to receive a reasonable standard of care;
- to receive the treatment, medication and equipment necessary for our clinical needs.

Standards for Better Health sets out the standards of care that all NHS services should provide. These standards also give us rights as to what we can expect from the NHS. There are seven categories, called 'domains'. Under each domain there are several core standards, which the NHS must be meeting already, and some developmental standards, which the NHS must work towards achieving over the next three to four years (Box 4).

Box 4. Examples of core standards in the seven domains

Safety Healthcare organisations keep patients, staff and visitors safe by having systems to ensure that the risk of healthcare-acquired infection to patients is reduced, with particular emphasis on high standards of hygiene and cleanliness, achieving year-on-year reductions in MRSA and *Clostridium difficile.*

Clinical and cost effectiveness Healthcare organisations co-operate with each other and with social care organisations to ensure that patients' individual needs are properly managed and met.

Governance Healthcare organisations undertake all appropriate employment checks and ensure that all employed or contracted professionally qualified staff are registered with the appropriate bodies; and require that all employed professionals abide by relevant published codes of professional practice.

Patient focus Healthcare organisations have systems in place to ensure that staff treat patients and their relatives and carers with dignity and respect; that appropriate consent is obtained when required for all contacts with patients and for the use of any confidential patient information; and that staff treat patient information confidentially, except where authorised by legislation to the contrary.

Accessible and responsive care Healthcare organisations enable all members of the population to access services equally, and offer choice in access to services and treatment equitably.

Care environment and amenities Healthcare services are provided in safe and secure environments that promote effective care and optimise health outcomes and that protect patients,

---

staff, visitors and their property and the physical assets of the organisation; and are supportive of patient privacy and confidentiality.

Public healthcare organisations have systematic and managed disease-prevention and health-promotion programmes that meet the requirements of the National Service Frameworks and national plans with particular regard to reducing obesity through action on nutrition and exercise, smoking, substance misuse and sexually transmitted infections.

Standards for Better Health also reminds the NHS of the targets (or commitments) it must be meeting now or be working towards. Details of these targets (or commitments) are included throughout this book in the relevant chapters.

RIGHTS FOR OLDER PEOPLE

All adults have the same basic entitlements to NHS services, but there are some additional rights for older people:

- Free flu vaccination – each year (usually in the late autumn and early winter). This is available to everyone aged 65 or over. You should receive a letter from your GP's surgery inviting you to come in. But if you don't get a letter, there is nothing to stop you from asking for an appointment. And you can refuse the vaccination – it must be available for you but you don't have to accept.

- Free pneumonia vaccination if you are aged 65 or over. This aims to protect you against pneumonia, septicaemia and bacterial meningitis. (Most people will need to take this vaccine only once in their lives.)

- You can ask for a free annual health check if you are aged 75 or over, if you have not seen your GP/health professional in the past 12 months. This takes place at your GP's surgery, but might be carried out by a nurse rather than your GP. If you find it hard to visit the practice because of medical reasons, ask for this check to be carried out at home.

19

- Free NHS prescriptions if you are aged 60 or over.

- Free medication check if you are 75 or over. This should be carried out every year – and is part of the National Service Framework for Older People. If you are taking four or more different medicines, your check should happen every six months. Your local pharmacist (the chemist) will carry this out. You may be given a leaflet before the check to help you think about the sorts of questions you might be asked.

- Free NHS eyesight tests if you are aged 60 or over.

Most NHS services are free. But there are charges for some, such as NHS dentistry, any glasses (spectacles) or contact lenses you may need, wigs and some other types of support such as elastic stockings or corsets. But there is also help with these health costs for people on low incomes – including older people. There is more about this scheme, and about any costs for NHS services, in Chapter 7.

Developments in healthcare mean that new rights are added from time to time. In August 2006, the Government introduced a new screening programme in England for bowel cancer. It started in the Midlands, and will be spread across the country over the next three years – so, depending where you live, you may not find this is available to you straight away. To start with, the programme will invite men and women aged between 60 and 69 for screening once every two years. Once this is available in your part of the country, you will be able to ask for bowel cancer screening if you are aged 70 or older. Your GP surgery should know if this is yet available in your area.

THE NHS'S RIGHTS

It may come as a bit of a surprise to learn that the NHS also has rights. More specifically, there are certain things that are expected of you by the people who work for NHS organisations.

For example, NHS staff have the right to expect not to be attacked – either physically or verbally. If you assault a member of staff, the NHS is within its rights to:

- Ask you to leave the premises – and escort you out of the door if needed.
- Call the police and press charges against you.

You will often find details about the type of patient behaviour that is unacceptable, on posters put up around NHS hospitals, GP surgeries or other clinics. You should always treat staff respectfully. This means not behaving in a way that is racist or sexist or causes other offence.

If you do offend a member of staff but did not mean to, the best thing to do is apologise and explain that no offence was meant. If you do not understand why a member of staff has taken offence, ask them or one of their colleagues to explain this to you. But even if you have offended a member of NHS staff, they should never retaliate against you in any way. If you feel they have retaliated, or are treating you unfairly or unkindly, you should raise this concern straight away with the person responsible for managing that member of staff.

Recently there has been some discussion about whether patients who fail to turn up for appointments (or who don't let staff know they can't keep the appointment) should be fined a sum of money. So far, this suggestion hasn't been accepted or introduced. Indeed, recent changes to NHS dentistry mean that dentists offering NHS care cannot now charge you if you miss your appointment. Nevertheless, if you cannot get to an appointment, make sure you ring or write to let the relevant staff know as soon as you can – and make sure your call or letter reaches them before the appointment is due. This way, they have a chance to offer the appointment to another patient. If an emergency means that you are unable to attend at the last minute, get in touch as soon as you can afterwards to explain this.

Finally, if you make a false claim for help with health costs, such as claiming you are entitled to free NHS prescriptions or eye tests when you should pay, under the Health Act 1999 you can be fined up to £100 plus the cost of the original treatment.

2

Asking For and Getting Help

There are lots of different ways you can ask for help because of a health worry – whether you think this is something that can wait or you need advice and help as a matter or urgency. They include:

- NHS Direct (NHS Helpline in Scotland);
- NHS Direct Online (the website of NHS Direct);
- NHS Direct Interactive (the digital television version of NHS Direct);
- GP surgeries and out-of-hours services;
- NHS walk-in centres;
- pharmacists;
- hospital accident and emergency (A&E) units – sometimes also called emergency departments (ED);
- 999 calls and emergency services;
- minor injuries units.

There are some private medical walk-in facilities, such as the Medi-centres at some of London's larger mainline train stations. Chapter 3 looks in more detail at primary care services such as GP surgeries, district nursing and out-of-hours services. Chapter 10 looks in detail at pharmacists.

NHS DIRECT ENGLAND

NHS Direct England provides the same service to everyone living in England.

It offers 'nurse-led' advice and information about health matters over the telephone. It works by your telephoning NHS Direct – in England the number is 0845 4647. This is not a free call; you will be charged as if you are making a local telephone call (the cost of your making the call will be added to your telephone or mobile bill as usual). You can ring to find out about:

- what to do if you or someone in your family is feeling ill;
- particular health conditions;
- local healthcare services, such as the nearest doctor, dentist or out-of-hours pharmacy;
- self-help and support organisations.

The NHS employs everyone who works for NHS Direct. You can ring at any time, 24 hours a day, all year round. Your telephone call will be recorded but all the information you give is confidential (see also Chapter 17). If you are asking for details of your nearest dentist or pharmacy, the person answering the call will give you this information; but if you are ringing with a health concern, you will either be put through to a nurse or you will be told that a nurse will ring you back. The nurse you speak to at NHS Direct will ask you about the health matter you are calling about – for example, she or he may ask you to describe any symptoms. They will then advise you on the best course of action – for example, if you are feeling ill with flu-like symptoms they may suggest how to look after yourself at home if this is appropriate (for example, stay in bed, drink lots of fluids), or advise you to visit your GP or hospital accident and emergency (A&E) department if things are more serious. If necessary, they can connect you so you can speak direct to the ambulance service.

If English is not your first language, when you ring NHS Direct you should make sure to give the English name of the language you need to speak in (for example, by saying 'French', or 'Urdu', or 'Welsh', or the name of whichever language it is that you want to speak in). If you stay on the line you should be connected to an interpreter who speaks your language; or you can ask someone who does speak English to ring for you, explain that a translator is needed, and then let you speak to the translator when he or she comes on the line.

Box 5. Textphone enquiries

There is also a textphone number you can use to contact NHS Direct. This is aimed at people who are deaf or hard of hearing or who have speech difficulties. The number to call, 0845 606 4647, is also charged at local rates and is available all the time.

NHS Direct says that textphone calls will be answered as soon as possible, but asks people who contact them on the textphone number to wait if they don't get a reply straight away.

There is more about NHS help for people with hearing difficulties in Chapter 6.

Everyone who contacts NHS Direct for advice about their health will be asked to give.their name, address, phone number and the name of their GP (doctor). NHS Direct says this is needed to provide safe treatment and care. As with all health records held in the NHS, these are confidential – they may be shared with other NHS professionals but only if this is needed because of the treatment involved, and only with your permission. Chapter 17 explains about getting access to any health records that the NHS holds about you (and explains what to do if you are acting on behalf of someone else).

Contacting NHS Direct can be helpful if you are uncertain what to do – for example, if you are not sure whether you should go to your GP or call an ambulance.

NHS DIRECT ONLINE

This is a website of information, as part of NHS Direct, available through a computer with Internet access. If you don't have such a computer, many public libraries provide computer terminals with Internet access. Some of these are available free; at others there may be a small charge to pay. There are also lots of local 'Internet cafés' around the country that you could use, although you will probably be asked to pay a fee (for example, it might cost £5 for you to go on the Internet for 30 minutes).

Many local libraries, and some local Age Concerns, offer free training sessions on how to use the Internet. This usually involves your accessing (looking at) a website as part of the training. You might want to try looking at NHS Direct Online (see page 282) in your training session.

The website includes a health encyclopaedia that covers more than 400 topics, including different illnesses and conditions, tests, treatments (and a separate 'best treatments' section) and operations. NHS Direct Online also provides a database of hospitals and community health services, GPs, dentists, optometrists and pharmacies, and you can use it to find the details of your nearest service. It is also possible to complete and submit an online form setting out a particular query, if you cannot find the information you need on the website. This will be researched by a health-information professional and you should receive a response within five working days – but if you are feeling unwell and need immediate advice, contact the NHS Direct telephone service instead.

You will also find a link on NHS Direct's website to HealthSpace, an online service provided by the NHS for people aged 16 or over in England (www.healthspace.nhs.uk). If you want, you can use this secure website to keep a record of your own health details. There are plans to use the HealthSpace website as one of the ways to access Choose and Book, the new appointments booking system – see page 153. If you have a digital satellite television, you can use this to access NHS Direct with your TV remote control's 'interactive' button.

NHS Direct Interactive

This is the digital television version of NHS Direct, and is available to anyone who has a digital satellite television. You can access this by pressing the 'interactive' button on the remote control, scrolling down the menu to 'NHS Direct Interactive' and pressing the 'select' button. You can also view it on the Internet (www.nhsdirect.tv).

GP surgeries and out-of-hours services

Chapter 3 gives more details about seeing a GP, including registering with a particular surgery and out-of-hours services. Chapter 13 looks at your rights to NHS care if you are away from where you usually live (for example, on holiday elsewhere in the UK). If you are not sure whether you should see a GP, you can ask NHS Direct for their advice, see a pharmacist or attend a walk-in centre (see below). If any of these professionals feels it is necessary, they will advise you to go to a GP.

NHS walk-in centres

NHS walk-in centres provide treatment for minor injuries and illnesses seven days a week. They are usually open from early in the morning until late evening. There is no need to make an appointment. An NHS nurse will see you. Walk-in centres can also provide details of out-of-hours GP and dental services, and details of other local health services, such as pharmacies. If your illness or injury is more serious, staff at the centre will advise you what to do – they may even call an ambulance on your behalf if needed.

There are 85 walk-in centres in England, with more planned. You can find details of the one nearest to you by looking in your local telephone directory or by asking NHS Direct.

Pharmacists

Pharmacists (or 'the chemist's') are experts on how medicines work. If you have any worries about the medicines you are taking, visit your nearest pharmacist, bringing the medicine bottle or packet with you so that he or she can see what you have been taking and when.

Pharmacists can also advise on common illnesses such as coughs and colds or on other health issues such as giving up smoking, and can also help you decide whether you need to see a doctor. You don't need to make an appointment to see a pharmacist but you may need to wait a few minutes if they are busy with other customers (for example, getting other people's prescriptions ready).

As well as independent pharmacy (chemist's) shops, found in most towns in the UK, major shops such as Boots The Chemist and Lloyds Chemists have pharmacy counters where you could also ask to speak to the pharmacist. Some supermarkets also have a pharmacy. Local newspapers often publish lists of the pharmacies offering out-of-hours services (usually on a rota basis: for example, one pharmacy offers this on a Tuesday night, another on a Wednesday and so on); or you can look in your local telephone book or contact NHS Direct for details.

See also Chapter 10.

HOSPITAL ACCIDENT AND EMERGENCY (A&E)

A&E is one of the departments (also sometimes called emergency departments, EDs) found in many (but not all) NHS hospitals. As the name suggests, they are intended for when emergency care is needed for serious injury or illness. The NHS regards an emergency as something that is a critical or life-threatening situation, such as:

- loss of consciousness;
- heavy blood loss;
- suspected broken bone(s);
- persistent chest pain for 15 minutes or more;
- difficulty breathing;
- overdose or poisoning.

If you are with someone who you think needs to go to A&E, you can either take them there yourself or you can call 999 for an emergency ambulance. If you are on your own, you may feel it is better to call for an ambulance than to try to get a lift from a friend or a taxi.

Calling for an ambulance won't necessarily mean that you are treated any more quickly when you arrive at A&E, however, as most departments assess you when you arrive and then treat the most urgent cases first. A&E units have a team of doctors and nurses and, because they are generally part of a hospital, can admit you to other wards if needed.

The usual advice, if you are going to an A&E unit, is not to eat, drink or smoke anything in case this delays any emergency treatment you need. A&E departments are open 24 hours a day, all year round. If you are not sure where your nearest A&E unit is, you can ask NHS Direct or look in the local telephone book.

999 CALLS AND EMERGENCY SERVICES

Most people know that to obtain an ambulance you should telephone 999. This is a free call. The operator will ask you whether you require the police, fire brigade or ambulance, and will then connect you. You can also be connected if you ring NHS Direct and they think your situation requires an ambulance. The major work of the ambulance services is to get patients who have been seriously injured to hospital (usually A&E units) as quickly as possible because the treatment they need can only be provided there.

In the last few years, ambulance services have been finding it harder to meet their targets because of a huge rise in the numbers of hoax or unnecessary calls. Ambulance Trusts do not have to respond to all calls. They do not have to respond to calls for people in non-urgent situations. For example, people who dial 999 and ask for an ambulance because they have a minor cut to their finger or earache will not automatically be sent an ambulance. Instead, Strategic Health Authorities and local Primary Care Trusts, together with the relevant Ambulance Trust, will have other options in place. This might involve local paramedics or an on-call doctor visiting and treating you at home, or (depending on why you have rung) it might be suggested you seek advice from NHS Direct or visit an NHS walk-in centre.

The ambulance service must respond to Category A or Category B emergency calls:

- Category A calls are for problems that are life-threatening, and the ambulance service aims to respond to them within eight minutes;

- Category B calls are where the problem is serious but not immediately life-threatening, and should be responded to within 14 minutes (in urban areas) or 19 minutes (in rural parts of the country).

Calls requesting the emergency services are often recorded.

Ambulances may be used to provide transport for complicated hospital admissions, discharges and transfers. This type of non-emergency work is carried out by the Patient Transport Service (PTS) – see Chapter 12. It also provides transport for hospital day care for older people, along with other people who need to attend a hospital for out-patient appointments or treatment and whose illness or disability means that other forms of transport are not an option. Patient Transport Service arrangements usually need to be booked in advance (and your need for this confirmed by a health professional, such as your GP). They are not available through the 999 telephone number. If your admission to or discharge from hospital is more routine, you will probably be expected to make your own arrangements – perhaps getting a lift from a friend or neighbour, or using a taxi. Voluntary organisations such as the British Red Cross can sometimes help people who cannot use or do not have access to public or private transport and need to get to a health appointment or return home from hospital.

MINOR INJURIES UNITS

An appropriate alternative to A&E for some people is a minor injuries unit, where treatment is led by nurses. These units are for patients with injuries such as:

- sprains, cuts and grazes;
- infected wounds;

- bites and stings;
- minor head injuries.

You do not need an appointment to visit a minor injuries unit but, if you are not sure whether A&E or some other route would be more appropriate, you can telephone NHS Direct and ask for their advice. These units tend to be part of a hospital – including hospitals with A&E departments. Unlike A&E departments, they are not all open all the time – for example, they may be open only between 8am and 10pm.

KEEPING HEALTHY

Although we all need some health services from time to time – even if this is only for flu vaccinations or check-ups with the dentist – most people would like to stay as healthy as they can for as long as they can. There is lots of information and advice available for anyone who wants to try to improve or maintain their health.

See also Chapter 20.

3

GPs and
Primary Care Services

M ost NHS services are divided into two types – primary care
and secondary care. *Primary care* is the term used to describe
treatment and care from general practitioners (GPs) and other
community-based professionals such as dentists, district nurses,
chiropodists and occupational therapists. *Secondary care* describes
the more specialist care that you would expect to find in hospital
– there is more about this in Chapters 11 and 12. This chapter
concentrates on some aspects of primary care. There is more about
occupational therapy in Chapter 7, and more about chiropody in
Chapter 9.

GP SERVICES

Since 1 April 2004, the vast majority of GPs have been working
to a changed national NHS contract. This is the contract that GPs
agree to sign with their local Primary Care Trust (PCT). It sets out
the services they will provide to NHS patients from their premises
(the surgery, health centre or clinic), and at the patient's home where
necessary.

Some GP surgeries are run by only one doctor – these are known
as solo or single-handed practices. This type of arrangement has
become less common in recent years, as it is felt that doctors (and,
thus, patients) benefit from working with other colleagues rather than

on their own; it can be popular with patients who prefer to have only one doctor involved in their care, although there will always be times when another doctor has to be seen because the solo GP is away or not on call.

Most practices are formal partnerships (as might exist in other businesses) owned by two or more individual GPs.

A few GPs are employed direct by the Primary Care Trust – they are sometimes called salaried doctors. Some GPs who are partners in their practice may also employ a doctor to work for them.

There are also GP services available through what is called the Personal Medical Service (PMS). This arrangement, which began in 1998, is another way of providing NHS general practice.

Everyone who lives in the UK is entitled to register with an NHS GP practice. This right is based solely on whether you live permanently in the UK, not what nationality you are or where your passport was issued or how much tax you have paid. This right includes people living in care homes (see Chapter 13).

Some people who are UK citizens no longer live in the UK but have decided to live abroad. They have different rights, discussed in Chapter 13.

Registering with a practice

Before April 2004 you would have registered with a particular GP at the surgery where he or she worked – and joined that GP's list of patients. If one GP's 'list' was full, you might be asked to register with a different GP at the same practice. When you rang for an appointment, you might well have been asked who your GP was, so an appointment could be made for you to see that doctor.

The current arrangements are slightly different. Instead of registering with one particular GP, you are now registered with the practice. This means it is the practice that holds the list of patients, rather than the individual GPs who work there. If you register as a new patient, you should be asked if you want to say which GP would be your 'preferred' doctor (you can also name a preferred practitioner who is not a doctor but works as part of the practice team, such as a specialist nurse). Your choice should be recorded in writing, and as far as possible you should be able to see that person when you make an appointment. But it doesn't give you a right to insist on seeing that doctor or nurse every time. If they are away, for example, or cannot fit you in when you are free, you will be offered an appointment with another doctor or nurse at the practice as appropriate.

The surgery will ask you to provide your address and other details when you register, including your NHS number. You will have been sent this by the NHS when you last registered with a GP practice. But it will not affect your registering now, if you cannot find the number. When you have registered, your last GP will forward on your medical records.

There is more about your health records in Chapter 17.

If you are having problems finding a surgery to register with, get in touch with your local Primary Care Trust. It is responsible for making sure you are registered. You can find it in your telephone book or by contacting NHS Direct (page 282).

Appointments

Everyone has the right to expect to be able to see a GP within two working days, or another primary care professional (such as the practice nurse) within one working day of requesting an appointment. The appointment might not be with your 'preferred' GP, however. This right to be seen does not mean you cannot make appointments further ahead, if this would suit you better.

You may find that your appointment with the GP will be expected to be concluded within 5–10 minutes. Some people take with them a list of questions or concerns they want to raise with the GP about their health, to make sure they remember everything they want to say. You may also find it helpful to write down what the GP has told you as soon as you can. It is very easy to get some details wrong when remembering what was said. If later on you can't remember an important point, you can always ring the surgery, explain you have forgotten and ask to speak to the doctor you saw if they are available when you ring. You can then ask the GP to tell you again what was discussed.

If you are taken ill when you are visiting somewhere else in the UK and need to see a GP, you can go to any NHS surgery and ask to be registered as a temporary patient. You 'count' as a temporary resident in the new area if you have been there for more than 24 hours but less than three months. In a medical emergency you can also ask a GP to provide treatment without needing to register. If you are taken ill away from home and don't know where the GP practices are and cannot find a local telephone book, ring NHS Direct to find out.

Changing practices

You can ask to change practices – in fact, you don't need to ask at the current practice. If you want to go to a different practice, ask the new surgery if they will take you on as a patient. If they agree, they will contact your last GP practice to ask for your notes to be transferred over. You don't have to let your previous GP know but it would be polite to do so.

Many people change practices because they move to a different area. Some people might decide to change practices because they are unhappy with some aspect of the surgery's care. It's always worth telling the practice manager, or a GP or nurse at the surgery, why you are unhappy. They may be able to resolve this with you. They should also tell you about the complaints system they must offer (see Chapter 16).

Being removed from a practice's list

Occasionally, a patient is asked to leave the practice. This might happen if a patient has been violent or abusive towards a member of staff or to other patients in the waiting area. If this cannot be sorted out, as a last resort the patient may be asked to find another practice. If this affects you, contact the local Primary Care Trust as well as the Patient Advice and Liaison Service (PALS). The Primary Care

Trust must provide general practice services for you; the Patient Advice and Liaison Service may be able to suggest ways you could receive this other than going to a particular surgery. Or it may be that alternative arrangements are offered together with some support or treatment to help with aggressive behaviour.

You should receive an explanation as to why you are being asked to leave the practice; many practices do so as this information can be helpful. But you cannot be asked to leave because of your age or because your health needs are high. If this happened, you would have grounds for a complaint – see Chapter 16.

The practice team

All surgeries offer the same sort of basic primary care medicine. This includes:

- diagnoses;
- prescribing medicine;
- health checks;
- referring you to other NHS services (such as to hospital);
- providing inoculations (eg flu vaccinations).

Different surgeries may offer other services as well, such as:

- minor surgery (eg removing a wart);
- cervical cancer screening.

Many practices also employ a nurse who carries out some screening and treatment services. In a few cases, he or she may also visit you at home, if you need regular monitoring or nursing help. Or the GP will arrange for the local NHS community nursing service to get involved. Some nurses have received extra training and can prescribe a limited list of medicines, or may be involved in the management of patients with long-term (chronic) conditions such as heart disease.

The surgery should have a leaflet that tells you what services are offered, and gives the surgery's opening hours, contact details and what to do if you are taken ill when the surgery is closed (see page 42). This should also tell you about the people working at the surgery, including their qualifications.

A few GP practices have arranged with their local social services departments to have a social worker available at the surgery. The social worker is employed by social services but runs specific sessions at the surgery or clinic, or has appointments available for you to see him or her there. If your GP thinks this would help you – perhaps because you need advice about care services or help with completing a welfare benefit application – they will suggest that you arrange to see the social worker. The idea behind having a social worker at the surgery is that this makes it easier for patients who might otherwise have to make a separate trip to social services' offices. Even if your surgery doesn't have a social worker based there, your GP might still suggest that you talk to someone from social services, if this is appropriate for you.

You may find other staff available to help as needed at the practice, such as nurse practitioners and specialist nurses to support patients with specific conditions such as diabetes or asthma. Practitioners with Special Interests (PwSIs) can be GPs, or nurses or other health professionals, who have an interest and expertise in certain conditions.

If you are registered with a practice, you are entitled to receive any of the services it provides for its NHS patients. This applies regardless of whether you are living in your own home, in a sheltered flat, with relatives in their home, or in a care home or in a care home offering nursing care (see Chapter 13).

Referrals

Your GP may prescribe medicine for you, or give you advice and information to help you deal with a particular health problem. Or he or she may want to refer you to a more specialised doctor. This will either be a consultant, often based at a hospital, or it might be a GP who is a GP with Special Interests (GPwSI). A GPwSI may work at the same surgery or be based at another clinic or health centre. They have chosen to specialise in care for a particular health area, such as dermatology (skin conditions – eg eczema), or ear, nose and throat conditions, with the aim of making it easier for patients to receive appropriate treatment more quickly.

Chapter 11 explains about being referred by your GP for hospital treatment.

Box 6. Second opinions

You have the right to ask for a second opinion – but you can't insist that one be provided. It is up to the doctor you ask (usually either a GP or a hospital consultant) to arrange this. Generally, most doctors will arrange for a second opinion for you. Indeed, your GP or consultant may decide they would like a second opinion if they are not sure what the problem might be, or are unclear why a treatment isn't working as well as it should. Asking for another professional's view should help. You can also ask for a second opinion on behalf of someone else, but you must have his or her permission to do so.

Because there's no automatic right to a second opinion, there are no time limits within which one must be provided. If a second opinion is needed because of a medical priority, an appointment with another consultant or GP will be made as soon as possible.

Your GP may also refer you to the local NHS community health services. In some areas, you can also contact the community health services yourself without involving your GP. The sorts of services they may provide include:

- a chiropodist (see Chapter 9);
- a physiotherapist (see Chapter 7);
- a mental health nurse (see Chapter 8);
- a hospice at home or Macmillan nurse (see Chapter 15).

Or your GP may refer you to the local intermediate care service (see Chapter 7) or to the district nursing or health visitor services (see page 43).

The GP may also refer you to the local continence service (Box 7). You may also get in touch with the service yourself, without a GP referral. There are two types of incontinence: urine (or bladder) and faecal (or bowel). Typical problems with urine incontinence include 'leaking', or not emptying your bladder fully each time, or needing to go to the toilet very frequently. Problems with bowel incontinence include being constipated or having diarrhoea.

Box 7. Continence services

Your local Primary Care Trust (PCT) must provide an integrated continence service. The PCT sets criteria to decide when it will provide free continence supplies and aids. These criteria must be available to the public. They apply whether you live in your own home, in a sheltered flat or in a care home (including those offering nursing care). There is more about NHS services for care home residents in Chapter 13.

The type of continence help the NHS can give includes:

- A diagnosis, so you know what is causing the problem.
- Advice about what to eat and drink, to help your bladder and bowels perform more effectively.
- Clothing that you can remove quickly and easily to aid your using the toilet.
- Reviewing your current medication to see if this is causing the problem or making it worse.
- Pelvic floor exercises to help your internal muscles and keep better control.
- Providing continence pads, aids and other supplies.
- Commodes are usually available, free of charge, from the Joint Equipment Stores (see page 99; sometimes also called the Community Equipment Store). The NHS or social services may offer a laundry service. The continence service will be able to tell you about this.

Since April 2005 GP practices have been able to commission some services for you direct, but it is up to each practice whether to do this. It means that the practice where you are registered as a patient can choose either to buy the NHS care you need or to refer you to the services commissioned (arranged) by your Primary Care Trust. Whichever arrangement is used should make no difference to the quality and speed of NHS treatment you receive.

Home visits

Your GP should visit you at home (including the care home where you live) if you are too ill to get to the surgery. If you cannot leave the person you provide care for in order to get to the surgery, because they are too ill to be left alone, ask your GP to visit you at home. When you ring the surgery, explain in as much detail as you can why you cannot get to the surgery, so that staff can decide whether or not to visit you at home.

The practice's leaflet should explain about home visits.

NHS SERVICES YOU CAN BE CHARGED FOR

Many primary care services are provided free of charge through the NHS. These include visits to the doctor or nurse, and any advice or treatment they provide. But you may have to pay for some services. These include several services you might ask your GP to carry out. They include some (but not all) travel or holiday vaccinations. They can also include medical reports for insurance and driving purposes. Ask your GP in advance how much the charge will be.

There are some services you might have to pay for because they are not always available from the NHS; for example, complementary therapies such as acupuncture, osteopathy, reflexology or homeopathy. Even if your GP thinks that one of these may help you, there is not much of this type of support available on the NHS. There may be some exceptions for people who are terminally ill or have severe, long-term conditions. Although there are no guarantees that the NHS will provide these therapies for you, you can always ask.

If a service is not available to you on the NHS, your GP may suggest alternatives or even tell you if he or she knows of a local practitioner. Note that if you are an NHS patient your GP should not put pressure on you to accept private treatment; they cannot recommend private practitioners. If you decide to find a local practitioner privately, you need to contact that person and arrange to see them in their private clinic, and pay whatever they charge. Make sure you know what this might cost before agreeing to a session. Many complementary therapists charge a larger sum for the first visit, as this tends to take longer than subsequent visits, because they use it to find out the detail of what has been happening for you.

Thirteen types of professional therapist are registered by the Health Professions Council (see page 278). These include physiotherapists and chiropodists. There are plans for acupuncturists also to be registered. In each case this requires an Act of Parliament to be passed, because to make it illegal to practise without registration there must first be a law requiring this.

OUT-OF-HOURS SERVICES

Since December 2004, Primary Care Trusts have been responsible for 'out-of-hours' primary care. It is up to GPs whether they want to provide out-of-hours NHS services. If the GPs do not provide this, between the hours of 6.30pm and 8am Monday to Friday, and the whole of weekends and Bank holidays, other arrangements may be in place. What is available varies from place to place, and may still involve GPs who have decided that they would like to provide an out-of-hours service.

There are out-of-hours services in all parts of the country, and your practice must be able to tell you what this is (in the practice leaflet, or perhaps in a poster at the surgery). Alternatively, you can contact NHS Direct, as they will be able to tell you the arrangements for your area (page 24).

COMMUNITY NURSING SERVICES

Primary Care Trusts provide the community nursing services in each area. They employ a range of district nurses to carry this out and, in some cases, also employ specialist health visitors (often called Health Visitors for the Elderly or for Older People. Most other health visitors work with babies and young children).

District nurses provide nursing care to people who live in their own home, in sheltered housing or in care homes (Chapter 13 has more about this). There is no minimum amount of nursing that you might receive at home – it all depends on your need for care and the priorities of your Primary Care Trust. District nurses can help with things such as:

- care of pressure sores (including taking steps to prevent them from happening);
- artificial feeding tubes;
- blood pressure and other monitoring.

They may become more involved in your care during periods of severe illness, or if someone is coming to the end of their life (see also Chapter 15). District nursing services from the NHS are free. District nurses are often supported in their work by 'community nurses'.

In recent years, the type of support that a community or district nurse might provide through the NHS has changed. Some care is now carried out, free, by healthcare assistants under the supervision of the district nurse. But some care provision has gradually moved over to social services departments. This often includes bathing services – where someone helps you take a bath because you cannot do this alone. However, if you feel that the NHS should be providing, free of charge, the type of support you are being asked to pay towards, you may want to contact Age Concern (see page 271) to make sure that what has been arranged is correct and to find out how to challenge this local policy.

Where social services departments arrange a service such as help to bathe, you may be asked to pay. Each department sets the amount it charges, but there are some rules about this.

Age Concern's leaflet Help with Care in Your Own Home *may be helpful.*

Sometimes people decide to pay privately for a nurse at home. It is up to you whether you want to do this, and it is up the nurse or the agency (if they work for an agency) how much this will cost. Agencies that provide nurses or care workers who carry out personal tasks must be registered under the Care Standards Act 2000. Nurses' agencies are registered with the Commission for Social Care Inspection (CSCI; see page 275 for contact details).

The agency should provide you with written details about its services, and you should agree a contract with it. Details of local private agencies can be found in your local telephone directory. Or you can contact the United Kingdom Home Care Association (UKHCA; address on page 286), whose member organisations provide care at home. UKHCA also has a leaflet, *Choosing care in your home,* which you may find helpful.

Community matrons

In January 2005 the Government announced the creation of a new NHS professional: the community matron. Community matrons work with people who have serious long-term conditions, such as diabetes, asthma and arthritis, and who live in the community. They provide one-to-one support, and co-ordinate all the person's care needs. They form part of the National Service Framework for Long-Term Conditions, which was published in 2005 (see page 16).

The Department of Health plans to have 3,000 community matrons in post during 2007.

PRIVATE DOCTORS

Some primary care doctors have their own, private, practices. In this case, you register with them as a private patient. This means you have to pay each time you see them, and you may also have to pay for any medicines they prescribe for you. It is up to doctors who practise privately whether to offer a repeat prescription service (see also Chapter 10).

How much you are charged is up to the doctor, as for any private business. Make sure you know how much the visits and other treatment and items cost before agreeing to them. If you have private healthcare insurance, ask your insurer whether the cost of private primary healthcare is included.

Dentistry

This chapter explains your right to an NHS dentist (and how to find one); emergency NHS dental care; and your entitlement to different types of dental care, such as check-ups, crowns and dentures. It also covers paying for NHS dental care, the role of other dental personnel and dentistry services provided in NHS hospitals. How to complain about dental services, dentists and dental staff is explained in Chapter 16.

It also briefly covers private dentistry in terms of cost and payments, standards and cosmetic treatment.

FINDING AN NHS DENTIST

In some parts of the country, finding an NHS dentist has become more difficult. Some people have found that their dentist, whom they might have visited for many years, has decided not to offer treatment under the NHS any more but will accept them as private patients instead.

Most dentists working in England do accept NHS patients. However, most dental surgeries are run by dentists as their own businesses, so it is up to each dentist whether or not to offer treatments under the NHS. Dentists who offer NHS treatment to patients do so under a contract with the NHS. In the past, this contract was with their

Strategic Health Authority, but since 1 April 2006 dentists have contracts with their local Primary Care Trust (PCT) to provide NHS dental care. Under this arrangement, the Primary Care Trust pays the dentists for the NHS treatment they provide.

Most NHS patients pay something towards the cost of their treatment – these amounts are set by government and are explained on page 54.

A small number of dentists are 'salaried'. This means they are full-time NHS employees. They often work for the local Community Dental Service. Salaried dentists are not allowed to offer private treatments to their NHS patients.

There are several ways you can find a dentist who provides NHS treatment. The first is to contact NHS Direct (see page 282). NHS Direct will be able to tell you about dental practices in your area that are taking on new NHS patients. Alternatively, if you have access to the Internet, you can visit the NHS website (www.nhs.uk) and select the option 'Dentists' to find your local dentist.

One of the difficulties people often face is that the nearest available NHS dentist is some miles from where they live. You can raise with the local Patient Advice and Liaison Service (PALS) any concerns you have about the lack of NHS dentists nearer to where you live. Each Primary Care Trust has a Patient Advice and Liaison Service you can contact (see page 227 for more details). There is no financial help available with the costs of travel to a dentist. If travelling to a dentist is a problem for you, contact your local Age Concern organisation for advice.

If you need a dentist to visit you at home, perhaps because you have a disability or have other health problems, make sure you tell NHS Direct this when asking for an NHS dentist. It will be able to tell you which dentists offer home visits.

Some dentists advertise themselves as taking on new NHS patients. These adverts might be in local telephone directories (under 'Dental services') or in your local newspaper.

Neighbours and friends in your area might be able to recommend the dentist with whom they are registered as NHS patients. You could then contact that dental surgery and ask if they are accepting new NHS patients.

In October 2004 the National Institute for Health and Clinical Excellence (NICE) issued guidance about how frequently you should see your dentist for an NHS check-up. For example, some people who have very good oral health (teeth, gums and mouth) may not need to go for a routine check-up as often as every six months – see below.

In the past, dentists accepted people as NHS patients for a period of 15 months. If you did not visit your dentist during this 15-month period, you could find you had 'lost' your status as an NHS patient because your dentist decided to remove you from his or her list.

The changes in NHS dentistry since 1 April 2006 mean that this system no longer applies. Dentists are no longer required to register the patients they accept for NHS treatment, although they may well keep their own lists of their patients as well as other records such as details of the dental treatment given. For everyone aged 18 or over the minimum time between routine checks should be three months and the maximum time two years. The basic rule of thumb is that the better your oral health the longer the time between routine check-ups. NICE has asked that local health communities review their existing practice and work out how quickly this change to routine check-ups can be put into place.

What it means in practice is that your dentist will agree with you how soon you should come back for a check-up or for further treatment. This might be within three months or perhaps not for another two years – the exact time will depend on the health of your mouth, teeth and gums, or whether you are in the middle of ongoing treatment, for example. But, regardless of what your dentist suggests to you, if something begins to worry you about your teeth or gums, make an appointment straight away – don't delay until the next check-up visit is due.

EMERGENCY NHS DENTAL CARE

If you are registered with a dental practice for NHS treatment,
that surgery should give you details of its emergency treatment
arrangements. If you can, try to contact your dentist during usual
surgery hours, as treatment will be easier if surgery staff are
available. The surgery's answerphone, which will be switched on
when the surgery is closed, should also give details of what to do if
you need emergency dental care out of normal hours.

Emergencies can arise for a range of reasons. They could include
raging toothache, a filling that has fallen out, a damaged crown or
more serious issues. Injuries or accidents to the face may require
emergency dental surgery in hospital. If you are at all unsure what to
do, or how serious your particular emergency might be, contact NHS
Direct for advice.

Some emergencies arise during usual surgery hours. But some may
arise at night or at weekends – what are often called 'out of hours'.

Since 1 April 2006, local Primary Care Trusts have been responsible
for out-of-hours and urgent NHS dental treatment. These
arrangements vary across the country. Urgent treatment may be
available from more than 50 Dental Access Centres in England,
or from the Community Dental Service, another local dentist or a
different arrangement. To find out what is provided in your area,
contact your local Primary Care Trust or NHS Direct (see page 282).

Even if you usually receive private dental care, you can still ask for
emergency NHS treatment.

HOME VISITS FOR NHS PATIENTS

Arrangements for people who cannot get to a dentist because of poor
health or disability vary from one part of the country to another.
If you are unable to visit a dentist's surgery, your local PCT has to
make sure you can still receive NHS dental care. These arrangements
vary around the country but might involve asking local dentists to
visit people at home or using the Community Dental Services.

People who live in care homes or sheltered housing have the same rights to access NHS dental care as everyone else. (Care homes may have their own arrangements; ask the care home manager about this. See also Chapter 13.) In rural areas there may be mobile dental services. NHS Direct will have the details of these local arrangements.

Anyone who receives NHS treatment at home will still have to pay the same charges that would have applied if they had visited the surgery (see pages 54–55).

NHS DENTAL TREATMENTS

As with any treatment, precisely what you need in the way of dental care will depend on the state of your teeth, gums and mouth. Dentists who undertake NHS treatment must offer you all the necessary treatment that is available under the NHS to make and keep your mouth healthy (your 'oral health'). It should also be 'within the competence of the dentist providing it' – a dentist should only offer you treatments that he or she is capable of providing.

There are, however, some treatments that are not available on the NHS. These include cosmetic treatments such as teeth whitening or tooth-coloured crowns on back teeth. If you want these treatments, you will probably have to pay privately for this (see later, under 'Private dentistry').

If you are a new NHS patient, your dentist will carry out an examination, inspecting your mouth, teeth and gums, and possibly will decide to take some x-rays or impressions of your teeth. Then he or she will explain the treatment options. If this involves a mixture of NHS and private care, the dentist will provide you with a treatment plan. This is free, and will include details such as the costs of the treatments being suggested. You should receive a written treatment plan if your dentist decides you need the sort of NHS dental care that is provided under Bands 2 or 3 (see page 55).

Your dentist should also provide other information for patients (see Box 8).

Box 8. Information from your dentist

Your dentist should:

- explain your treatment options and let you know what can be provided on the NHS or privately;

- make sure you know how much your NHS and/or any private treatment will cost;

- provide you with a written treatment plan (including costs) if you are receiving both NHS and private care;

- display a poster in the waiting room about the charges for NHS treatment;

- discuss with you how often you need to attend;

- provide a leaflet with information about the dental practice and the services it provides.

Cancelling appointments

Your dentist cannot charge you if you miss an appointment for NHS treatment. If you continue to miss appointments, however, they may decide not to offer you treatment. In that case, you would need to find another dentist.

You should try to give your dentist as much notice as possible if you cannot keep an appointment. Even if you do not know there is a problem until the day of the appointment itself, it is always better to telephone and cancel if at all possible.

ORAL HEALTH

Although most of us think of going to the dentist in terms of our teeth, dentists are expert in the health of our whole mouth (oral health). They often detect early signs of oral cancer, for example, or other serious health problems. Even if your teeth appear to be fine, following the advice of your dentist should help you maintain and improve your overall oral health – such as dealing with gum disease. A dentist can also refer you to more specialised NHS services if needed – for example, to see an NHS consultant at an ear, nose and throat (ENT) hospital department.

DENTAL PROFESSIONALS

Dentists usually employ dental nurses and assistants to help them with their work. Dental nurses may make up the formula used in fillings, for example, and assist in a variety of other ways. There are also other dental professionals.

The General Dental Council (GDC) keeps up-to-date registers of dentists, dental hygienists, dental nurses, dental technicians, clinical dental technicians, dental therapists and orthodontic therapists who are qualified to practise dentistry in the UK. These are called The Dentists Register and, since 31 July 2006, the Dental Care Professionals Register. It is illegal for dentists, dental hygienists and dental therapists to practise without being registered with the GDC – except for doctors who are registered with the General Medical Council and are working in non-NHS dentistry. From 31 July 2008, it will be illegal to use the titles 'dental nurse' or 'dental technician' without being registered with the GDC.

PAYING FOR NHS DENTAL CARE

For many years (almost since the beginning of the NHS), the NHS has been asking patients to contribute towards the cost of the care they receive individually. These are standard amounts that all patients pay for NHS dental care – except for some people, who may pay less (or nothing at all) because they have a low income. The NHS Low Income Scheme applies to all adults – not just older people – and is explained on pages 97–98.

There are some NHS dental treatments for which no one pays:

- removing stitches;
- repairs to dentures;
- writing a prescription (although you may still have to pay for the prescription itself, if you are under 60 – see page 141).

53

Dentists do not usually charge for adjustments to NHS treatments if these are needed within a short time of the original treatment. Examples include a tooth still being uncomfortable a few days after a filling or dentures needing adjusting in the first few weeks after they have been fitted. However, if dentures become loose several months after being fitted and need to be readjusted because of natural changes to the gums, this may count as a new course of treatment. If so, there will be further charges to pay – ask your dentist about this when your dentures are first being fitted.

HOW MUCH DOES NHS DENTISTRY COST?

The costs of NHS dental treatments, like other NHS charges, are set by the government of the day. This means that they are the same no matter where in England you live. The total amount you pay will depend on:

- the actual treatment you receive;
- which of three new 'bands' of charges your treatment comes under;
- whether you are eligible for any help with these costs (as set out on pages 93–94).

On 1 April 2006, the government introduced a new system of charges for NHS dentistry. This is based on three fixed 'bands'. Each band relates to one course of treatment. Even if you have to visit your dentist several times over one course of treatment, you will still pay only one charge. Only one of the bands applies at a time – which one you have to pay will depend on the type of treatment you receive. From 1 April 2007, you might have to pay:

- *Band 1: £15.90* This applies if you receive an examination, diagnosis and preventative advice. If needed, this cost would also cover X-rays, scale and polish, and planning for further treatment.
- *Urgent and out-of-hours care will also cost £15.90.*

- **Band 2: £43.60** This charge covers all the treatments included in the £15.90 charge and the costs of extra treatments such as fillings, root canal treatment or tooth extractions.
- **Band 3: £194.00** This charge includes all necessary treatment covered by the £15.90 and £43.60 charges plus more complex procedures such as crowns, dentures or bridges.

If you needed more treatment at the same charge level within two months of seeing your dentist, it would be free of charge. For example, if you had a filling you would be charged £43.60; if you needed a second filling (even in another tooth) within two months of this, you would not have to pay anything more.

If you are referred to another dentist for part of your treatment, you will still pay only one amount. You pay the dentist who referred you. If you are referred to a specialist for a new course of treatment (such as orthodontics, or if you need sedation), you will pay one charge to the specialist dentist. Your dentist might also need to charge you for any treatments you received before you were referred to the specialist service.

The maximum amount anyone has to pay for any single course of NHS dental care in England from 1 April 2007, is £194. Before this new system was introduced, the most you could pay was £384. Governments tend to revise charges for NHS dental care each year, usually around April or May. You can always check current charges with your dental surgery or contact Age Concern's Information Line (see page 271).

Your dentist collects the amount that you pay for your NHS dental care. Dentists are allowed to ask you to pay before the treatment is provided.

PRIVATE DENTISTRY

There is no state help with the costs of private dentistry. This makes it very important that you know how much you might have to pay for any dental care you receive privately before you agree to start the treatment.

Everyone is entitled to receive NHS dental care; but some people have decided – either as a positive choice or because they have not felt able to accept the NHS service offered to them – to become private patients. Many dentists offering NHS treatments also offer private care – this can become confusing, so be clear about whether the treatment you are agreeing to will be provided through the NHS or privately. Your dentist should provide you with written information about this, and about any costs.

Unlike the charges for NHS dentistry set out above, it is up to each dentist how much they charge for private treatment. The amount you will be asked to pay may vary from one dentist to another. These costs are likely to be more than the NHS would charge. Do make sure that you are certain how much you will be asked to pay before agreeing to go ahead.

Sometimes it may be difficult for a dentist to give you an exact cost – some procedures may be easier than expected, or the dentist may discover unknown problems once they start the treatment. But you could ask the dentist for the 'worst case' and 'best case' scenarios – in other words, ask what the highest cost would be as well as the lowest cost. This will give you as good an idea as possible of how much you might have to pay.

There are some health insurance companies that offer dental insurance plans to cover at least some of the costs of private dental treatment. Some dentists will take on patients who are members of particular schemes – your dentist will be able to tell you about this.

DENTISTRY IN HOSPITAL

The vast majority of people receive primary dental care – that is, they see their dentist in his or her local surgery or practice. Some NHS dentistry is, however, provided in hospital. There are 14 specialist NHS Hospital Dental Services in the UK. The treatments they offer include:

- removal of some wisdom teeth;
- work to teeth and gums following facial injury, or for a disability that affects the jaw;
- any dental treatment that requires a general anaesthetic.

Your dentist or your GP can refer you to NHS hospital dental services if he or she thinks this is necessary. You might also be admitted to hospital in an emergency – for example, if you were involved in an accident that resulted in severe facial injuries. If you receive NHS dental services as a hospital in-patient, you will not have to pay for this.

You may not have to pay anything if you are attending an NHS Hospital Dental Service as an out-patient, although there may be a charge for dentures and bridges. Make sure you ask about any charges before treatment begins.

ANAESTHETICS

There are lots of different ways that dentists can make treatments pain-free. They might use creams or injections to numb the area, for example. Or a general anaesthetic might be used to sedate you during treatment, particularly if you are having a lot of treatments in one go (such as having lots of teeth extracted during one session).

Dentists also use a technique called *conscious sedation*. This means that you are given drugs that stop you feeling pain but you are able to understand what is happening and respond to questions that the dentist asks. Private dental clinics that provide general anaesthesia are regulated under the Care Standards Act 2000. This means they are registered and inspected by the Healthcare Commission (which also inspects such services from the NHS).

PUBLIC HEALTH

Primary Care Trusts are responsible for dental public health. This means they have a duty to assess the overall picture of dental health in each area and to commission services to meet its need. There might be particular problems locally – for example, very poor dental health among some schoolchildren, or particular groups of older people, or homeless people. Examples of the services a Primary Care Trust might commission include health-promotion schemes reminding people to have their teeth checked, or explaining what 'good oral health' looks like, or trying to improve people's access to NHS dental services. Or they may look at schemes to fluoridate local water supplies. You can ask your Primary Care Trust what steps it is taking with regard to dental public health in your area.

5

Eye Services

This chapter explores eyesight, including free eye tests and getting and paying for equipment such as contact lenses, contact lens solution and spectacles. It looks at referrals to eye specialists; your rights if you have or your family has a history of glaucoma or diabetes; and referrals for surgery.

It also considers paying privately for treatments such as laser treatment to correct short sight, paying privately for glasses and contact lenses, and getting a guide dog and other support.

SIGHT PROBLEMS

There are a number of different sight problems. Some affect both children and adults; others are more likely to happen as we grow older. Common problems include (in alphabetical order):

- *Astigmatism* Both distance and near vision are affected. People with this may have headaches or be very sensitive to light.

- *Cataracts* More than half of people aged over 65 are likely to have some cataract development at some stage. Cataracts occur when part of the eye – the lens – becomes cloudy. This cloudiness stops light passing through the lens to the back of the eye, and vision becomes dim or blurred. Over time, vision may change colour (becoming more yellow), or you may see double images, or have particularly poor vision in bright light.

- **Diabetic retinopathy** Diabetes can affect the blood vessels in the retina, as well as affecting sight in other ways (it is one cause of cataracts).

- **Glaucoma** When pressure inside the eye becomes raised, the optic nerve can become damaged. This reduces the field of vision (how widely we can see) and the ability to see clearly.

- **Long sightedness (hypermetropia)** With long sight, light is focused beyond the retina and the eye has to compensate to re-focus. This makes it difficult to see things close up. Reading may become very difficult and, for older people, there can also be blurred distance vision.

- **Macular degeneration** The macula, which is at the centre of the retina, can become damaged and stop working. Because this often happens in later life, it is also called *age-related macular degeneration.*

- **Presbyopia (ageing eye)** As we get older, the lens of the eye thickens and begins to lose flexibility. As a result, we lose the ability to focus on objects that are close up.

- **Short sightedness (myopia)** This happens when light is focused in front of the retina and causes anything some distance away (eg a cinema screen) to look blurred. Near vision, however, is usually clear – for example, there are usually no problems in reading a book.

There are many treatments and solutions for problems such as those listed above. They range from glasses (spectacles) or contact lenses that correct your vision to surgery to remove cataracts (commonly carried out as day surgery, where there is no need for an overnight stay).

Eyesight can change quickly or slowly. Sometimes we are not aware straight away that damage is happening to the eye. So it is important to get your sight checked regularly, and to see an eye care professional as soon as anything about your eyesight begins to change.

Sɪɢʜᴛ ᴛᴇsᴛs

Everyone aged 60 or over is entitled to a free sight test on the NHS. Tests are carried out by local optometrists. Even though we still call them 'the optician's', if you go to a high street practice, you will have your eyes examined by either an optometrist or an ophthalmic medical practitioner (OMP) – see Box 9.

Box 9. Different terms for 'sight professionals'

There are a number of terms used to describe different professionals specialising in sight. 'Optician' is a term we are all familiar with, but in fact it describes:

- *Ophthalmic opticians* (also called optometrists), who are qualified to examine eyes, recognise disease, and prescribe and fit spectacles (glasses) and contact lenses.
- *Dispensing opticians* are qualified to fit spectacles, and may have additional qualifications to enable them to fit contact lenses, too (in which case they may call themselves 'Contact lens opticians').
- *Manufacturing opticians,* who make spectacles.

Everyone who examines eyes or fits and dispenses (gives out) spectacles and contact lenses has to be registered to do this by the General Optical Council.

This registration means that these professionals have adequate training, qualifications and practical experience. It is an offence to practise as a dispensing optician without being registered. If someone is found guilty and convicted, they can be fined up to £5,000.

There are also other terms you may come across:

- *Ophthalmologists* specialise in the treatment of eye diseases.

continued over

Box 9 continued

They are medically qualified and work mostly in eye hospitals and hospital eye departments.

- *Orthoptists* work with ophthalmologists to assess squints and double vision, for example, before treatment. They are then involved in monitoring the treatment.

Ophthalmic medical practitioners often work in practices called Medical Eye Centres. They are doctors who have chosen to specialise in examining eyes. Many optometrists run their own, private, businesses. Some work for larger chains such as SpecSaver, or run the optical services in larger chemists' stores, such as Boots The Chemist.

When you make an appointment, make sure the optometrist knows this is for an NHS sight test. The test may include checking the pressure in your eyes as well as your ability to read letters at long and short distances. Tests for older people may also include conditions such as glaucoma and cataract.

If you are the parent, brother, sister, son or daughter of someone with glaucoma, and you are aged 40 or over, you are entitled to a free NHS eye test. If you are under the age of 60, and have either been diagnosed as having glaucoma or been told by an ophthalmologist that you are at risk of glaucoma, you are also entitled to a free NHS sight test. Leaflet HC11 *Help with health costs,* which can be obtained from the post office or the optometrist or the Department of Health (see page 275), explains who else is eligible for free NHS tests. This includes people under the age of 60 with diabetes, and people registered as severely sight-impaired.

When you go for your sight test, tell the optometrist if you are entitled to a free NHS test. If you are claiming because you are aged 60 or over, you may need to take with you an official document that proves your age. Examples of such proof include your birth certificate, passport, a travel concession card (eg your train or bus pass), or your NHS medical card (this is the card given to you when you first register with a GP as a patient). You will need to fill in a form, GOS1, to claim your free NHS sight test. Your optometrist will give you this form.

In recent years, the Government has been trying to reduce the numbers of people falsely claiming free NHS tests. This is why people are now asked for proof. If you make a claim but are in fact not eligible for a free sight test, you could end up being fined up to £100 as well as having to pay the original fee for the eyesight test. In some cases you could even face prosecution, under the Health Act 1999.

Although most people have their sight test carried out at the optometrist's premises, he or she could visit you where you live. They can (but do not have to) provide a free NHS sight test to you at home if you are not able to get to their premises because of ill-health or disability. Ask your optometrist if they offer this service. If you have difficulty finding someone who will visit you for a free NHS test at home, contact NHS Direct for help. If your eye test is carried out while you are an NHS patient in hospital, this will be free of charge.

Most advice suggests that people under the age of 70 should have their sight tested every two years. If you have diabetes, your doctor or optometrist may recommend that you have a sight test every year. The Department of Health recommends that people over the age of 70 should also have their eyes tested every 12 months. If you are not sure how often you should visit, ask the optometrist when you next have your test.

At the end of the test, the optometrist will give you a 'prescription', using another form – GOS2. This describes what you might need in the way of glasses (spectacles) or contact lenses. You can take this prescription and use it to buy glasses or contact lenses at any opticians – you do not have to use it where you had your sight test. This prescription is free but it is not like a medicines prescription: you may still have to pay for your glasses – but see page 94, as you may be eligible for help with these costs.

GETTING GLASSES OR CONTACT LENSES

If your sight test indicates that you need glasses or contact lenses, you may be eligible for some help with the cost if you are on a low income (see page 97). Two leaflets produced by the Department of Health help explain this system: leaflet HC11 explains about optical vouchers and it says who is entitled to help with health costs; leaflet HC12 has information on the current value of optical vouchers. If you need complex lenses, you may also be able to get help with the cost, whatever your income. You will also be entitled to a free eye test.

There are some types of glasses you can buy 'over the counter'. These are ready-made reading glasses that are designed to correct presbyopia (see above). They can be sold by anyone – you don't have to buy them from an ophthalmic or dispensing optician (see Box 9). But they are limited in two ways: firstly, there is a maximum prescription (or 'strength') of +4 Dioptres in each lens and, secondly, the right and left lenses will be identical.

LOSS OF OR REPAIRS TO GLASSES OR CONTACT LENSES

There are a few circumstances in which your Primary Care Trust (PCT) may help with some of the costs of repairs to glasses, or offer replacements if you lose your glasses or contact lenses. They do this by issuing you with a voucher towards the cost of repair or replacement. They do not offer cash or pay your bill. If you hope to obtain such financial assistance, you must make sure first that the PCT will definitely help you before going ahead with any repairs or replacements. Ask your optometrist for form GOS4; this will tell you what to do to get NHS help with these costs.

You should note that the NHS may help you only if they agree:

- the loss or damage was due to illness;
- you can't get any help through an existing warranty, insurance or after-sales service;

- you would be entitled to an NHS voucher for glasses or contact lenses.

OTHER SUPPORT

If, during your sight test, the optometrist finds problems that may not be solved by your having glasses or contact lenses, he or she may do one of two things:

- If your eyesight is impaired (eg your field of vision is affected so that you cannot see very much around you), the optometrist may suggest that you contact social services to find out if there is help they can give you. The optometrist may give you a form that you complete and send to your local social services department. If you are visually impaired (partially sighted) or blind (including being registered blind) you may be entitled to a range of other support, including low-vision aids.

- If there are other problems, the optometrist can refer you to a consultant ophthalmologist (a doctor specialising in eyes) at a hospital eye clinic. This might be because you have cataracts, or a weeping eye, or some other problem that may require further attention and possible treatment.

Many people who experience a sudden and major loss of vision go to an optometrist rather than their GP. The optometrist can refer you as an emergency to the hospital eye clinic. If this happens, he or she may also give you a simple form, LVI 2003. This is for you to use to get in touch with your local social services department. It also contains information about other sources of advice and support.

It is up to you whether you use this form. If you do send it to social services, someone from that department will get in touch with you to see what help they can provide.

If you decide not to send the form to social services but are referred to the hospital eye clinic, you may find that clinic staff also ask if they may refer you to social services, for a social care assessment.

Again, it is up to you whether or not to accept this. If you agree, the hospital clinic will send social services a form called RVI 2003.

Social services may be able to help you with information about community services for people whose vision is impaired, emotional support, practical advice and rehabilitation training (you may be eligible for a Blue Badge, for example, which would entitle someone driving you in their car to park in a disabled parking bay). Exactly what is on offer from social services will depend on the criteria your local department has set.

For more information, contact Age Concern's Information Line (details on page 271).

Your sight loss may mean that you are no longer able to drive – your optometrist, hospital consultant or GP will be able to advise you. You may need to contact the Driver and Vehicle Licensing Agency (DVLA; contact details on page 276), which issues driving licences, to tell them about your changed eyesight.

If you have lost some or all of your vision, you may be considered to have a disability. As a result, you might be able to get other support, such as:

■ a reduced-cost BBC (TV) licence;

■ disability-related benefits.

In terms of NHS services, you have the right to receive information on your treatment options, as well as information (eg leaflets) meant for any member of the general public, in Braille, large print or audio, for example (as needed).

For some years the NHS and private health providers have had to make 'reasonable adjustments' to remove physical barriers to your receiving services, under the Disability Discrimination Act 1995. Since October 2004 this has included making sure there are no physical barriers to their premises that stop you from using their service or make it unreasonably difficult for you to use it. This means removing, altering or avoiding a physical feature, or providing the service in a different way.

This also applies to other services, goods and facilities available to the general public. It means not being discriminated against by your being unable to use restaurants and shops, for example. This might happen if you cannot read the price labels or menus because of your sight difficulties. Restaurants and shops can comply with the Act by making this information available to you in large print or Braille, or by having one of their staff read these out loud to you.

Voluntary organisations may be able to offer support. For example, the Guide Dogs for the Blind Association (contact details on page 278) may be able to suggest options ranging from helping you to learn to use a long-handled (or 'white') cane to your having a guide dog.

If you have a guide dog and need to use a taxi, you have a right to expect licensed taxi cabs (black cabs) and private minicabs to accept you as a fare, under the Disability Discrimination Act 1995. A taxi driver or minicab driver can refuse to carry a registered guide dog only if the driver has a medical exemption certificate issued by the licensing authority. The driver must display the exemption certificate at all times. You can find out more about the Disability Discrimination Act and what it means by contacting the Disability Rights Commission (DRC; address on page 276):

Other charities, such as the Royal National Institute of the Blind (RNIB; contact details on page 284), offer goods and services, such as their Talking Books service.

SCREENING FOR PEOPLE WITH DIABETES

The Diabetes National Service Framework (NSF) promises that, by the end of 2007, every Primary Care Trust will offer eye-screening services to people with diabetes. The NHS was given a target to offer screening for diabetic retinopathy to at least 80% of people with diabetes by 2006; everyone with diabetes has a right to this screening by 2007. If you have diabetes and want to find out about arrangements for this in your area, contact your local Primary Care Trust. The charity Diabetes UK may also have useful information.

HOSPITAL EYE SERVICES

One of the most common reasons for an older person to be referred to the hospital eye service is that they have a cataract that needs removing. The target for cataract treatment is that people should not have to wait more than three months from being referred to receiving the treatment. Many cataract operations are now carried out as day surgery, under local anaesthetic. This means you will not have to stay overnight in hospital, but can return home the same day.

In some areas, there are specialist NHS eye hospitals. In other areas, eye services are part of general hospitals. In some parts of England, Primary Care Trusts have contracts with *diagnostic and treatment centres* (DTCs) to provide cataract surgery and after-care on behalf of the Primary Care Trust for NHS patients. Diagnostic and treatment centres are often run by private companies. As such, they have to be registered and inspected by the Healthcare Commission.

OTHER PRIVATE TREATMENTS

Some treatments, such as laser eye surgery to correct short sight, are rarely if ever available on the NHS. If you want this type of surgery, you need to find a private clinic that will carry it out.

Make sure that you understand what the procedure involves and how much it will cost. You can always ask the advice of your GP or optometrist if you are unsure about this type of treatment. Costs vary, but remember that the price you are quoted may be only for one eye. If both eyes need treating, make sure that you know in advance what this will cost.

6

Hearing Services

This chapter looks at your rights to support from the NHS in terms of hearing tests, equipment and paying for hearing aids – and also considers these issues in respect of private hearing services. It tells you whom to contact to find out about entitlements to other equipment and support in the event of hearing loss or deafness – such as 'hearing dogs', British Sign Language and Typetalk.

INTRODUCTION

The overall health of our ears can affect both our hearing and our balance. As with many other health issues, some people will reach older age with an existing hearing impairment or loss. For others, the quality of their hearing will only begin to reduce during older age. Different terms are sometimes used to describe people with hearing difficulties – these include deaf, deafened, hard of hearing, sensory impairment or sensory loss (the last two terms are also sometimes used to describe people who have lost some or all of their eyesight).

Both loss of hearing and deafness are classed as disabilities – which means that the Disability Discrimination Act 1995 applies to you (see page 67). If your hearing is impaired, you may be eligible for disability-related benefits and other support.

For more information, contact Age Concern's Information Line (details on page 271).

LOSING HEARING

Many people who first begin to lose some of their hearing in older age do so because of a condition called *presbyacusis*. As we grow older, the specialised cells in the innermost part of our ears (the cochlea) start to die. Sounds become less clear to us as a result. Common signs that you may be losing some of your hearing include:

- Hearing people talk – but thinking they are mumbling because you cannot make out what they are saying.

- Needing people to repeat things to you several times before you understand what they're saying.

- Needing to have your TV or radio on much louder than is needed by other people in the same room.

- Finding it difficult to follow conversations when you are in a group of people or in a noisy environment such as a pub or café.

- Finding it difficult to hear what people say to you on the telephone.

DIAGNOSIS

If your hearing has changed in any way, the first thing to do is see your GP. They will begin by looking in your ears using an instrument called an otoscope. They may want to check to see if a build-up of wax in your ear is causing the problem. If so, they can arrange for you to have your ears syringed. This is usually done by a nurse based at the surgery.

Your GP may carry out some other tests. These can involve using a tuning fork (used to tune musical instruments to particular notes) to find out a bit more about the type of problem you are experiencing, or they may test your hearing in other ways. If there is a problem, the GP will probably want to refer you to specialist hearing services

– either the ear, nose and throat (ENT) department of a hospital or the audiology department (or audiology clinic) in a hospital.

If you are referred to the ENT department, that department will get in touch to make an appointment for you to see an ENT consultant (the specialist doctor). Chapter 11 describes how soon you should be seen after you have been referred. The consultant will probably ask you whether there is any family history of deafness and may do some tests. Depending on the reason(s) for your hearing loss, he or she may then refer you in turn to the audiology department.

If you are over the age of 60, the chances are that your GP will refer you straight to the audiology department rather than get you to see the ENT consultant first. This is because the audiology department tends to be the most appropriate part of the NHS to deal with hearing loss for most older people. In this case, not going to the ENT department first helps to speed things up for you. But if you are worried about this, ask your GP to explain.

AUDIOLOGY TESTS

The audiologist (the professional working in the audiology department or clinic) tests your hearing using an audiometer. This is a piece of equipment that produces a range of sounds and you will be asked to say which of them you can hear. The audiologist uses these results to see if a hearing aid would help you. There is a wide range of hearing aids available, both on the NHS and privately. They will improve your hearing – but your hearing will not be fully restored.

NHS HEARING AIDS

NHS hearing aids are provided free of charge. This includes digital hearing aids for new patients. These digital aids look similar to the older, analogue, hearing aids that people wear but the Royal National Institute for Deaf People (RNID) says they give a better sound quality. One of the reasons is that it is possible to modify a digital hearing aid very precisely, to give a very good 'fit' with your particular hearing difficulties. They are also often designed to reduce steady background noise (eg traffic noise). This can make it more comfortable for you to concentrate on your conversation. They can also be programmed for different environments – for example, to suit someone whether they are at home watching the TV or out shopping in a busy supermarket.

If you already have an analogue hearing aid, there may be a wait before you are reassessed for a digital aid, using criteria set by your Primary Care Trust. National targets for diagnosis and fitting hearing aids are expected to be in place by 2008.

Do bear in mind that digital hearing aids are not suitable for everyone's hearing problem. An analogue hearing aid may be a better option for you.

When you see the audiologist, ask how soon you will receive your hearing aid. Once it has been fitted, you may need to go back to the clinic after a few weeks for adjustments to the aid.

Bear in mind that your hearing aid is lent to you by the NHS. It is not your personal property, so you must not try to sell it. It may have to be returned to the NHS if you no longer need it for any reason.

PRIVATE HEARING TESTS AND AIDS

You can also choose to pay for a private hearing test, and buy a hearing aid from a private hearing-aid dispenser. They often have shops in the high street, or you can find their details in your local telephone directory. You might decide to 'go private' if you want a hearing aid fitted very quickly, or there is a particular design you want that isn't available on the NHS. Private hearing tests cost around £25. If you find somewhere that doesn't charge, be aware that this may mean you are not given a copy of the results of your hearing test (an audiogram). You will need a copy of your audiogram if you decide to buy a hearing aid from a different dispenser from the one who carried out the test.

If you are thinking about buying a hearing aid privately, it is still worth seeing your GP first. He or she can advise whether further medical tests are needed. Your GP may also be able to give you information about hearing-aid dispensers in your area.

Sometimes private hearing-aid dispensers have a base in an NHS hospital; or you might want to arrange to see the NHS audiologist privately if he or she has a private practice. A private hearing aid can cost anything from £595 to £3,500. They may last for up to five years – but you will need to buy another aid when your current one fails. If you have private medical insurance, make sure that this policy covers the cost of hearing aids before you order the device.

The RNID (contact details on page 284) advises you not to respond to advertisements in newspapers or on television or radio offering free or cheap hearing devices. This is because you may find that you are on the receiving end of high-pressure sales tactics; at present you won't have as many rights as a consumer if you contact the company and they visit you at home at your invitation (there are proposals to tighten up this area of consumer law in the future).

The RNID produces a leaflet – Hearing aids *– that you may find helpful.*

TINNITUS

Tinnitus is a common hearing problem that can happen at any age. It is the condition where people hear noises in their ears or in their heads – noises such as ringing, whistling or buzzing.

Equipment known as sound or noise generators can be useful for someone with tinnitus. They work by helping to mask the noise you hear – for example, by producing a 'shhh' or soothing noise. Some devices can be fitted in your ear; others attach to a hearing aid. They are available free as part of NHS tinnitus treatment in hospital. Ask your GP or consultant about this.

They can also be bought privately from hearing-aid dispensers but they can be expensive. Try to find a dispenser who will offer you a trial period of at least 30 days. That way you can test it out in as wide a range of settings as possible to make sure it will be of some benefit.

The RNID runs a specialist helpline for people with tinnitus. The charity the British Tinnitus Association (contact details on page 273) also offers advice, leaflets and support.

Hearing dogs

As with guide dogs for people with sight loss, 'hearing dogs' are provided by charities. The main charity involved is Hearing Dogs for Deaf People. The dogs help people with no or little hearing by touching the person with a paw to alert them to household sounds such as telephone, doorbell and alarm clock as well as public fire alarms and bomb alerts. Sometimes they are also called 'assistance dogs'.

It is up to the charity whether it thinks you would be suited to a hearing dog. If you have a hearing dog, under the Disability Discrimination Act 1995 you should be able to take it with you into hotels, restaurants and shops – just as with a guide dog for a blind person. There may be some exceptions, though, if there is a good reason why a dog should not be accepted – such as areas where food is being prepared. If you have a registered assistance dog and need to use a taxi, you have a right to expect licensed taxi cabs (black cabs) and private minicabs to accept you as a fare, under the Disability Discrimination Act 1995. A taxi driver or minicab driver can refuse to carry a registered guide dog only if the driver has a medical exemption certificate issued by the licensing authority. The driver must display the exemption certificate at all times.

For further information, contact Hearing Dogs for Deaf People (details on page 279).

You may also want to contact the charity Sign Community (details on page 285) to find out about the services they offer to deaf people. Or the charity Hearing Concern may be of interest. They offer volunteer-led hearing clubs (contact details on page 279).

British Sign Language

There are various courses available to people who would like to learn to 'speak' British Sign Language (BSL). Your local education authority (LEA) may run day or evening classes. Social services may be involved with running BSL classes for people who have recently lost some or all of their hearing. There may also be lip-reading courses available. Contact your local council. RNID may also have further suggestions.

Typetalk and SignTalk

Typetalk is a service that supports people with hearing or speech difficulties to communicate with hearing people. It is run by the Royal National Institute for Deaf People (RNID) and funded by British Telecom (BT).

People with hearing or speech problems can use a special telephone – a textphone – to 'talk' to other people and organisations. Typetalk provides a link between the two – a Typetalk operator. The operator reads out loud to the hearing person the words typed by the textphone user. As the hearing person replies, the Typetalk operator types what is said for the user to read the response on the textphone display panel.

To find out more about Typetalk and how to join, free, contact RNID Typetalk (details under Royal National Institute for Deaf People, page 284).

Some older people also find that sending and receiving text messages via a mobile telephone and using email are useful ways of communicating with both hearing and hard-of-hearing or deaf people.

SignTalk is another service run by the RNID. This is a video relay service that uses a personal computer with a webcam (a camera used to broadcast over the Internet) to link together someone who uses British Sign Language with a hearing person using a voice phone (not a textphone). They communicate through a BSL interpreter.

Because the interpreter and the BSL signer can see each other over the video (webcam) link, the interpreter can then 'translate' BSL into the spoken word for the hearing person on the telephone. SignTalk is currently available Monday through Friday, 9am to 5pm. Contact the RNID for further details.

COCHLEAR IMPLANTS

A cochlear implant is a device for people with severe to profound deafness for whom hearing aids do not help. It involves an operation to the middle ear, under general anaesthetic, carried out in a hospital ENT department. The implant system stimulates the auditory nerve, and helps people to gain awareness of environmental sounds, understand speech without lip-reading and perhaps to use the telephone. Whether a cochlear implant is right for you is up to your consultant. You may also want to contact the charity National Cochlear Implant Users Association (NCIUA; address on page 282) if you have or think you should have an implant.

Therapies, and Other Support

This chapter looks at a broad range of support from therapists, including physiotherapists, occupational therapists (OTs), music and arts therapists, speech and language therapists, dietitians and practitioners of complementary therapies. It describes how to access this type of support through the NHS, and whom else to approach.

It also explores buying these services privately, as well as looking at three aspects of the National Service Framework (NSF) for Older People:

- falls clinics and other falls services;
- stroke services;
- intermediate care.

Other types of support, such as wigs and wheelchairs from the NHS and help with costs, are also explored in this chapter.

Support for people with mental ill-health or distress is included in Chapter 8; bereavement counselling is discussed in Chapter 15.

TYPES OF THERAPY

There are lots of different types of therapy services provided by a range of therapists. We tend to think about therapeutic support in one of two ways:

- for physical ailments and problems – for example, physiotherapy or speech and language therapy;

- to support people with mental ill-health (such as counselling services and art therapy).

The word 'therapy' is sometimes also used to mean helping people feel better able to manage aspects of modern life, such as stress. This meaning is often used in connection with complementary therapies.

Many types of therapy cross over these two aspects. For example, helping someone with the practical skills of everyday life, such as being able to lift your arm to brush your hair after having had a stroke, can be very effective in improving how you feel about yourself and your life as well as helping you regain physical abilities.

Most therapists need to be registered with the Health Professions Council (HPC). These are:

- art, music and drama therapists
- biomedical scientists
- chiropodists and podiatrists
- clinical scientists
- dietitians
- occupational therapists
- operating department practitioners
- orthoptists
- paramedics
- physiotherapists
- prosthetists and orthotists
- radiographers
- speech and language therapists.

People who are not registered are not allowed to use these professional titles. To do so would be a criminal offence, for which they could be prosecuted. Registration under the Health Professions

Council is a relatively recent requirement and replaces previous state registration schemes. As a result, few therapists now use the term 'state registered' – so don't be concerned if the title of the therapist you see does not include those words. The important point to establish is that they are registered with the Health Professions Council (see page 278).

OCCUPATIONAL THERAPISTS (OTs)

The College of Occupational Therapists describes the role of OTs as enabling people to achieve health, well-being and life satisfaction through taking part in occupation. The type of 'occupation' varies from person to person but covers the usual daily tasks and activities that meet our need to look after ourselves and enjoy taking part in society.

In broad terms, there are three main ways that occupational therapists (OTs) work with older people:

- Advising people on how to manage on a practical basis in their own home; this can include using the stairs, lifting pots and pans in order to cook, or advice about having grabrails or a stairlift fitted.

- Helping people to look after themselves physically, such as re-learning how to wash their hair or to cook. (There is more about this later in the sections 'Intermediate care' and 'Stroke services'.)

- Giving support to people with mental health difficulties, helping them to take part in different hobbies and leisure interests or through reminiscence sessions (see also Chapter 8).

OTs can be employed either by the NHS or by the local authority social services department. Those with social services departments are often involved in work to adapt the homes of people with physical disabilities or ill-health to help them to continue living there for as long as possible. Such adaptations are often paid for through a means-tested system. This means you might be asked to pay something towards the cost of the work, based on your income and savings. There are several different systems, but if you are advised by an OT employed either by your local council or by the NHS that an adaptation will cost less than £1,000, this will be carried out free of charge. The advice from OTs is also free.

To find out more about help with housing adaptations, you can:

Contact your local Home Improvement Agency – sometimes called Care & Repair or Staying Put scheme (often run by a voluntary organisation but sometimes by a department in your local council).

Contact your local council's housing department.

OTs employed by NHS hospitals can advise you on whether you can safely leave hospital or if some adaptations might be needed at home before your return. They might also advise about equipment needed to help you, on either a temporary or a permanent basis. For example:

- a walking stick or frame;
- a wheelchair;
- hand-held items to help you to put on your shoes or to pull up stockings, tights or socks.

Equipment stores providing this type of support are run jointly by the NHS and local social services departments (see page 99).

Box 10. Getting to see an OT

Your route to an OT depends on the sort of help you are looking for.

If you want advice on adaptations to your home, this is most likely to be via your local council. You won't be asked to pay for the OT's visits or advice if they are employed by the council but in some areas there are long delays getting to see an OT this way.

This has been a problem for some years, due largely to a shortage of qualified OTs willing to take on these roles. As a result, some local councils have begun to use occupational therapy assistants

---

(OTAs) to advise people on more routine adaptations, such as handrails. They may also set up contracts with a voluntary organisation to provide and fix the rail, if this is needed, through Handyperson or similar schemes. Your local Age Concern should be able to tell you about arrangements in your area.

Older people with mental health problems are most likely to see an OT via their GP. They may do so as part of attending an NHS day hospital (see Chapter 8).

If you are in hospital, advice from an NHS-hospital OT will probably be sought on your behalf by the consultant in charge of your care. This could involve you and the OT going to your home on a short visit, to make sure that you will be able to manage things when you are discharged from hospital.

If no one suggests you should see an OT while you are in hospital, ask your consultant or the ward sister if this can be arranged, explaining why you think this is needed. (There is more information about coming out of hospital in Chapter 12.)

As with many services, there must be an appropriate reason for you to see an OT. Although you have the right to ask to see an OT, this does not mean that you will see one.

Private OTs

There may be some OTs working privately in your area. If you decide to see a private OT, you will have to pay them: make sure you know before your visit how much this will be. Remember that, to be able lawfully to call him- or herself an OT, the person must be registered as such with the Health Professions Council.

Bear in mind that, even if you see an OT privately for advice about housing adaptations, if you need to apply for a grant to pay for the work, it may still be necessary for the council's own OT to visit you – so this won't necessarily speed things up for you. It's also very unlikely that you'll be able to claim the cost of seeing an OT privately (for this or other reasons) from either the NHS or your council.

ART, MUSIC AND DRAMA THERAPY

Art, music and drama therapists should be registered under the Health Professions Council, regardless of whether they are employed by the NHS or run their own private practices or work within charities. Registered professionals can also use the term 'art psychotherapist'.

These three therapies use different approaches to encourage people to express their feelings and emotions through music or drama or art such as drawing and painting. Each therapy has its own separate training.

Although there are art therapists, music therapists and drama therapists employed in the NHS, provision of this kind of support is quite patchy across England. You would need to be referred by either your GP or a consultant to receive this through the NHS. Some charities offer these therapies to older people who already receive other services from them. For example, some charities that run nursing homes for older people with profound levels of dementia or other mental disability or ill-health may offer regular music therapy sessions to their residents. But deciding to do this is up to the charity concerned. (For more information, see also Chapters 8 and 13.)

SPEECH AND LANGUAGE THERAPISTS

Speech and language therapists (SLTs) specialise in communication disorders or difficulties. These disorders might arise because of a stroke, for example, or a head injury or difficulties such as:

- Parkinson's disease, multiple sclerosis (MS), motor neurone disease (MND), dementia;
- cancer of the head, neck or throat;
- mental health difficulties;
- stammering;
- hearing problems.

Speech and language therapists diagnose and assess speech and language problems, and work with people to increase their communication abilities to the maximum possible. They also work with people who have difficulties in swallowing and eating and drinking. This can particularly affect people who have had a stroke (see also 'Stroke services', page 90).

Speech and language therapists often work for the NHS in hospitals, running in-patient and out-patient services. They can also provide NHS support in community settings, such as health centres or people's own homes. It very much depends on the individual's need and on local arrangements.

Speech and language therapists are often also involved with intermediate care services, alongside OTs. You will see an NHS speech and language therapist by being referred to them:

- by your GP;
- by a hospital consultant;
- through the local intermediate care arrangements.

Professional speech and language therapists must be registered with the Health Professions Council.

Some speech and language therapists work privately. As with other services, if you arrange this privately you must be prepared to pay the amount set by the therapist. There is no 'national rate' for private therapy, so the amount can vary from one professional to another.

PHYSIOTHERAPY

Physiotherapists (physios) use a range of techniques to restore or improve movement of the body. They treat common problems such as back pain and muscle sprain but can also help people to deal with incontinence, osteoporosis and depression.

Your GP is the person most likely to refer you to an NHS physiotherapist if he or she thinks this is necessary. Again, you have the right to ask for a referral.

Physiotherapists can run their own private practices and clinics – again, you would have to pay for treatment you arrange privately. Physiotherapists must also register with the Health Professions Council.

DIETITIANS

Registered dietitians (RDs) provide advice about nutrition and health. This includes advice about what food to eat, as well as dealing with food-related problems such as allergies and ill-health. They may also work closely with speech and language therapists; for example, if patients are finding it difficult to swallow food or liquids. Many dietitians work in the NHS but there are some who practice privately. Only those who are registered with the Health Professions Council are legally allowed to call themselves a 'dietitian'.

COMPLEMENTARY THERAPIES

There is an enormous range of complementary therapies. This section looks at five of the most commonly found therapies:

- acupuncture
- osteopathy
- chiropractic
- reflexology
- homeopathy.

Acupuncture

Acupuncture is a form of traditional Chinese medicine that can trace its origins back more than 2,000 years. It involves inserting very fine single-use needles into points around the body that in acupuncture relate to the particular physical or mental symptoms being described. There are different methods of working. Some practitioners leave the needles in for several minutes before they are removed, whilst others remove the needle immediately.

People seek acupuncture for many different reasons, including pain control, to help with the side effects of chemotherapy, and for insomnia and depression.

There is currently no formal system to register acupuncturists, although there are plans to do so in the future. In the meantime, many acupuncturists are members of the British Acupuncture Council, for which they must have reached particular standards of professional education.

Some NHS doctors and physiotherapists are also trained in particular acupuncture techniques.

Osteopathy

Most patients pay privately for osteopathy but some GPs will and do make NHS referrals. Osteopaths must be registered by law with the General Osteopathic Council (GOsC). The GOsC keeps a Statutory Register of those who are allowed to practise osteopathy.

Osteopaths diagnose and treat problems to do with muscles, joints, ligaments and nerves. They do this by gently manipulating the damaged part of the body. They can also advise on ways to prevent problems from happening again.

Chiropractic

Chiropractors must be registered with the General Chiropractic Council (GCC). Chiropractic is concerned with the diagnosis and treatment of 'mechanical' problems with the musculoskeletal system – such as lower back pain. The aim is to manipulate the affected part of the body so that it will work normally again.

Although your GP may suggest that a chiropractor might help you, there is no guarantee that this will be funded by the NHS. It is much more likely that you will be asked to pay privately.

Reflexology

Reflexology is based on the idea that different parts of the foot reflect the tension and congestion being experienced by other parts of the body. Reflexologists concentrate on the corresponding area of the foot, gently applying pressure with their hands. Some reflexologists also use this approach on the hand.

There are plans to regulate reflexologists. At present there are National Occupational Standards for reflexology that have been developed by Skills for Health, which is a skills sector council that is licensed by the Department for Education and Science and is a part of the NHS.

Homeopathy

Homeopathy is an unusual complementary treatment in that there are five NHS homeopathic hospitals in the UK. Your GP would need to refer you to one of these hospitals. Treatment is mostly used to treat chronic (long-term) conditions such as asthma, and involves people taking much-diluted doses of plant and mineral extracts. The idea behind homeopathy is that 'like cures like'. Very small and diluted doses of the substance causing the symptoms of poor health are taken by mouth, to stimulate the body to build its own defences.

Homeopathic products are widely available in health food stores and other outlets. They are regulated under the Medicines for Human Use (National Rules for Homeopathic Products) Regulations 2006, which came into effect on 1 September 2006.

Box 11. Paying privately

If you are paying privately and have a private medical insurance scheme, or a 'cash back' treatment plan, check whether this covers contributions towards physiotherapy or any of the other therapies or support discussed in this chapter. If so, you may be able to use these sums towards the costs of buying this support privately.

If you do not have this kind of plan, make sure you know how much the therapist will charge before you agree to make the appointment.

FALLS SERVICES

The NHS has to provide 'falls clinics' (or services), under Standard Six of the National Service Framework (NSF) for Older People. The two main aims in this standard are:

- to reduce the number of falls that result in serious injury;
- to make sure that anyone who does fall receives effective treatment and rehabilitation.

Falls in older age are a major cause of disability. They also result in a large number of deaths each year among older people. Injuries from falls, such as a fractured hip, can seriously reduce an individual's independence and, in some cases, may result in their having to move into a care home far sooner than if they had not fallen. Reducing the number of falls, and of injuries from falls, has been a major government target for some years.

People fall for lots of reasons, including:

- poor eyesight (see Chapter 5);
- rushing to the toilet because of incontinence (see Chapter 3);
- dementia (see Chapter 8);
- loss of leg (muscle) strength and ability to balance;
- side effects of some medication.

Since April 2005, every Primary Care Trust must offer a falls service across local health and social care systems (sometimes called an 'integrated service'). This is provided free of charge to you. The actual services provided may vary from area to area but they typically offer two things. The first is support to help prevent falls. This might include:

- exercise classes to help people improve their balance and strength;
- advice from chiropodists on suitable footwear;
- information packs;

- talks and demonstrations on how to reduce your risk of falling at home and when out and about.

The second element of a falls service is to provide support for people who have already fallen and, because of the increased risk, may fall again. Examples include providing hip protectors (these go over the top of underwear and look a little like very padded pants) for older people most at risk of falls (such as those living in care homes offering nursing) and specialist hospital services where people receive intensive occupational and physiotherapy support following surgery on fractured hips (fractured neck of femur). You may find that there may be a charge for items such as hip protectors; the National Institute for Health and Clinical Excellence (NICE) has decided not to recommend that the NHS provide hip protectors because of insufficient evidence as to the benefit of these items.

The criteria for deciding who can have this support are set by each Primary Care Trust, depending on how it judges what should be organised locally in order to meet the national target of reducing falls. For example, in one area, older people who have attended the local hospital A&E department because of a fall are referred by hospital staff to their local falls-prevention service. In another area, older people who have fallen in the last year can refer themselves to a local falls clinic so that they can be assessed on the risk that they might fall again, and receive support and advice as needed. Your Primary Care Trust may offer something quite different.

In some areas, services to help prevent falls are linked with broader work to promote older people's overall health (see Chapter 20).

To find out more about falls services in your area:

- *ask your GP (Chapter 3);*
- *contact NHS Direct (Chapter 2);*
- *contact your local Patient Advice and Liaison Service (PALS) at the Primary Care Trust (PCT);*
- *ask your local Age Concern (you can find it by looking in your telephone book, searching on Age Concern's website*

or telephoning Age Concern's Information Line – contact details on page 271).

■ *There are two other charities you can contact for more information. Help the Aged (page 279) has a range of leaflets and other information about preventing falls, and runs the National Preventing Falls programme. The National Osteoporosis Society (page 283) also has a variety of advice and information available on osteoporosis, one of the particular risk elements for falling.*

INTERMEDIATE CARE

'Intermediate care' is a term used to describe services that provide a structured, time-limited period of rehabilitation to help people recover as much independence as possible. Typically, this offers you a 'bridge' of support between your being in hospital and going home or moving to a care home. Intermediate care is provided under Standard Three of the National Service Framework for Older People. The aim is to:

■ provide integrated services to promote faster recovery from illness;

■ prevent unnecessary hospital admissions;

■ support timely discharge from hospital;

■ maximise independent living;

■ prevent premature or unnecessary admission to long-term residential care.

In recent years, the NHS and local councils have been given money to invest in intermediate care services. But the services are not available for everyone – to be eligible, you have to meet the local criteria.

Intermediate care includes support provided to people in their own homes as well as actual 'intermediate care beds' where people might stay for short periods of time (some beds are in hospital settings, others are in care homes or sheltered housing schemes).

Typically, intermediate care provides intensive occupational therapy, physiotherapy, speech and language therapy, and other practical support and advice – including rebuilding people's confidence. It can involve a wide range of professionals across health and social services, as well as from the private and voluntary sectors. It is given for a maximum of six weeks for each person, and is free.

Local arrangements for accessing intermediate care services vary. This means you could be referred to it by your GP, by a hospital consultant or another NHS professional or by someone working for social services – perhaps a social worker or care manager. Most people are referred following a stay in hospital or arrival at a hospital A&E department after a fall or other emergency. In some areas, intermediate care teams work with ambulance paramedics to help avoid older people being taken to hospital unnecessarily, by quickly setting up appropriate support at home.

Intermediate care services have tended to focus on people's physical needs and home environment, but new approaches are being developed to support people's mental health as well. In particular, in some areas there are now services for older people with dementia, to help reduce the chances of their needing to go into hospital.

STROKE SERVICES

Standard Five of the National Service Framework for Older People aims to reduce the number of people who have a stroke and to make sure that those who have had a stroke have prompt access to integrated stroke care services. This means that people who are thought to have had a stroke:

- can get this diagnosed, using any necessary equipment such as a CT scan;
- are treated appropriately by a specialist stroke service;
- subsequently take part in a multi-disciplinary programme of secondary prevention and rehabilitation (with any unpaid, informal or family carers).

Since April 2004, you have the right to expect that every GP practice:

- identifies and treats patients who are at risk of having a stroke;
- follows the local agreements for the rapid referral and management of the care of people with transient ischaemic attack (TIA, a sort of mini-stroke);
- has identified patients who have had a stroke and is treating them in line with local agreements;
- has established 'clinical audit systems' for stroke, to identify any patterns in stroke patients and their treatment needs.

In broad terms, the 'local agreement' means what the specialist stroke services and GPs in an area have agreed to do for patients in primary care.

You also have the right to expect every NHS general hospital caring for people with stroke to have a specialised stroke service, and to be referred to this if you are admitted to hospital following a stroke or have a stroke while in hospital. (See also Chapter 11.)

COMPLAINTS

Any complaint about the NHS – whether about a service it provides or because it's not providing a service you think is needed – can be made through the NHS complaints system. You can also complain about individual NHS staff through this route. This is explained in Chapter 16.

OTHER SUPPORT

As well as help from therapists, the NHS provides a range of other support.

Wigs and support stockings

The NHS provides wigs and fabric supports to some patients. 'Fabric supports' means something that helps to support your spine or abdomen, or an item such as a surgical bra. You might need a wig if you experience hair loss as a result of illness – for example, following treatment for cancer.

The NHS provides these free if you are in hospital as an in-patient. If you are an out-patient (going to an NHS clinic for appointments), you may be asked to pay a prescription charge for these items. In this case, you may be entitled to reduced charge or a free item, depending on your income. There is no charge if you are exempt because you receive a war pension.

There is more about help with these costs in the free leaflet HC11 *Help with health costs,* published by the Department of Health. You can get copies at a post office, or from the staff at the hospital or clinic. See also page 275.

Home oxygen

Some people with conditions such as severe emphysema will need to have a supply of oxygen at home, to help them breathe, prescribed for them by a hospital specialist. This is provided free of charge by the NHS.

Oxygen cylinders used to be supplied by local pharmacists, but since 1 February 2006 supplies have been handled by a specialist oxygen supply company. This service is still part of the NHS, and there is no charge to patients. Although GPs can still prescribe oxygen for short-term needs, if you have ongoing problems you may find that you are seen instead by a hospital specialist. The specialist will write out an NHS prescription setting out your needs. These details will be sent to the oxygen supply company for your area. This company will then contact you, and decide on the range of equipment needed to support you, including types of cylinders that you can take with you if you want to go out somewhere (sometimes this is called 'ambulatory oxygen').

The British Lung Foundation (contact details on page 272) has information about different lung diseases, and the help available.

HELP WITH **NHS** CHARGES

Although many NHS services are free to people aged 60 or over, there are some charges that apply to:

- dentistry;
- spectacles and contact lenses;
- travel to and from hospital;
- wigs and other 'support' items.

If you are on a low income, however, you may not have to pay anything – or you may only have to pay a reduced charge for these services. The Department of Health has a freephone advice line, giving information on NHS charges (see page 275).

NHS dentistry

You do not have to pay for NHS dental treatment if you or your partner (someone whom you are married to or live with as if married) receives:

- Pension Credit, guarantee credit;
- Pension Credit, guarantee credit with savings credit.

Pension Credit is a system of state financial support for people over the state pension age. Whether you qualify depends on your income from all sources (including your state pension) plus any savings you have. You are not eligible for exemption from NHS dental charges if you are over the age of 65 and receive just the savings credit element of Pension Credit (that is, you do not also get the guarantee credit element), but you may still be able to claim some help on the grounds of low income – see 'NHS Low Income Scheme' on page 97.

Anyone under the age of 60 who receives Income Support (IS) or income-based Jobseekers Allowance (JSA IB) is entitled to free NHS dental treatment.

If you qualify for free dental care through any of these routes, show the surgery (either the receptionist or the dentist) your 'award notice' each time you start a new course of NHS treatment. Your award notice is the letter you received from either the Pension Service or the JobCentre Plus office, saying that you receive the relevant benefit.

You may be eligible for some help with dental costs on the grounds of low income, via the NHS Low Income Scheme (see page 97). As well as being eligible on the grounds of low income, you may qualify for help if you receive a war disablement pension and you need dental treatment because of the disability for which that pension was awarded.

Help with the costs of glasses and contact lenses
If you receive the 'guarantee credit' component of Pension Credit, you will be eligible for vouchers towards the cost of glasses or contact lenses, if it is decided you need these following your NHS eye test.

The optometrist who carried out the NHS eye test will write a prescription that shows the type of lenses you need. You can take a copy of this prescription away with you.

If you are eligible for help towards the cost of glasses, the optometrist will also give you an optical voucher. If you need a pair of glasses for reading and another for distance, you will be given two vouchers. Your optometrist may ask you to fill in form GOS3 for this voucher, at the time of your appointment.

The value of the voucher varies, depending on the type of lenses you need. The stronger the lenses, the more the voucher will be worth. Vouchers can be used towards the cost of single-vision, bifocal, varifocal or contact lenses.

If you have an HC2 certificate under the NHS Low Income Scheme (see page 97), you will be entitled to the full value of the voucher for your type of lens. However, if the glasses you want cost more than the value of the voucher, you will be expected to pay the difference yourself.

If you have an HC3 certificate, this will tell you the maximum amount you should contribute towards the cost of your glasses. For example, if the certificate says you should contribute £22 and the glasses you want cost £46.50, your voucher will give you £24.50 towards the cost of your glasses.

If you have lost or damaged your glasses or contact lenses as a result of an illness, and you have an HC2 or HC3 certificate, ask your dispensing optician if you can get help towards the cost of replacement or repair. They will give you form GOS4, which will explain what to do. You should note that there is no help available towards the costs resulting from general wear and tear.

Help with the cost of wigs and support items
Wigs and support items are free to you if:

- you are a hospital in-patient;
- you or your partner receive the guarantee credit element of Pension Credit;
- you are a war pensioner, the wig or fabric support is needed because of your war disablement and you have a war pension exemption certificate.

As outlined on page 92, if you are an out-patient (going to an NHS clinic for appointments), you may be asked to pay a prescription charge for these items. If you have a low income, you may be entitled to pay a reduced charge or even pay nothing through the NHS Low Income Scheme – but you must apply for this help (page 97).

Even if you are not entitled to a free wig, you can still get one from the hospital at a subsidised rate. In this case, hospital staff will give you a form to give to your wig supplier to offset the cost. The procedure is explained in the Department of Health leaflet HC12 *NHS charges and optical voucher values.*

You may prefer to choose a wig from a hairdresser or wig supplier, although this can be a bit more expensive. VAT (Value Added Tax) does not have to be paid on wigs when hair loss is caused by cancer treatment. You will need to fill in a VAT form, which most shops will give you, when you buy the wig. The tax cannot be claimed back at a later date.

Help with the costs of travel to hospital

If you are a war pensioner, the cost of travel to an NHS hospital for treatment overseen by a consultant is free if the treatment you are having is for the condition or disability for which you receive this pension. There are also special arrangements for people living on the Isles of Scilly, which are explained in the Department of Health leaflet HC12 *NHS charges and optical voucher values.* Otherwise, you will need to apply for help through the NHS Low Income Scheme (see page 97).

If you have an HC2 or HC3 certificate, the hospital is responsible for reimbursing your relevant travel costs. You should always speak to the hospital staff before travelling if you have questions about the help you may receive.

If you need someone to travel with you for medical reasons, a doctor or other appropriate health professional will have to agree that this is the case before your companion's travel expenses will be paid.

You must use the cheapest means available at the time you need to travel. The hospital decides what is necessary – this tends to be either public transport or a private car (this cost is then based on fuel used) or voluntary car schemes. Taxis are an exception, so if using a taxi is your only option, discuss this with the hospital before you travel, to make sure that they agree about this cost. You can also speak with hospital staff if it would be difficult for you to pay for your transport and then claim it back. They can consider sending payment in advance.

Under the NHS Low Income Scheme, the HC2 certificate will entitle you to a full refund of reasonable costs. An HC3 certificate will show

how much you should contribute towards transport costs each time you need to go to the hospital.

There is no help towards the cost of travel to visit someone in hospital.

NHS Low Income Scheme

You apply to the NHS Low Income Scheme by filling in and sending off form HC1. Your dentist or optometrist may have copies of this form, or you can obtain it from your local Pension Service office (this is your local social security office – find it in your telephone book).

For copies of leaflets, you can also telephone (free) the Department of Health's Health literature line on 0800 555 777. The leaflets to ask for are:

- *HC1* Help with health costs – *this is the claim form you will need to fill in.*
- *HC5 – this is the claim form you must complete if you are seeking a refund.*
- *HC11* Help with health costs – *this leaflet explains whether you are eligible to claim.*
- *HC11 (LP) – this is a large-print version of the HC11 leaflet.*

If you live in a care home and receive financial support from your local social services department to pay for this, you will need to fill in a different form – HC1 (SC). If you live in a care home but pay for this in full yourself, you may be eligible for help under the NHS Low Income Scheme, depending on how much savings and income you have. You should note that you will not be eligible for this help if you live permanently in a care home and have savings above £21,000.

The form explains what counts as a low income; it also tells you what you need to provide in the way of information to support your claim, and where to send the form once you have filled it in. If you qualify for help, you will be sent one or other of two certificates:

- Certificate HC2, which entitles you to full help with costs such as NHS dental charges and optical lenses (for spectacles or contact lenses); or

- Certificate HC3, which entitles you to some help. The certificate you receive will tell you the maximum amount you will have to pay, which will also depend on the cost of the treatment. For example, if your certificate says you must pay for the first £30 of any dental treatment and the treatment comes under Band 2 of the dental charges and so costs £43.60, you will pay £30 and the dentist will claim the remaining £13.60 from the Low Income Scheme via the Primary Care Trust.

Ideally, you should apply before your current course of treatment comes to an end. But it is possible to claim for a refund for NHS charges you have paid recently – see below.

If you are aged 60 or over, your certificate usually lasts for five years. If you have a current certificate, take this with you when you go to the dentist, for new glasses or to hospital. Remember to apply for a new certificate – it is not renewed automatically. Do this by completing another claim form (HC1) four weeks before your current certificate comes to an end (remember that you will need a different version of the form if you are in a care home).

Refunds of NHS charges

You may be able to claim a refund for NHS charges you have paid in the past three months. You might be eligible because:

- You are on a low income – but you have not yet applied for a certificate.

- You are exempt from NHS charges but did not tell the dentist or dispensing optician at the time (perhaps because you did not realise that you were exempt).

- You did not provide proof as needed by the dental surgery, hospital or dispensing optician's (eg you did not take with you your certificate or your letter confirming that you receive the guarantee part of Pension Credit).

If you have a valid certificate but left it at home, the dentist or dispending optician is entitled to ask you to pay the full relevant NHS charges there and then. This is because you must show your entitlement at the time of the treatment or when buying the spectacles or arriving at hospital for treatment, not afterwards. In this situation, it is up to you to apply for a refund.

You make a claim for a refund on form HC5. This is available from your local post office or Pension Service office (you could also ask about it at your dentist's surgery or at the optician's).

If you do not hold a valid certificate, you will need to complete form HC5 and form HC1 described above. You will also need to send in your receipt from the dentist or dispensing optician – so make sure you always keep these. And you need to apply within three months of paying the charge.

JOINT EQUIPMENT STORES

Equipment is one of the areas where the NHS and local social services departments have to work closely. There will be a Joint Equipment Store in your part of England, run jointly by the local Primary Care Trust and local social services department. These are sometimes called Integrated Equipment Stores.

You do not have to pay for any free-standing equipment from this 'store'. Minor adaptations such as grabrails or a handrail to the stairs are also free up to a maximum cost of £1,000 (this amount includes any costs to fix equipment in place). Equipment that might be provided includes:

- pressure-relief mattress;
- commode;
- shower chair;
- raised toilet seat;
- equipment for deaf or hard-of-hearing people (eg a telephone with a flashing light).

You may have to be assessed by either an occupational therapist or a physiotherapist before you can receive equipment from the Joint Equipment Store. Equipment can also be requested by district nurses and the local continence service.

If you need help with larger adaptations to your home, such as a walk-in/wheel-in shower, you may be asked to pay towards the cost. There are various forms of financial support available from your local council (not the NHS).

For more information, contact Age Concern's Information Line (details on page 271).

If you live in a care home – particularly in a care home offering nursing care – the home will be expected to provide equipment for basic handling, lifting and mobility. But you have the same rights to equipment and aids as if you were still living in your own home. If you need specific items that would not be suitable for (or are not needed by) other residents, these may be lent to you by the local Joint Equipment Stores. You could ask the care home manager to get in touch with the equipment store on your behalf.

Wheelchairs and walking frames

If you have a long-term need for a wheelchair, including an electrically powered wheelchair, the NHS will provide this on what is in effect a long-term loan basis. This means that the wheelchair doesn't belong to you – the NHS will expect it to be returned when it is no longer used, even if it was specially designed just for you. Your GP or a hospital consultant can refer you to be assessed by the local NHS service for a wheelchair. If it is agreed that you should have an NHS wheelchair, the NHS will be responsible for its repairs and maintenance (provided this is not needed because the wheelchair has been misused or not looked after properly).

Sometimes, instead of the NHS providing you with a wheelchair, it will offer you wheelchair vouchers. These vouchers are worth the equivalent of a standard chair, and you can put this towards the cost of a wheelchair that costs more than the NHS will provide free of charge. You can do this through the NHS or use the voucher with a private wheelchair company.

If you need a wheelchair for a short time, the NHS may lend you one. If not, organisations such as local British Red Cross branches and Age Concerns can sometimes lend wheelchairs on a short-term basis (see pages 273 and 271 for contact details).

In some parts of the country there is a long wait for the NHS wheelchair service. If this affects you, you could contact your local Patient Advice and Liaison Service (PALS) for help. The Limbless Association also has information for people who need to use a wheelchair (see page 280 for contact details).

You may also find a Shopmobility scheme near you. The schemes lend manual and powered wheelchairs, and powered scooters, to people who need these in order to be mobile around their town.

To get walking aids such as a frame or a stick from the NHS, you will first be assessed by a physiotherapist (see page 83). As well as assessing what you need, the physiotherapist will be able to show you how to use the equipment safely.

8

Mental Health

This chapter considers commonly experienced mental ill-health – permanent, temporary and fluctuating conditions such as dementia, depression and schizophrenia. It looks at how a diagnosis is made, your rights to drug treatments, access to support, compulsory treatments and after-care services. It also describes decision-making in situations where a person lacks the 'mental capacity' to decide for him- or herself, and safeguards for someone who is detained in hospital.

Some people find the phrase 'mental health' a difficult one to use. This may be because of concerns about the stigma that can be attached to these types of illnesses and disabilities. Others feel that the word 'mental' is too often used as an insult or that it applies only to the tiny number of people in the UK who might behave violently as a result of their illness. But within the NHS 'mental health' is used widely to describe services and support for people with all these types of illnesses and disabilities.

MENTAL ILL-HEALTH

There is a wide range of types of mental ill-health. Those most commonly connected with older age include dementia and depression. But many people under the age of 60 are also depressed, and some may develop particular types of dementia at younger ages.

Schizophrenia, for example, tends to develop in younger people but in some people it does not appear until older age.

Mental health problems can be:

- temporary, or
- permanent, or
- fluctuating.

An example of a temporary problem might be anxiety caused as a side effect of medication. A permanent problem could include dementia. Depression is an example of a condition that may fluctuate – that is, it may change from one day to the next.

Three of the more familiar mental health problems – dementia, depression and schizophrenia – are explored below. But there are many other examples of poor mental health:

- alcoholism
- anxiety
- delusions.

DEPRESSION

The term 'depression' is often used to describe a huge range of feelings, from feeling low to having a severe problem that interferes with everyday life. But depression is not the same thing as being unhappy. People with severe depression may experience very low moods and loss of any interest and pleasure in life, as well as feeling worthless or guilty.

Although depression can affect anyone, older people are more likely to be affected than any other age group. There are many reasons for this, including being widowed or divorced, increased physical difficulties, feeling isolated, side effects from medication, and neurobiological (the workings of the brain) changes to do with getting older. Even retiring from paid work can, for some people, trigger a period of depression.

Diagnosis

As with any illness, getting a diagnosis is the first step. It can be difficult to diagnose depression if it occurs alongside other illnesses and disabilities such as dementia (see below), stroke, cancer or other physical problems. But this doesn't mean it should go undetected. If you (or someone you know) are becoming withdrawn or feel very unhappy, lack energy or have lost interest in everyday life, or are experiencing some other change in your behaviour or attitude towards life, this should all be explained in a visit to the GP.

If you are feeling desperate to the point of thinking about suicide and want help, it is really important that you explain how badly you are feeling. You could:

- Telephone NHS Direct – if needed, they will call an ambulance for you, to take you to hospital.

- Telephone your GP or go to the surgery – explain how you are feeling and ask to speak to a doctor straight away. If you do not feel well enough to get to the surgery, telephone and ask for a doctor to visit you at home as a matter of urgency.

- Telephone the emergency services on 999, tell them how you feel and ask for an ambulance.

- Go to the nearest hospital A&E department.

If you don't want any help from the NHS at this time, you could contact the charity Samaritans. They will talk to you in confidence, which means that what you say stays private, and you won't have to tell them your name or where you live if you don't want to.

The Samaritans also has over 200 local groups, many of which are open to visitors who need to talk to someone in person. You don't need to be feeling suicidal to contact Samaritans. They can offer support to people in many different circumstances. You can also write to the Samaritans if you are in a crisis and need to write about how this feels. If you give a return address, your letter will be answered. And you can get in touch with them by email. (See page 284 for contact details.)

You could also contact other help lines – such as SANELINE, which is run by the charity SANE (see page 284 for contact details).

Other organisations also offer support to people with mental ill-health. For example, the Mental Health Foundation has several factsheets about different mental illnesses, including depression. You may also want to contact the organisation Depression Alliance, which offers information and advice for people with depression, as well as other support. (Contact details are on pages 281 and 276.)

Treatment and support

There are lots of different approaches that can help with depression but they won't all help everyone. Even though one of the difficulties for someone with depression is that it can be very hard to find the energy or interest to try different options, it is worth persevering to find what will help you. For some people this will be medication (perhaps antidepressants; the National Institute for Health and Clinical Excellence has issued guidance on the use of some antidepressants as a treatment for depression), whilst for others it will be a combination of changes to their diet, physical exercise (such as a regular walk or yoga exercises) and having something meaningful to do – perhaps activities organised by an occupational therapist, if the depression is more severe (see below).

Some people find what are often called 'the talking therapies' very helpful. These include particular approaches such as cognitive behavioural therapy (CBT). This involves your seeing a counsellor trained to use techniques to help you learn about and change your approach to situations in your life. Usually, you meet with the counsellor for fixed appointments, perhaps for half an hour or an hour each time, once a week for a period of several weeks. Sometimes CBT sessions (or other therapeutic approaches) are available on the NHS – ask your GP what is available locally and whether this would be helpful for you. The Government has announced plans to increase the number of trained counsellors available for people. Chapter 15 has information about counselling for people who have been bereaved.

You could also look into paying privately for therapy (Box 12).

Box 12. Private therapy

There are many different approaches to psychological therapy, sometimes also called psychotherapy. You need to find the one that you feel is most suited to you. You should also find a counsellor or psychotherapist you feel comfortable with. Counsellors and therapists should be able to give you some information about the approach they use. You can always book one session to start with, to get a feel for the approach and the person. A good counsellor will understand if, after this first session, you decide that their style or their approach is not right for you.

First sessions often last for longer than subsequent, or later, sessions. This is because the therapist needs to start by hearing from you the reasons why you have come to see them. If there is a lot to explain, this may take some time.

It's not unusual for a first session to be one hour, or an hour and a half, long. The next sessions tend to be shorter, perhaps half an hour or an hour in length. They may take place once a week, or more or less frequently – this will be something for you and your therapist to discuss.

Therapists and counsellors charge different amounts. Some offer a reduced rate if you are on a low income but it is up to each professional to decide whether to do this. You and the therapist will agree how many times you should see them. Bear in mind that, as with many forms of help, good therapists will not suggest that you keep seeing them indefinitely. They will want to work with you so that you reach a point where their help is no longer needed, or perhaps needed only very occasionally.

Don't be afraid to tell the therapist if you need to limit the number of sessions because of the cost. If he or she knows you can afford only a small number of sessions, together you can work out how best to use that time.

You may well reach a point where you no longer feel the need to see the therapist. But if something happens to change that

continued over

Box 12 continued

– perhaps another period of depressions arises – and you feel that going back to the therapist would help you, get in touch and ask about making another appointment. You should not feel that you have failed if you need help at some later stage – after all, you don't feel you've failed if you are physically ill more than once and need to see your GP each time.

Your GP may be able to suggest a therapist or counsellor you could approach. Or contact an organisation such as the British Association for Counselling and Psychotherapy (BACP; details on page 272), which will help you find a trained therapist in your area.

In some areas, the NHS, charities and other not-for-profit organisations work together to provide different types of support for people with depression. Examples include local walking groups, taking part in the Green Gyms run by the British Trust for Conservation Volunteers (BTCV; contact details on page 273), or becoming a volunteer, or taking part in a local Time Banks UK initiative. Time Banks work by people helping each other in whatever way is possible and needed (contact details on page 286).

You can also find out about other volunteering opportunities from your local Age Concern.

Whether or not these types of support are available or suitable for you, your GP may refer you for:

- assessment by a consultant;
- out-patient clinic;
- day care;
- hospital stay;
- support from a community mental health nurse (formerly called community psychiatric nurse, or CPN).

These types of support would most probably be provided through your local NHS psychiatric services (Box 13), although some social services departments and voluntary organisations offer day services for older people with depression and other mental health problems.

Box 13. NHS psychiatric services

Psychiatry is a branch of medicine. It looks at disorders to do with people's behaviour and emotions, whether or not these are thought to be due to a particular disease of the brain. Within the service, you may find:

- Psychiatrists – doctors who diagnose and treat a wide range of mental health difficulties.

- Old age psychiatrists (psychogeriatricians) – doctors who have particular knowledge of older people's mental health problems.

You may also come across geriatricians, doctors who specialise in the physical illnesses and disabilities of older age; or neurologists, doctors who have expertise in disorders of the brain and the nervous system.

There are specialist hospitals that offer particular treatment and care for people with mental ill-health. These are usually called psychiatric hospitals.

Depression and dementia

The relationship between dementia and depression is quite complex. The symptoms of dementia and depression – including withdrawal from social activities and general apathy – are very similar. As a result, someone who is severely depressed may be misdiagnosed as having dementia. On the other hand, a person with dementia may also become depressed.

Just as it is possible to have more than one physical illness or disability (for example, to have diabetes and arthritis), so it is possible to have more than one mental health problem. In these situations it can be important to make sure that medication to treat one illness does not, because of any side effects, make worse any other mental health illnesses. Your GP or pharmacist should be able to advise about this.

DEMENTIA

The term 'dementia' describes more than 100 different brain disorders that result in a loss of brain function and which usually get worse over time. The most common types of dementia are:

- Alzheimer's disease;
- vascular dementia (resulting from brain damage caused by tiny strokes);
- Lewy body dementia (caused by abnormal collections of protein, called Lewy bodies, in the brain's nerve cells).

Typical symptoms include confusion, memory loss (especially short-term memory) and problems with speech and understanding. People may become agitated, or find it difficult to go about their usual daily business.

Having any of these symptoms does not necessarily mean you have dementia, however. For example, memory loss can also be a symptom of depression or stress. Similar symptoms can also arise as a result of problems with your thyroid or because of vitamin deficiencies.

Diagnosis

Getting a diagnosis is very important. You shouldn't be tempted to diagnose yourself or to assume that the confusion of someone you know must be because of dementia.

The first thing to do is see your GP and explain what has been happening. Ask them to tell you about the range of reasons that might be causing the problems. If your GP thinks that the possibility of dementia should be considered, they may refer you to a specialist consultant (perhaps an old age psychiatrist – a psychogeriatrician). The consultant will most probably see you at an appointment at a hospital out-patient clinic. Just because you are referred, however, does not mean you definitely have dementia.

There are various tests that may be carried out in order to diagnose your condition. They might include asking you some straightforward questions or getting you to do a simple task such as moving an object from one part of the room to another. A brain scan may be carried out, and blood samples taken.

Having a diagnosis of dementia can, like many diagnoses of ill-health, come as a huge shock. You may well want to talk to someone about this, and about what it means for you. The Alzheimer's Society (contact details on page 271) offers a telephone helpline for people (and their relatives/carers) with all types of dementia, not just Alzheimer's. They also have local groups, provide services, and offer information and advice.

Treatment and support
There is no medication at present that can cure dementia, but there is some medication that can, temporarily at least, slow down the progression of the disease.

The National Institute for Health and Clinical Excellence (NICE) has recommended that donepezil (Aricept), rivastigmine (Exelon) and galantamine (Reminyl) should only be available on NHS prescription for those with moderate Alzheimer's disease, and if:

- treatment is started by a doctor who specialises in the care of people with dementia;
- people who are started on the drug are checked every six months, usually by a specialist team;
- the check-up includes a test called the Mini Mental State Examination (MMSE) and an assessment of the person's behaviour and ability to cope with daily life;
- the views of carers on the person's condition are discussed at the start of drug treatment and at check-ups;

- the drug is stopped if the person's MMSE score falls below 10 points, or if the drug isn't working;

- the least expensive of these three drugs is prescribed first. If this is not suitable for the person with Alzheimer's disease another drug can be chosen.

(Note that, at the time of writing, this recommendation is subject to further, legal, challenge. Contact Age Concern's Information Line or the Alzheimer's Society (details on page 271) for more information.)

Initially, only a consultant can prescribe these drugs on the NHS. Your GP has to refer you to hospital so that the consultant can assess you. If the consultant thinks the drugs would benefit you, they will write the first prescription. After this, your GP can write prescriptions for these drugs as usual, unless the consultant decides you should come back to hospital for regular check-ups and have your prescriptions drawn up then.

As with many other drugs, it is possible to obtain these through a private prescription. Bear in mind that, as well as the cost of the drugs, you may have to pay your GP for writing a private prescription as well as the pharmacist's fee for dispensing the medicine privately (see Chapter 10). But no one in the NHS should put you under pressure to buy these treatments privately.

Some patients experience side effects from these treatments. As with all medication, you need to agree to take it after having considered the side effects, risks and benefits with your doctor. If any side effects cause you concern, see your GP as soon as you can; or talk to the pharmacist who issued the medicine.

The other types of drugs that are sometimes prescribed to older people with dementia are medicines called *neuroleptics*. These act as tranquillisers, and are sometimes used as a way of controlling behaviour such as 'wandering' among people living at home or in care homes. But there are misgivings about using the drugs in this way, and many organisations suggest other approaches that can be used. The Alzheimer's Society has further information on this.

Aside from drug treatments, there are services to support you. Chapter 13 describes some of the different care options that you might want to consider for the longer term. However, with the right support, many people with dementia can remain living at home for a long time.

Day hospitals and day care

Day care services can play an important part in supporting someone with dementia, as well as any family (unpaid, or informal) carers who may be involved. This type of support may also be available for older people with depression or other mental illnesses.

Day services may be provided in hospitals by the NHS or in centres run by social services departments or voluntary organisations. There are very few privately run day care services for older people with dementia.

Your GP can refer you to the day hospital. This may also form part of what the consultant recommends you receive from the NHS, after your assessment and diagnosis.

Day hospitals are typically open to patients between 10am and 4pm on weekdays, although some hospitals are expanding this service to offer longer hours, separate morning and afternoon sessions, and weekend openings.

What is actually offered at each day hospital varies but may include time in a small group undertaking an activity or taking part in reminiscence work (perhaps with just one member of staff). Many people attend for the whole day, in which case you will probably also be offered lunch.

Your going to the day hospital may help the consultant and nursing staff to gain a much more detailed picture of how dementia is affecting you, by spending time with you over a period of weeks. If you cannot get to the hospital yourself, the Patient Transport Service may provide door-to-door transport. This is often part of the local Ambulance Trust's service. Attending at the day hospital, and the transport to get you there, is free to you if it is all provided by the NHS.

By contrast, you may be asked to pay towards the costs of any day support arranged by social services or a voluntary organisation.

Some support may be provided to you in your own home from community mental health nurses (see Box 14), or perhaps from social services or a voluntary organisation. In some parts of the country, 'outreach' services have been developed, particularly for older people with dementia or depression (see page 108). This involves someone visiting you at home (perhaps once or twice a week) for a couple of hours, during which you and the worker share an activity. The type of activity will depend on your interests – for example, it could be completing a jigsaw or crossword, painting, recording your life history or looking at photographs. Outreach services such as these tend to be aimed at people who are so ill that they cannot attend a day hospital – for example, if the nature of their illness makes it extremely difficult for them to spend time with groups of people.

Box 14. Community mental health nurses

Community mental health nurses (sometimes also called by their former name 'community psychiatric nurses' or CPNs) specialise in support for people with mental ill-health, and tend not to carry out any physical nursing.

They may visit you at home as part of the overall assessment and to help check how you are; or they may visit to provide support for you in your everyday life.

They work with people of all ages and with all types of mental health difficulties. Your GP will be able to tell you whether you can contact the community mental health service direct and ask for their help or if you need to be referred by the GP or hospital consultant. Community mental health nurses are part of the NHS, so this support is provided free.

There are many other approaches to supporting older people with dementia. These include music therapy and gentle swimming exercises – both of which offer enjoyable and soothing experiences. There has also been a lot of work in recent years looking at how best to communicate with someone who has dementia. The research has uncovered several different ways this can be achieved, including 'non-verbal' forms of communication such as the way the person moves and other types of body language. The Dementia Services Development Centre at the University of Stirling (page 275) has researched this aspect.

SCHIZOPHRENIA

There are a number of more rare mental health problems that affect older people, including delirium, anxiety and late-onset schizophrenia.

Sometimes there is hostility and anxiety towards people who have been diagnosed with schizophrenia. This is often because of a belief that everyone with schizophrenia is violent. But this is not the case. Only a tiny number of people with schizophrenia ever commit a violent act. In the UK, the vast majority of violent crimes are committed by people who don't have this illness.

People often think that schizophrenia is to do with having a 'split personality'. But the illness is really to do with serious, or major, changes to what we believe and how we experience ordinary, everyday life. We all need to make sense of the world around us in order to function and get on with our lives. We're so used to doing this that we don't always realise just how much information our brain has to deal with to make sense of, for example, our getting on a bus and going shopping in a busy supermarket. During a schizophrenic episode, the person's experience and interpretation of the outside world are so affected that they can lose touch with reality. They may see or hear things that are not there and act in unusual ways in response to these hallucinations. These episodes can be very frightening for the person as well as for anyone witnessing this. They can last for weeks at a time.

Schizophrenia usually develops when someone is in their late teens or early 20s but can also start in an older person. Although the causes are unknown, episodes of schizophrenia seem to be connected with changes in some brain chemicals. It is thought that stressful experiences (and some recreational drugs, such as cannabis) may trigger an episode.

Diagnosis

Doctors sometimes talk about the 'positive' and 'negative' symptoms of schizophrenia. Positive symptoms are abnormal experiences such as hallucinations, feeling that your thoughts are being taken over, or delusions. Delusions are unusual beliefs, such as believing that someone is trying to kill you. These can be extremely frightening. It is important to remember that, for the person experiencing the delusions, these beliefs and feelings are real.

Although these positive symptoms are often the most dramatic, it is usually negative symptoms that cause the most problems. One reason for this is that negative symptoms last longer. They include tiredness, loss of concentration and lack of energy. People may have little or no motivation to do anything, and may struggle to manage household chores as a result.

Treatment and support

Most people with schizophrenia are prescribed medication to reduce the positive symptoms. These may be prescribed for long periods of time, and can have unpleasant side effects.

However, not everyone needs drugs – or doesn't need to take them all the time. Some people find that, with other support (perhaps from a community mental health nurse) they are able to cope well with experiences such as hearing voices.

There are some differences in how older people with a 'psychotic' illness (such as schizophrenia) access support services, compared with older people with other mental illnesses such as dementia and depression.

Like the word 'mental', 'psychotic' is sometimes used as an insult. But it is a proper medical term. To be psychotic means you have a psychosis – a severe mental illness. The *New Shorter Oxford Dictionary* defines a psychosis as:

'a severe mental illness, derangement, or disorder involving a loss of contact with reality, frequently with hallucinations, delusions, or altered thought processes'

Sometimes, people in a severe phase of schizophrenia need to be admitted to hospital, under the Mental Health Act 1983. This will be because of serious concerns about their current health. Anyone who is severely mentally ill might need hospital treatment, not just people with schizophrenia. People can become patients under the Mental Health Act voluntarily (just as we agree to go into any hospital for treatment), or the Act can be used to require someone to be in hospital because of concerns about their safety or that of other people. This doesn't just apply to people with schizophrenia – it can apply to someone with depression, for example, or other mental health problems.

Some people with schizophrenia who want to make sure they have a say in what happens to them while in hospital carry 'crisis cards' or set up an 'advance decision' (sometimes called an 'advance directive'), which make their wishes known (see page 127).

If you (or someone you know) experience the symptoms of schizophrenia, the first step will be to contact your GP, who can prescribe any medication needed. The GP can also refer you for other psychiatric help, including that provided by the local NHS Community Mental Health Team. In an emergency, if you are not sure what else to do, you can go to the Accident and Emergency department of your local hospital or dial 999 and ask for an ambulance to take you there. Or if you are already in contact with a community mental health nurse, you may have details of the team that can help in a mental health crisis, in which case you could contact them.

If you are diagnosed as having schizophrenia, you may want to contact the charity SANE (address on page 284).

Older people who are severely ill with a psychotic illness such as schizophrenia may need a package of treatment, care and support. Their care plans should be worked out according to the National Service Framework (NSF) for Mental Health – not the NSF for Older People. This involves what is known as the Care Programme Approach, which applies to everyone over the age of 16 who is under the care of a consultant psychiatrist. But this approach should be just as thorough for people over the age of 65 as the Single Assessment Process (SAP) used in all other cases where older people have health and care needs (see pages 171–172).

MENTAL HEALTH LEGISLATION

Most people have heard about 'being sectioned' under the Mental Health Act 1983. The term 'sectioning' refers to the differently numbered clauses (or sections) in the Act. These set out the various ways in which someone can be detained in hospital as well as receive other services because of mental health needs.

Services provided under the Mental Health Act are free – regardless of whether they come from the NHS or via social services. This is particularly important in terms of what are sometimes called 'after-care services': support provided after a period of compulsory treatment (or 'detention') in hospital, and might, for example, involve moving permanently to live in a care home. In 2003 an important ruling about after-care services was published by the Local Government Ombudsman. This reminded local councils that no one should pay for after-care services until they are formally 'discharged' from this support – which happens when both the health and social services agree it can take place. There have also been some important court cases repeating what should happen after you are discharged in this way. If you have been receiving after-care services after compulsory hospital treatment for mental ill-health and are now being asked to pay towards future care services, you might want to check that the correct system is being applied. Contact Age

Concern's Information Line (see page 271) for further details if this affects you.

Being detained

Being detained can be a frightening experience that may come at a time when you are already very confused and agitated. But there are rules about this that must be followed.

You cannot be detained under the Mental Health Act until three people – two doctors and an approved social worker (ASW, a social worker specialising in mental health) – agree this is needed. The approved social worker then applies for the 'sectioning'.

One other person can apply for you to be 'sectioned' – your nearest relative. The Mental Health Act lists, in strict order, the people who may be considered as your nearest relative. The list starts with your spouse/person you live with as your partner, then goes on to adult children, and then parents. In your case, whoever is highest on the list is your 'nearest relative'.

Sectioning is usually done in one of two ways. The first is called a 'section 2 detention', because it comes under section 2 of the Mental Health Act 1983. This is when you have a mental disorder and it has been decided that you need to be detained for assessment either for your own safety or for that of other people. You can be detained for up to 28 days and this cannot be extended, although you can be further detained under section 3 of the Act (see below). Your nearest relative must be told about this type of detention.

You can also be detained if you have a:

- mental illness
- mental impairment
- severe mental impairment
- psychopathic disorder

and you need to be detained for your own safety or that of other people, and treatment cannot be provided unless you are in hospital.

This is sometimes called a 'section 3 detention'. You can be detained for up to six months before this must be reviewed; after that, it will be reviewed at least once a year. If you are going to be detained in this way, the approved social worker must tell your nearest relative before it happens. Your nearest relative can object, in which case the approved social worker has to come up with some other solutions that would meet your mental health needs.

You can start with assessment through a section 2 detention and then have a period of compulsory treatment through a section 3 detention.

You have the right to consult a solicitor, although your detention won't be delayed while you contact someone. But a solicitor would be able to give you legal advice about asking to be discharged from the section, for example. You will need a solicitor who knows about mental health law. This is not a free service, however, and you may be asked to pay something towards it, depending on your income. The exception is for appeals to the Mental Health Review Tribunal (see page 121), which are free. The charity MIND has information on solicitors specialising in mental health law and about financial help with these costs (contact details on page 281).

You may also find it helpful to have an advocate. This is nothing to do with the law. An advocate is someone who will find out what you want and then speak for you, perhaps at meetings or other discussions. MIND may also offer advocacy support.

Under both types of section you can be prevented from leaving the hospital ward, but you can be given permission to leave by the 'responsible medical officer' (RMO). Your consent to any treatment should be sought; however, some treatments can still be given to you even if you do not give consent:

- When you are incapacitated, which means you are unable to consent (see page 125).
- If you or someone else is in immediate danger; in this case, you can be given a limited amount of treatment to deal with this immediate danger.

- Medical treatment for mental disorder while you are detained.

The types of medical treatment you can be given without your consent include most treatments and care available on a psychiatric ward, such as nursing care and medication. It could include physical restraint. It can also include treatment that cannot be given without your co-operation, such as 'talking' treatments. It is not clear, however, that physical treatment, such as blood tests (associated with some psychiatric drugs), would be included. You might want to seek legal advice if this type of treatment is being proposed and you object to it. There are no time limits for this medical treatment.

There are also three exceptions to this arrangement:

- Psychiatric drugs can be given to you for three months. After that, an independent doctor, sent by the Mental Health Act Commission, must decide whether this treatment should continue. This doctor is called a 'second opinion appointed doctor' (SOAD) – but this has nothing to do with other types of second opinion.

- Electro-convulsive therapy (ECT) cannot be used without your consent unless a second opinion appointed doctor has decided this treatment should be given to you (although in an emergency, ECT can be given before the second opinion appointed doctor arrives).

- Psychosurgery, such as a lobotomy, cannot be given without your informed consent and a second opinion that this surgery is in your best interests.

While compulsorily in hospital, you have some other rights:

- The right to apply to the Mental Health Review Tribunal, asking them to review the decision about your being discharged. This right is often used by people who feel much better following treatment and who disagree with the view of their doctors that they should remain in hospital.

- The right to complain about any aspect of your care to the Mental Health Act Commission (MHAC). This is a Special Health Authority and is independent of the hospital. The Commission will probably expect you to use the hospital complaints procedure in the first instance (see Chapter 16).

You can also still handle your own money and make other decisions while in hospital (such as voting in local or general elections), unless there is a question about your mental capacity to do so (see page 125).

There is another way of being detained. This applies to people who are mentally ill and have been charged with, or found guilty of, a criminal offence. It is not dealt with in this book.

It is important to remember that many people also receive treatment in psychiatric hospitals and units as voluntary patients. This means they are free to discharge themselves at any stage, just as they would be if they were in hospital because of physical ill-health. It also means that no treatment can be given without their consent – just as would be the case for treatment for physical conditions.

In 2006, the Government published a draft Mental Health Bill. This aims to replace the current legislation (although it must first pass through the usual Parliamentary processes). Among other changes, the draft Bill seeks to change the law regarding compulsory treatment. Instead of only being able to require someone to receive treatment in hospital, it sets out proposals whereby doctors could require patients to comply with treatment being received in their own homes. This would include being required to take medication as directed, or to receive other treatment. It is not clear, at the time of writing, whether (or when) this Bill might become the law. You should note, though, that the Government has been looking to introduce similar legislation for the past few years. Contact the mental health charity MIND for further details (see page 281).

CONSENT AND DECISION-MAKING

There are many references to consent throughout this book. We need to give our consent before almost all NHS services (and other health treatments) can go ahead – except for compulsory detention in hospital and emergency treatment in some situations (see page 158).

We are free to go ahead and agree to treatment – or to refuse this, even when we know that by refusing we may hasten our death.

This treatment could be an operation or taking medicine or having physiotherapy or any other of the NHS's services. As long as we can express our views and make our own decisions, the wishes of other people – whether they are doctors, relatives, religious leaders, campaigning groups or anyone else – cannot be imposed on us.

But problems arise when we are not able to either give or refuse to give our consent, or when we cannot express our views.

The Bournewood case

In the autumn of 2004, the European Court of Human Rights gave a final ruling on a case that had already gone through the UK's courts, taking some years to do so.

What has become known as 'the Bournewood case' involved a man who was not able to express his wishes regarding his current treatment and longer-term care because of autism. A doctor, who had been called out when he became agitated at a day centre he attended, admitted him to hospital. His two paid carers, with whom he lived, went to court on his behalf when the hospital was still refusing to discharge him two months later.

He had not been detained under the Mental Health Act 1983. But doctors ruled that, as he was 'compliant' with being in hospital, he did not need to be formally detained. His carers argued that, because he was not able to express his views, his compliance at being in hospital should not be viewed as agreeing to be there.

The European Court ruled that his human rights had been breached because he had been deprived of his liberty. Doctors and other health professionals had taken full control over his liberty and treatment. Had the man been detained (sectioned) under the Mental Health Act, he (or someone acting for him) would have had the right to a review of his continuing hospital stay. But because he was 'voluntarily' in hospital, it was only the professionals who had already decided he should remain there who would review his care.

This case is very important for anyone – including any older person – who is not able to consent to or refuse or to express his or her views about treatment because of a lack of 'mental capacity'.

There is now a legal definition in England and Wales of 'mental capacity' (Scotland already had its own law on mental capacity). This is set out in the Mental Capacity Act 2005, which came into effect in two phases during 2007.

Mental capacity

'Mental capacity' means having the ability to make your own decisions. Most of us can make most decisions for ourselves, although we often seek advice and information from others to help us do so – whether from solicitors or financial advisers, doctors, friends, charities or other sources.

We may all be uncertain from time to time about whether we are making the right decision. Being able to make your own decisions means you may get some of them wrong. You may look back and wish you had done something differently. But at the time you were able to understand what you were deciding about. This included understanding, as well as you could at the time, the implications of making that decision as well as the implications of not making it. You were able to understand the issues, gather information and seek advice, and you were able to express your decisions, whether in writing or verbally or by some other means.

Some people are able to make some, but not all, decisions. For example, someone might be able to decide what to have for lunch and where to sit while eating it – but be unable to decide whether the person they sit next to every day is to be trusted to look after their gold watch. This isn't because they are uncertain about these things but because:

- they cannot understand all the aspects of this situation; or
- they cannot comprehend the implications of their decision (one way or another); or
- whilst they may be able to show you through body language, facial expressions or other means, what clothes they have decided to wear, they cannot express more complicated matters – even with help and support.

Mostly the inability to communicate a particular decision is a result of disability, illness or accident. Occasionally, it is one of the side effects of prescribed medicine. Sometimes people can make all their own decisions at some times but not all the time – for example, if they have an illness or disability that fluctuates and so affects their decision-making abilities.

Most older people have been making their own decisions throughout their lives. It is the onset of an illness, disability or accident (such as a head injury) that tends to affect their ability to continue to make all these decisions.

The Mental Capacity Act 2005 defines a person to be lacking mental capacity 'in relation to a matter if at the material time he is unable to make a decision for himself in relation to the matter because of an impairment of, or a disturbance in the functioning of, the mind or brain.' This impairment could be permanent or it may be temporary (see Box 15).

Sometimes, if people know they have a condition such as dementia that means their ability to make their own decisions may reduce over time as the disease progresses, they decide to write down now what they want to happen in certain circumstances. They do so using an advance decision or an advance statement or a Lasting Power of Attorney.

Box 15. The Mental Capacity Act 2005

One of the important aspects of this Act is that it starts by presuming that people have the capacity to make their own decisions. In other words, someone has to be assessed as *lacking* this – you don't have to start by proving that you have mental capacity.

There are provisions in the Act that also make clear that no one should be viewed as lacking capacity simply on the basis of their age.

There are five important principles on which the Act is based. The first presumes that people have mental capacity. The other four are:

- the right to make unwise decisions;
- support to make one's own decisions;
- decisions made on behalf of someone must be in their best interests;
- the least restrictive intervention should be used.

There are also provisions for people who lack family or friends to speak for them: when a decision must be made about a serious medical condition, or the NHS or local council is involved in making arrangements about where the person lives, that person must have access to an independent advocate. This new Independent Mental Capacity Advocates (IMCA) service came into effect in England in April 2007.

Since 1 April 2007, any carer who ill-treats or willfully neglects a person lacking mental capacity will be committing a crime under the Act. The definition of 'carer' includes all health staff.

The details about how the Act is to be used in practice is contained in a Code of Practice, published by the Department for Constitutional Affairs (DCA).

Advance decisions

Advance decisions (sometimes also called 'Living Wills' or advance directives) are different from advance statements (see page 128).

Advance decisions offer you an opportunity to refuse particular medical treatments in advance.

If you decide to refuse treatment that is offered, the doctors must abide by this – even if they wish you had made a different decision. However, if you are no longer able to decide, doctors can look at your advance decision to see what types of treatment you have said earlier you would refuse and the circumstances in which you would refuse them.

The part of the Mental Capacity Act 2005 that covers advance directives for people in England comes into effect in October 2007. The Code of Practice (which describes how the Act works) says that only advance directives (or decisions) that involve a decision to refuse life-saving treatment must be written down. You may prefer, however, to write down all aspects of your advance decision – this would be your choice.

Advance decisions are not popular with everyone. But you do not have to make one, nor should you do so if you have any doubts about them. If you do make an advance decision, most advice suggests that you review it every few years and update it as needed. You may want to talk to your GP or hospital consultant before you draw this up or make any changes.

Make sure that other people know it exists and how to get hold of it – especially anyone whom you have nominated for a Welfare Lasting Power of Attorney (page 130). You may decide to always carry a copy with you, in your bag or wallet. You may also want to tell your GP, or a hospital consultant if you are under their care, about the advance decision you have made.

Even if you have made an advance decision, it comes into effect only if there is a time when you cannot make that sort of decision. If you still have the mental capacity to decide, you will be asked to do so as usual.

Although some people think that making an advance decision is only to do with refusing care at the end of your life, your advance decision can cover any medical treatment. You might want to make sure that everyone knows you would always refuse to have all your teeth taken out, for example; or that you would never accept eye surgery under local anaesthetic (although you might agree to this being carried out under a general anaesthetic) because you have a fear of people touching your eyes.

The Alzheimer's Society and MIND have further information about advance decisions, including how to record these.

Advance statements

Unlike an advance decision, which allows you to record your refusal of medical treatment in advance, an advance statement is a way for you to record your wishes and views. This is about you saying what you would like to happen, and what is important to you in all aspects of life – not just medical care. For example, you might use an advance statement to record your favourite things to eat, television programmes to watch, and hobbies and interests.

In the summer of 2004, a case was brought against the General Medical Council (GMC) concerning their guidelines on end-of-life treatment, which are followed by doctors in the UK. The case was brought by Mr Burke (who has a neurological condition that will get progressively worse). He had made an advance statement that he wanted everything possible done to prolong his life, if at the time he is no longer able to express that view.

In 2005, the Court of Appeal ruled that it would be lawful for doctors to refuse him artificial nutrition and hydration once he has lost competence to determine his own best interests. In 2006, the European Court of Human Rights declined Mr Burke's application to have this ruling overturned. If you have queries about the implications of this case, contact Age Concern's Information Line (see page 271).

None of us has an absolute right in law to insist that all and every medical treatment is provided to us by the NHS. This doesn't change when we are at the end of our lives. Some people do not want to have life-prolonging treatment and, when they have the capacity to make that decision and say so, this has to be respected. One example of this was the case of Miss B (see page 8). She had the mental capacity to refuse to continue the artificial support she was receiving, knowing that this would hasten her death. In contrast, other people who have the capacity to decide, or to communicate their decisions, might decide that they do want everything possible done.

If you have particular views about the end-of-life treatment you would want for yourself but are worried that your wishes won't be followed (or known about), you may want to think about recording this view in an advance statement. As with advance decisions, you should make sure that people close to you and/or involved in your care know it exists and, preferably, have at least some idea of what it says.

There are other ways advance statements can be used. For example, you can use them to record details about your life such as what you have done and what has been important to you. Or you might want to nominate someone to be consulted when decisions have to be made (such as deciding about medical treatment) – but you should make sure the person agrees to this.

You cannot use an advance statement to:

- Demand care that the health professionals involved in your care consider inappropriate for you.
- Ask for anything that is against the law – such as euthanasia or help to commit suicide.

Lasting Power of Attorney

New arrangements, called Lasting Powers of Attorney (LPAs), come into effect in October 2007 under the Mental Capacity Act 2005. This is where you nominate someone (or more than one person) to make decisions for you if you reach a point where you cannot make decisions yourself.

These replace the previous system of Enduring Powers of Attorney (EPAs). There are some major differences between the two schemes. EPAs covered only money issues; from October 2007, two LPAs may be set up, one covering finances and a second covering matters of health and welfare (this latter is called a Welfare Lasting Power of Attorney). The same person can hold both LPAs for one person, or you could choose to ask different people to take on the separate LPA functions. But you must obtain the consent of the person you are asking to become your 'attorney'. An LPA cannot be used until it has been registered with the new Office of the Public Guardian, also in place from October 2007.

There are other new arrangements under this Act, including the ability for the new Court of Protection to appoint 'deputies' in situations where someone was not able to set up an LPA before losing mental capacity.

Age Concern's leaflet Help with Legal Advice *may be helpful.*

OTHER ISSUES

If you have been diagnosed with a mental illness, you may be eligible for disability benefits; you may also be entitled to reductions in the amount you have to pay in Council Tax. You may want to contact any of the organisations mentioned in this chapter for further advice and information about the effect of your diagnosis on different aspects of your life. For example, if you are diagnosed with dementia, you are obliged to tell the Driver and Vehicle Licensing Agency (DVLA); but you may also be eligible for the Blue Badge parking scheme for people with disabilities.

9

Chiropody and Foot Care

This chapter looks at how to get NHS chiropody services, and what to do if these services are not provided. It also explains about private chiropody (including finding a chiropodist and paying privately), and toenail-cutting services. It explains different terms that you might come across, and looks at some of the links between foot care and certain diseases and illnesses.

CHIROPODISTS AND PODIATRISTS

The first thing you may notice, when looking for a professional to help look after the health of your feet, is that two terms are used – 'chiropodist' and 'podiatrist'. Some people say that 'podiatry' is simply the American term for 'chiropody'. Others say that podiatry is a particular type of chiropody, where the professional focuses on the bones in someone's feet and what might be called the 'mechanics' of walking – how we actually walk (sometimes also called 'biomechanics'). This chapter uses the terms 'chiropody' and 'chiropodist'.

Chiropodists diagnose and treat abnormalities and diseases of the lower limb. They can also advise on preventing foot problems and on proper foot care and footwear; and can perform minor surgical procedures such as nail surgery.

In the UK, people must be registered with the Health Professions Council to be able to call themselves 'chiropodists' (or 'podiatrists'). This registration means that people have reached a certain standard in their professional training. It is against the law to call yourself a chiropodist (or podiatrist) if you are not registered in this way. This applies whether people are working in the NHS, in a charity or in the private sector (perhaps running their own business).

People who work in beauty salons offering nail-cutting services and pedicures cannot call themselves chiropodists unless they are registered as such with the Health Professions Council. They can call themselves 'foot care professionals' or 'pedicurists' instead.

This arrangement replaced an earlier system of state registration. Some professionals may still use 'SRCh' or 'State registered chiropodist' after their name, but you should always look for someone who says they are registered with the Health Professions Council, or holds one of the following qualifications:

- MChS (Member of the Society of Chiropodists and Podiatrists)
- FChS (Fellow of the Society of Chiropodists and Podiatrists)
- FPod(S) (Fellow of the College of Podiatrists or the Society of Chiropodists & Podiatrists).

If you think the chiropodist has behaved badly or the standard of care has not been good, you can contact the Health Professions Council. This applies both to private chiropodists and to those who work in the NHS. If you are concerned about the NHS treatment you have received, you can also use the NHS complaints procedure – see Chapter 16.

Other terms
There are two other terms that you may come across, depending on the type of help you need with your feet:

- orthotics
- prosthetics.

An *orthosis* is something that either corrects how you walk or helps you to walk or place your feet more easily. This could include a built-up shoe (if one leg is longer than the other), or a brace that supports your leg or foot if it is twisted in some way. Someone who works with orthoses is likely to be called an orthotics technician – and 'orthotics' may be the name of the department or organisation where they work.

Prosthesis is the name for something that replaces a missing part of your body – for example, an artificial replacement leg or hand. In foot care, a prosthetic technician may work with chiropodists and orthotic technicians if, for example, someone has one artificial foot and needs appropriate footwear for this and their other foot.

In hospitals, the department that concentrates on matters to do with your bones and joints is likely to be called 'orthopaedics'. If you need help with your legs and feet, your GP or an NHS chiropodist will refer you.

If you have problems finding shoes, slippers or other footwear because your feet are different sizes, or are swollen or particularly sensitive or there are other difficulties, the Disabled Living Foundation has information sheets that may help you (contact details on page 276).

WHY IS FOOT CARE IMPORTANT?

Chiropodists will tell you that your feet are one of the most vulnerable parts of your body. They are certainly likely to be one of the most used areas of the body. Foot care is important for three main reasons:

- The condition of our feet can alert professionals to other health problems, such as diabetes or poor circulation which, if untreated and severe, can result eventually in part of the foot or even leg having to be amputated.
- We are likely to walk more if our feet are healthy and strong.

- Healthy feet are important in keeping our balance and, thus, avoiding falling over.

Finding a chiropodist

There are many reasons why people need to find a chiropodist. You may have particular health problems with your feet, perhaps because of another medical condition such as diabetes. Or other disabilities may make it difficult for you to bend to get close enough to care for your feet; or you may have difficulty using nail scissors because of arthritis in your hands. Or you may want to have your feet checked and get some advice on how best to look after them or what footwear to buy.

People who like to have pedicures and other, more beauty-based, treatments are more likely to want to find a pedicurist rather than a chiropodist. Pedicurists may come to your home or offer treatments in beauty salons. You have to pay for these sorts of treatments. You can find a pedicurist in the local telephone directory, under the heading 'Beauty treatments' or 'Beauty salons'. They are likely to have been trained in different types of beauty therapy, including giving pedicures – but you can always ask about their training when you make the appointment.

Chiropody from the NHS

Over the last 20 years the amount and type of chiropody services provided by the NHS have changed quite significantly. As explained in Chapter 1, this is an example of there being no absolute right for every person in England to receive chiropody care. It is also an example of the differences around the country as to how much help is available from the NHS and who receives this. Each area sets its own 'rules' or criteria, and these can vary. In order to receive NHS chiropody, your reason for needing it must 'fit' the local criteria. If the NHS provides this, you will not have to pay for it.

You should be able to find out about NHS chiropody services and eligibility criteria from your GP or your local Primary Care Trust.

The obvious starting point for your getting NHS chiropody will be that you are experiencing some kind of problem with your feet or you have a health condition that could affect your feet – and, in turn, your overall health. An example of this is Type 2 diabetes.

Diabetes and other medical problems

Type 2 diabetes is where the body cannot produce enough insulin – or the right kind. This sort of diabetes may not develop until after you have reached the age of 40.

If it is severe enough, diabetes can lead to poor circulation, resulting in foot ulcers and sores. In extreme circumstances, someone with diabetes may face losing part of their foot or even leg. This is why foot care is particularly important for people with diabetes. In 2004, the National Institute for Health and Clinical Excellence (NICE) issued guidelines to the NHS on foot care for people with Type 2 diabetes. This stressed:

- That people with diabetes should have their feet and lower legs examined regularly (this might form part of their annual medical check-up).

- This examination should: check for changes in skin colour, for ulcers and sores, the flow of blood in the foot, and footwear (to make sure this is not creating pressure); assess the person's level of risk for developing foot problems in the future; agree a 'care plan' of what needs to be done.

The guidelines also say that if any NHS professional reports a change in the condition of your feet – such as a change of colour (to black, red, blue or white), or new swelling, ulcers or broken skin – you should be seen by the appropriate health team within 24 hours.

If you have diabetes and have any concerns about the condition of your feet, you could:

- make an appointment to see your GP or the nurse (who may run a clinic for people with diabetes) at the GP surgery;
- contact your district nurse, if someone already visits you;

- contact the NHS chiropody service where you live (it may be called 'podiatry' or 'foot care' in your area);
- contact NHS Direct or your local Patient Advice and Liaison Service (PALS) and ask them whom you should speak to or see locally, if you cannot easily do any of the first three, above.

Or you might want to contact the charity Diabetes UK, which runs a telephone advice service (address on page 276).

If you have foot problems because of other medical issues (such as problems with circulation as a result of heart disease), ask your GP or the surgery's nurse for advice. The GP should be able to tell you about local NHS chiropody services, and to refer you, if needed.

If you have recently had a fall and have been referred to your local NHS Falls Prevention Service, you may find that it runs clinics that include input from a chiropodist (see Chapter 7). Or there may be a Healthy Living Centre in your area that offers foot clinics or sessions with an NHS chiropodist.

Depending on where you live, chiropody may be available from different parts of the NHS – perhaps your local community NHS Trust or one of the examples mentioned above. If you cannot easily find out about your local NHS chiropody service, do keep trying: ask your local Patient Advice and Liaison Service or NHS Direct for help with this. Every part of the country provides some chiropody – the question you need answering is how much and where from in your area.

NAIL CUTTING

The number of nail-cutting services provided by the NHS has been reducing for some time. These may be needed by people who can't reach their toenails, or can't see to cut them, or can't hold nail scissors.

Some areas do still have an NHS nail-cutting service but you may find that this is not offered very often. For example, an NHS chiropodist may be available to cut your toenails but only every few months and only as part of other health treatments for your feet. Most people's nails need to be cut more often – perhaps every six weeks.

Many parts of the country, however, do not offer nail cutting through the NHS unless you have a health condition that puts you 'at risk' of foot-related problems. Instead, there may be a simple nail-cutting service available through a local voluntary organisation. Contact your local Age Concern to see if such a service is offered in your area. Unless it is funded by the NHS, though, you may be asked to pay towards this.

If you feel that you need a nail-cutting service from the NHS but you are told it is not available from the NHS in your area, or you feel that what is on offer from the NHS isn't enough, you can:

- Complain to your local Primary Care Trust, which is responsible for providing and arranging NHS services in your area via the Patient Advice and Liaison Service. (Chapter 16 tells you about complaining.)
- Ask your GP if they will make the case for nail-cutting services locally – or consider providing this in their surgery.
- Contact a campaigning charity, such as Age Concern England.
- Write to your MP and ask him or her to raise this with the Secretary of State for Health.

Most of these suggestions are to do with campaigning to achieve change in the future. There is more about this in Chapter 18. Although campaigning is important, you may still need help with cutting your toenails now. If you are using other local health and social care services, such as a local Falls Prevention Service (if you have recently had a fall), or a day centre, or are living in a care home, you may find that a nail-cutting service is provided as part of this support. Whether this is provided by the NHS, and so is free to you, is another matter. If it is not but there is a local nail-cutting service provided by a voluntary organisation, that organisation will tell you how much you might be asked to pay towards the service.

Whatever NHS chiropody exists in your area should be available to you no matter where you live –in your own home, or in a sheltered flat, or in a care or nursing home. And, like all NHS services, it should not matter if you could afford to pay privately for chiropody. NHS chiropody has to be based on your need for this service matching up with the local criteria. In the end, although you may also want to complain and campaign, if you cannot get NHS chiropody, you may have to look outside the NHS for chiropody. (See also Chapter 13.)

PRIVATE CHIROPODISTS

Chiropodists have to be registered whether they work in the NHS or privately. Many will have attended the same training courses. Some private chiropodists may even have previously worked in the NHS. The big difference is that private chiropodists run their own businesses – and they charge the people who use their services.

When you arrange to see a private chiropodist, you will have to pay them yourself. How much you pay will vary, depending on:

- whether they come to where you live or you visit their clinic;
- the type of treatment you need.

If you arrange to see a private chiropodist, make sure you know how much you will have to pay before you go. Knowing this should mean there are no nasty shocks at the end of the session – and no embarrassment for you or the chiropodist.

At your first appointment, the chiropodist should give you some idea of whether you should see them again, and how often. Some people can feel that, because the chiropodists charge for these visits, they will be trying to get you to visit as often as possible because then they will earn more. But this should not be the case – especially if the chiropodist is a skilled professional. Their training means they expect to see you as little as possible. This is because part of their job is to help you get better or to manage the problem more effectively.

If you have concerns about the chiropodist you are seeing, or the advice you are being given, try to see a different chiropodist in your area. But remember that you will still have to pay for the advice and treatment you have received, plus the advice of the second chiropodist.

Organisations you might like to contact, if you have questions about the registration or training of chiropodists, are: the Health Professions Council, the Society of Chiropodists and Podiatrists, the British Chiropody & Podiatry Association, the Associated Chiropodists and Podiatrists Union, the Institute of Chiropodists & Podiatrists, and the Alliance of Private Sector Chiropody and Podiatry Practitioners. These organisations are listed in the Appendix.

Pharmacy

This chapter looks at your rights to receive medicines on prescription. It describes the role of pharmacies (or chemist shops) and pharmacists, and also looks at who can prescribe and what is available on prescription from the NHS.

NHS PRESCRIPTIONS

Everyone aged 60 or over who is entitled to NHS prescriptions receives the items listed free of charge. The amount that younger adults pay in England for their NHS prescriptions is set by government; some of this group may qualify for help with these charges if they are on a low income. Some younger adults receive free prescriptions – for example, those who have certain conditions such as diabetes and those who cannot get out of their home alone.

If you are 60 or older, you do not have to pay for any drugs or other treatments that you receive on the NHS. But you do have to pay for:

- items on private prescriptions;
- 'over-the-counter' treatments (see Box 16).

Box 16. Over-the-counter treatments

The NHS may not prescribe some items for you. These may be
types of medication you can buy 'over the counter' (without
a prescription) from pharmacists (also called 'the chemist').
Typical 'over-the-counter' drugs and treatments include ordinary
pain-killers (eg aspirin or paracetamol) – although your GP may
prescribe these for you, in which case there will be no charge if
you are aged 60 or older – cough syrup and throat sweets.

The types of drugs (medications) available on prescription from
the NHS change over time. For example, some of the treatments to
help you stop smoking that, five years ago, you had to buy yourself
(such as some nicotine replacement patches) are now available
on the NHS. The Prescription Pricing Authority (a division of the
NHS Business Services Authority) and the Secretary of State for
Health regularly update this 'NHS list', and give this information to
everyone who prescribes NHS medicines. This includes the drugs
and treatments that the National Institute for Health and Clinical
Excellence (NICE) has said should be provided by the NHS. The
broad rule of thumb about the 'NHS list' is that the NHS prescribes
what it accepts has a medical benefit. This is usually medicine – pills,
ointments, injections – but it can include other treatments such as
oxygen supplies for people with severe breathing problems.

Note that oxygen cylinders for use by NHS patients at home are
no longer delivered by local pharmacies but by specialist oxygen
companies. Further information is available from the British Lung
Foundation (contact details on page 272). Oxygen supplies are
provided free of charge to NHS patients.

All drugs have to be paid for, however, one way or another. So even
if you don't pay for the items on your NHS prescription, the NHS
still has to buy the drugs and other treatments from the companies
that make them. In each area, this 'drugs bill' is the responsibility of
your local Primary Care Trust.

Primary Care Trusts and GPs work together to make sure that patients receive what they need within the budget available for the cost of drugs. This means that the doctor may prescribe what are called 'generic' medicines. Generic medicines are those marketed without a brand name. An example of brand and generic medicines that might be familiar to you are the pain-killers Nurofen and ibuprofen. Nurofen is the brand name; ibuprofen is the generic name. They have different names but they have the same main ingredient. You might be prescribed a generic drug rather than a particular brand whose name you know. One reason for this may be that the generic medicine is cheaper than the brand name drug. But you should still receive the drug that is right for your condition, so, if you have queries, ask the person who is prescribing it for you (see below). You could also ask the pharmacist (chemist) who will give you the drugs when you hand in your prescription (see page 149).

Sometimes doctors may decide to 'prescribe' a course of treatment that isn't about taking a drug. They may believe that a different approach would help improve a patient's health, such as:

- joining a walking group;
- going to a Stop Smoking Clinic.

This type of support may be available to you free of charge from the NHS in your area, but your doctor has to recommend you (refer you) in order for you to be able to take part. It is this recommendation that doctors mean when they talk about this kind of 'prescribing'.

TAKING MEDICATION

As with all other treatments, for the vast majority of people it is up to you whether to take the drugs you have been prescribed. There are occasional exceptions, and these are described in Chapter 8. But you need to be clear that there are likely to be consequences for you if you do not take your medicines. You need to be given information about this (see Chapter 17). The most likely outcome of your not taking prescribed medication will be that you do not get better, or at least not very quickly. But you can still choose to refuse to take the medication, even so.

If you are thinking about not taking prescribed medicines, however, do make sure that you talk through your reasons with your GP and/or the pharmacist first. They will work with you to find a solution that helps your health as well as addressing any concerns.

When you take your medicines, it is important that you:

- take only medication that has been prescribed for you;
- take only the dosage prescribed for you (how often, and how much each time).

It's particularly important that you don't take medication meant for other people. Even if someone else has the same illness or disability as you, there are lots of factors that are taken into account when prescribing medicine. This means that what you need may be very different from what someone else receives.

There are devices available to help people who find it difficult to remember to take their tablets. These are usually on sale at local chemist's shops. One design is a small box divided into seven sections, one for each day of the week. If at the start of each week you put out the pills you need to take in the correct sections, you will be able to see at a glance whether or not you have taken that day's dosage. Other designs allow you to put out pills for different times on each day of the week. Some people find a simple approach, such as setting an alarm clock to go off at the time a pill must be taken, and putting this next to the pills that must be taken, can also be helpful. There are also pill boxes that have an alarm built in. But if you (or someone you know) are struggling with this, talk to your GP or your local pharmacist to see if they have other ideas. If you are disabled (as set out in the Disability Discrimination Act 1995) and have difficulties taking medicine as a result, your pharmacist will provide appropriate aids to help you. The Disabled Living Foundation also has advice and information about taking medicines (contact details on page 276).

There is also a new information initiative involving the Royal National Institute of the Blind (RNIB). This is making the Patient Information Leaflet given out with medicines (often inside the box the medicine comes in) available on audio cassette and also in large print. Ask your pharmacist for details.

If it is difficult for you to collect your prescribed medication (perhaps because your illness or disability means you are unable to leave your home), ask your GP and pharmacist about help available to get your medicine. If there are other difficulties, such as sight problems that mean you need a large-print label stating how often to take your medication, ask the pharmacist for help with this.

If other professionals are involved in caring for you, such as home care workers who come to you at your home or staff in the care home where you live, they should keep a record of the medicine you have taken each day.

PRIVATE PRESCRIPTIONS

If you see your GP as a private patient and need any medication, you will be given private prescriptions. This means that you pay the chemist for the cost of the drugs prescribed. The chemist will also ask you to pay them a small dispensing fee for their services – this amount varies. You can ask your doctor how much the drugs you are being prescribed will cost.

WHO CAN PRESCRIBE?

It may surprise you to know that there are various professionals who are allowed to prescribe:

- doctors
- dentists
- nurses
- physiotherapists
- chiropodists
- optometrists

- radiographers
- pharmacists.

There are limits to the types of drugs that can be prescribed by these different professionals, and only nurses and pharmacists who have had extra training to prescribe are allowed to do so.

Physiotherapists, radiographers, chiropodists and optometrists can prescribe, if they have had extra training, once the medication has initially been prescribed by a doctor.

It might well be that the healthcare professional you are seeing knows you need a certain drug or treatment but they cannot prescribe this for you unless they have undergone the necessary training. Instead, they have to refer you to your GP (or to the consultant if you are in hospital).

REPEAT PRESCRIPTIONS

When you are coming to the end of the drugs you have been taking, you may need another supply. You can get this by asking for a 'repeat prescription' from the health professional who prescribed the medicine you are just finishing. Usually this just means that you go to the surgery (or clinic) and collect another prescription for the same drugs without needing to see anyone. But if your health has changed at all since you last saw someone, or you think there were any side effects from the medicine you have been taking, you should make an appointment to talk to someone about this – probably your GP.

Some GP practices have introduced new systems for repeat prescriptions, whereby you ring a separate telephone number and leave a message. Others are beginning to use the computer-based (electronic) patient-record system to transfer repeat prescription details direct to a particular pharmacy. In some areas, patients can already get repeat prescriptions from their local community pharmacy for up to a year before they need to see their GP again. There are plans to have this service available in all local pharmacies in England by December 2007. But you will still be able to collect your repeat prescription from your GP's surgery and then take it to your local pharmacy, if you prefer.

Doctors who see patients on a private basis will have their own system for repeat prescriptions. It is up to them whether or not to provide a repeat prescription. They may ask you to pay a small fee for this, and will probably want you to put your request in writing.

If you are older and need a repeat prescription, you may in any case be asked to come into the surgery or clinic. The National Service Framework for Older People recommends that NHS patients over the age of 75 should have their medication reviewed at least once a year. Those over the age of 75 who take four or more medicines should have a medication review every six months. One of the reasons for this is that people in this age group who take four or more different types of drugs are more likely than anyone else to have a fall. Another reason is that, if you need to take this amount of medicine, you may benefit from some regular checks on your health. A medication review makes sure that the right medicine and/or dosage is being given.

Some community pharmacists also offer a free medicines use review (MUR) as part of NHS care. An MUR aims to find out if there are any problems taking medication. This may be particularly helpful for people with long-term conditions or who are taking several different medications. In these different reviews, a pharmacist will:

- review all the medicines being taken and see whether there are any overlaps between medicines or if one medication is affecting another;
- explain more about the medicines you are taking;
- discuss any problems with the medicines being taken;
- improve the effectiveness of medicines by discussing how and when they are taken.

Ask your local pharmacy if they offer this service.

SIDE EFFECTS

If you experience any side effects while taking medication, contact your GP and pharmacist straight away for advice on what to do.

You can also report side effects using what is called the Yellow Card scheme. Fill in a Yellow Card, which you can obtain from your pharmacy or GP surgery, and post it to the address shown on the card (no stamp needed). Copies of the card may also be ordered free of charge by telephoning the Medicine and Healthcare products Regulatory Agency (MHRA) or by downloading a copy from its website (contact details on page 280).

WHEN YOU ARE AWAY FROM THE UK

If you are going to be out of the UK on holiday or on business, there are some restrictions about medicines that you may need to know about.

Firstly, there are some drugs that you are not allowed to take out of the UK, whether or not you are being prescribed these on the NHS. Your GP or pharmacist will be able to advise about this, or you can contact the Drugs Branch of the Home Office (see page 279) and ask about it.

Secondly, your GP can write you an NHS prescription for a maximum of three months' supply. If you are going to be out of the UK for longer, your GP can write you a private prescription. As well as paying for the cost of the medicine and the chemist's fee, you will probably have to pay your GP for writing the prescription.

Thirdly, you can ask your GP to prescribe drugs to take abroad 'just in case' – for example, antibiotics in case of a stomach bug. But this type of prescription is not available on the NHS. Again, your GP can write you a private prescription for this type of medicine, which you will have to pay for.

Chapter 13 has more information about healthcare while you are away from the UK or if you move to live abroad permanently.

PHARMACISTS

Pharmacists specialise in the actual medicines that we take. They are trained professionals, and must be registered with the Royal Pharmaceutical Society of Great Britain in order to practise. We talk about pharmacists *dispensing* medicine. This is because part of their work is to make sure that the right medicine is given (or 'dispensed') to you.

Pharmacists work in many different settings. They may be employed direct by the NHS and work in a hospital, for example. Or they may run their own pharmacy business and provide some pharmacy services to the NHS under a contract. Or they may work for large chains of shops such as Boots The Chemist or Lloyds Chemists, or for supermarkets.

One of their most important roles is to make sure that medicines (whether on prescription or bought over the counter) are supplied safely and correctly. They can also advise on the different aspects of taking medicines, such as side effects and dosage. Pharmacists can also help with:

- Disposing of medicines that are no longer needed or are 'out of date'.
- Repeat dispensing.
- Suggesting other healthcare professionals you should talk to.
- Giving advice for minor problems such as:
  - allergies (including hay fever);
  - aches and pains (including toothache and mild rheumatic pain);
  - infections and viruses (such as coughs and cold sores).
- Recommending over-the-counter medicines.
- Offering advice on healthy eating and stopping smoking.

The Department of Health is looking at proposals to develop Pharmacists with Special Interests (PhwSIs). This would involve local community pharmacists taking on some of the more specialist roles currently available only in hospital. The idea behind this change is to help patients to access support more easily, nearer to where they live, without the need to attend out-patient clinics.

Out-of-hours pharmacies

It is up to your local Primary Care Trust what arrangements it makes for out-of-hours pharmacy services. 'Out-of-hours services' means local chemist's shops that are open to dispense medicines when other pharmacies are shut – typically in the evenings, weekends and Bank holidays. You may also find that pharmacies in supermarkets are open for longer – for example, into the evenings.

In many areas this involves a 'duty rota', where pharmacies take it in turns to be on duty at night or at the weekend. Most local newspapers print details of out-of-hours pharmacy arrangements, or you can find out what is available in your area either by ringing NHS Direct (see page 24) or by searching on its website (www.nhsdirect.nhs.uk).

Going to Hospital

This chapter looks at going into hospital for treatment, whether as an in-patient (where you stay at least overnight) or as an out-patient at a clinic or for day surgery. It also describes going overseas for NHS-funded treatments, discusses the situation for private patients and looks at different aspects of being in hospital.

There are three ways of being a hospital patient:

- *As an out-patient* If you are referred for diagnosis by, or a second opinion from, a hospital consultant, or for tests to help with this diagnosis, you are an out-patient. You won't stay overnight. Your visit may take only a few minutes or, if you are having lots of tests and investigations carried out (such as X-rays or brain scans), you may be there all day. You may also be referred to an out-patient clinic or other service. This could include hospital day services for older people with dementia (see Chapter 8), or physiotherapy sessions (Chapter 7), falls services (Chapter 7) or 'stop smoking' clinics (Chapter 3). See also page 167.

- *As an in-patient* This is where you need to stay in hospital at least overnight. Much of this chapter looks at being an in-patient in hospital.

- *As a day patient* This is where surgery is carried out in the daytime, and you don't need to stay overnight. See page 166.

BEING ADMITTED TO HOSPITAL

If you are going to be staying in an NHS hospital, there are two ways you can be admitted:

- the unplanned way, via Accident and Emergency (A&E) in the hospital;

- for surgery that has been planned for you – this is usually called *elective surgery,* and is not emergency treatment.

There are national targets for both A&E and planned (or elective surgery) admissions to hospital that the NHS must meet. One of these targets is that you should be seen at an A&E department within four hours of your arriving. Once you have been seen, and depending on why you have come to A&E, staff will tell you which of the following will happen next:

- the problem is minor and you can go back home because nothing needs to be done; or

- the problem is best dealt with by your GP or another NHS primary care service; or

- you will be treated there and then and, because this treatment will be enough, you will then be free to make your own way back to where you live; or

- an appointment will be made for you with an out-patient clinic – for example, for a further assessment, medical test or diagnosis; or

- you will be admitted straight away for further hospital treatment.

Unlike A&E admissions – which might happen because of a medical emergency, such as someone falling over and breaking their arm or hip – elective surgery involves planned treatment. An example is having an operation to remove a cataract. This is also an example of a type of surgery that can often be done during the day (see page 166). This means you don't have to stay in overnight but can return home after a short rest.

Targets

There are several targets about hospital treatment that you should know about. These apply whether or not you need to stay in hospital or have day surgery. From December 2005, nobody should wait more than six months to go into hospital for treatment.

By March 2008, there should be a maximum of 18 weeks between your GP referring you to hospital and the hospital providing the treatment you need. This 18-week period includes the hospital carrying out all the tests that might be needed to diagnose your condition.

Since March 2007, no patient should wait for more than 20 weeks for in-patient treatment, or 11 weeks for an out-patient appointment (see Box 17). No NHS patient should wait more than 13 weeks for all diagnostic tests to be completed.

There are two targets for people with cancer. The first is that, if your GP suspects you have cancer, they can make an urgent referral to the local NHS cancer services. The referral is to find out whether you have cancer. If you are diagnosed with cancer, since December 2005 you should wait no longer than two months from the urgent referral being made to your receiving treatment for the cancer. The two-month period allows for the diagnosis to be confirmed – but if you are diagnosed with cancer, you should receive treatment for it no later than one month afterwards.

There is also a target about treatment for people with cataracts. No one should wait more than three months for their cataract operation.

All these targets are set by the government of the day.

Box 17. Choose and Book

There are two parts to this government programme: the first is about choosing the hospital and the second is about making the appointment.

continued over

Box 17 continued

Choosing the hospital
The first part of Choose and Book is about having a choice of which hospital you might go to, if your GP has decided to refer you to hospital and the referral is not urgent.

Remember that this is about NHS care, so the hospital must be either an NHS Trust (or NHS Foundation hospital) or private (or voluntary) healthcare provider that has a contract with the NHS for the particular treatment you need.

Each Primary Care Trust has produced a booklet for patients, *Choosing your hospital*. This lists the hospital departments at each hospital, information about public transport, and details about the most recent performance ratings for each hospital, for example.

Hospital performance ratings range from 'excellent' to 'poor'. Issues covered include waiting times for in-patient and out-patient care, hospital cleanliness and MRSA infections (see page 163). You can also look at each hospital's website, if you have access to the Internet, for more information.

You have a right to choose which hospital you might go to, from at least four hospitals or clinics offering the planned (or 'elective') medical care you need, that already have arrangements with your PCT to provide health services. But you do not have to choose, if you don't want to. You can ask your GP to decide on your behalf.

Booking an appointment
The NHS must make sure that every hospital appointment booked is for the convenience of the patient.

In some areas, GPs have access to a computer system that shows which hospitals offer the treatment you need, the likely waiting times to see the specialists, and a list of available appointment times and dates. If you choose the hospital while you are with your GP, he or she could book your appointment online there and then.

If your GP does not yet have access to this computer system, or if you want to take some time to think over which hospital you would prefer, your GP will explain how to book your appointment.

This might involve you (or someone doing this on your behalf):

- asking the practice manager at your surgery to make the appointment for you;

- telephoning Choose and Book Appointments Line on 0845 608 8888 (local-call rate – this service is available 7am–10pm, every day);

- using the Internet, through the website (www.healthspace. cbintroduction.aspx).

Before the appointment is made, your GP or one of the other staff at the surgery will give you an appointment letter. This will contain a reference number and password – you will need both whether you or your GP books the appointment.

You can change the appointment by telephoning the Choose and Book Appointments Line if something happens in the meantime to stop you going on the original date. You can do this whether you have made the booking yourself or the GP has made the appointment from the surgery.

If English is not your first language, when you contact Choose and Book you should say which language you would prefer to speak. Choose and Book will arrange for an interpreter on the telephone to help you.

Once your appointment has been booked, the hospital or clinic will send you details confirming the time and date. They will also send you any other information, such as whether you can drink or eat before the appointment.

More information about Choose and Book is on the website (www.chooseandbook.nhs.uk).

It is important to remember that the targets set out on page 153 are all about NHS services. They don't apply to private healthcare treatments that you buy yourself in the UK. However, the targets do apply to private healthcare services that the NHS has agreed to pay for on your behalf. This is because, when the NHS pays, you 'count' as an NHS patient, even if the treatment is provided by a private health company.

NHS HEALTHCARE GIVEN OVERSEAS

In some areas, and for a very small number of patients, the NHS has arranged for treatment to be carried out in a European Economic Area (EEA) country. This has been one of the ways in which the NHS has cut waiting lists for operations. These arrangements are made by local Primary Care Trusts.

Some criteria apply to overseas treatment paid for by the NHS. The first is that the clinic or hospital must provide a good-quality service. Another is that the patient must be well enough to travel (this must be no more than a three-hour flight from the UK). Follow-up checks and treatment are carried out in the UK. Because the NHS has arranged and paid for the treatment, everything (including the flight) is free for the patient. But if you wanted to take someone with you, and there was no medical reason for this, they would have to pay for their flight and accommodation. In any case, patients travel together in small groups, with at least one person (sometimes more, depending on patients' medical needs) from the NHS in support.

If you are offered overseas treatment paid for by the NHS, you do not have to accept. You can ask the NHS to arrange care for you in the UK, as usual. You can also ask your local Primary Care Trust to arrange overseas treatment for you, in an EEA country, but it does not have to agree to this. It is not clear, however, whether many Primary Care Trusts will be offering this option in the future, given that waiting times for many treatments have been reducing.

In 2006, the European Court of Justice ruled on a case where a 75-year-old woman had paid privately for a hip replacement operation in France, because the wait for NHS treatment was longer than her doctor advised was clinically appropriate in her case. The European Court ruled that, even if the waiting time for an operation is within agreed targets, if this is longer than clinically advised for a particular NHS patient, the NHS should refund the costs of treatment obtained privately. Note, however, that the European Court has ruled only on the legal principle; to obtain a refund, the patient would need to use the UK's courts.

Do be aware that this ruling applies to the details of this particular case; it does not mean that the NHS must pay for all and any private operations carried out overseas or at home. In 2007, the Department of Health issued guidance to the NHS. This states that, if a patient is assessed as requiring NHS treatment but faces an undue delay, the patient is entitled to seek that treatment in an EU (European Union) country. In such a case, the NHS would be expected to reimburse the patient – but only up to the equivalent cost of the NHS treatment. If the private treatment costs more, the patient would have to pay the difference. This arrangement applies only when it is patients who request treatment abroad – not to instances where the NHS is already arranging this.

PRIVATE HEALTHCARE

How quickly you receive private treatment depends on you and the particular clinic. Private and voluntary sector hospitals and clinics are regulated and inspected by the Healthcare Commission (see page 10). If you have a complaint about the private healthcare treatment you have received, you can take this to the Healthcare Commission if you are unhappy with the response from the clinic or hospital (see page 10). You can also complain about individual health professionals to the relevant body that registers them (see Chapter 16).

If you receive private healthcare that then goes wrong and you go to the NHS with this problem, the NHS has the right to ask the private clinic to pay for the costs of the later NHS treatment.

CONSENTING TO TREATMENT

As with all healthcare, you must agree to hospital treatment before it can go ahead. This is called giving your consent. You will be asked to sign a consent form, usually quite soon after you arrive in hospital. This sets out what you are agreeing to.

Make sure you take the time you need to read and understand what you are being asked to sign. If there are sections you don't understand, ask the doctor or nurse to explain them to you.

If you come into hospital as the result of an accident, there may not be time for you to give consent, if emergency treatment is needed. Or you may come into hospital unconscious or unable to say what you want to happen. In such a situation, the hospital staff will do whatever is needed to save your life and stabilise your condition. But if you have a valid Lasting Power of Attorney or advance decision that sets out the treatments you do not want, this should be respected. There is more about this on pages 127–130.

You may also have made an advance decision saying that you want everything possible done to prolong your life – see page 129. These must have been written down, signed and witnessed. Make sure that other people know this exists. You could tell your GP and give them a copy but you may also want to tell people close to you, and possibly carry a copy with you.

For more information about ways of expressing and recording your views, contact Age Concern's Information Line (details on page 171).

You do not have to make either a Lasting Power of Attorney or an advance decision. If you have any uncertainties about drawing up either of these documents, or you object for other reasons, you should not make one. The decisions that are made on your behalf must be in your 'best interests' – see Chapter 8 and Chapter 17.

People often think that, if a relative or their spouse or partner is taken into hospital and cannot consent to treatment, they will be asked to decide, as next of kin (Box 18). But the law is not so clear about this subject. There is no absolute right for you, as next of kin, to decide what should happen – but your opinion should be sought. At the moment, it is up to doctors to decide, together with the whole clinical team treating your relative.

If the medical decision is about withholding or withdrawing treatment, and you disagree with it because you think the person would disagree, you can go to the law courts to ask for a judgment. In the meantime, treatment should continue to be provided. There is more about this in Chapter 15.

Box 18. Next of kin

There is no absolute legal definition of who is your next of kin, but usually this is taken to mean either:

- your spouse (someone you are legally married to), or
- a close blood relative.

Gay and lesbian couples can officially cement their relationship through the local register office, under the Civil Partnerships Act 2004. Although the Act does not specifically set out 'next of kin' rights, it should help such couples in this respect. Problems can arise if, for example, you live with someone of the opposite sex as your partner but you are not married. Generally, though, if you live with your partner as if you are married, he or she would 'count' as next of kin.

You can also nominate your next of kin. When you go into hospital for planned treatment, you will almost certainly be asked to say who your next of kin is and to give their contact details. It is entirely up to you whom you choose, but make sure that the person knows they are listed in this way. Even if you are married and have children, if you feel closest to a cousin or a friend (for example), you could decide to nominate that person as your next of kin. It really is up to you.

Sections or clauses in the Mental Capacity Act 2005 make it much clearer who can – and who cannot – make healthcare decisions on behalf of people who do not have the mental capacity to do this for themselves at the time (see pages 125–126).

After your treatment, hospitals will usually give only your family information about how things have gone. However, even though someone is part of your family, you may not want them to know about what is happening. You can always tell the ward staff whom they should, and should not, give out information to. They should respect your wishes. If they do give information to someone when you have asked them not to, or refuse to give details to someone you have said must be told, you can make a complaint about this (see Chapter 16).

Road traffic accidents

If you have NHS hospital treatment because you are the victim of a road traffic accident, and if you then go on to claim and receive personal injury compensation, the NHS has the right to pursue the insurer for the cost of your treatment. But you will not be asked to pay – the insurer pays the NHS's charges and the treatment is still free to you.

OTHER FACTORS IN HOSPITAL

Mixed wards

Most hospitals have been working for some years towards having single-sex wards – separate wards for men and for women. But mixed wards of both men and women still exist. If you would rather be on a single-sex ward, ask staff if it is possible. If this is important to you, it might be one of the questions you want answered before choosing one hospital over another for planned surgery.

In some specialist wards (such as intensive therapy units, or ITUs), it may not be possible to offer separate wards. Instead, there may be separate bays for beds for men and for women.

If you find there is no option but to be placed on an NHS mixed ward, you could complain about this (see Chapter 16).

Hospital food

Attempts have been made over the past few years to improve hospital catering. Many catering services were contracted out to the private sector during changes to the NHS in the 1980s and since. This means that most of the food in hospitals is provided by private companies whose staff are not part of the NHS.

There have been concerns about the malnourishment of older hospital patients for many years. This is an aspect of NHS hospital care that many organisations and individuals have been actively campaigning to improve. (See also Chapter 18.)

Good food is an important part of patients' health and recovery. Some hospitals assess patients to check whether they are poorly nourished, so that steps can be taken to improve their diet and overall health while in hospital. Some hospitals now offer a ward kitchen, where food can be available 24 hours a day rather than the fixed mealtimes usually offered.

Nurses and healthcare workers have been reminded of the importance of helping patients to eat – for example, taking the cling film off sandwiches or removing the foil lid from small pots of yoghurt.

If you have particular dietary needs – for whatever reason – be sure to tell the ward staff as soon as you can. If you know you are going into hospital and will be staying, ask your GP or your local Patient Advice and Liaison Service about letting them know in advance.

Religious and spiritual needs

When we think about hospital services, most of us think about our physical health. But as individuals we may also have spiritual or religious needs. The Human Rights Act 1998 gives us all individual rights to religious observance. Respecting our religious beliefs is also one of the important principles of the NHS. It is found in *The NHS Plan* and in the various National Service Frameworks.

All NHS hospital Trusts must have a multi-faith facility. There should be a code of conduct on the sharing of 'sacred space' – this is usually a part of the hospital (for example, a room) that is put aside to be used by patients of all denominations and religious beliefs.

This used to be called the hospital chaplain service. But you might find it is now called something like chaplainry and spiritual caregivers or faith community representatives. This change is to represent the very wide range of faiths held by people living in the UK. Whatever it is called, you may well find that it is linked with the hospital Trust's bereavement service (see page 219).

Telephone and TV

Many hospitals still have day rooms where you can sit and watch television or read. Most wards also have a payphone, or there will be one nearby. You may be asked not to use mobile phones in hospital. However, there are now mixed views as to whether mobile phones do interfere with the smooth running of some hospital equipment, including health equipment used by other patients, as was previously thought. Ask the hospital about their current policy on this.

There is a facility where you can arrange to have a telephone and TV by your bedside. Called Patient Power, it is run by private companies. You have to pay for this even if you are an NHS patient. There is usually a daily amount to pay to watch the television, and a charge for the phone calls that you make. People who phone you may find this costs them more than usual. But it is up to you whether you have this. If you do have it, make sure you know how much it will cost you and ask about the cost of calls made to you on this system.

There have been concerns about the cost of making telephone calls to patients in hospital. In 2006, Ofcom (the Office of Communications, which regulates the telecommunications industry) published a report into the matter. As a result, the Department of Health and the providers are looking at ways to reduce these costs.

Volunteers in many hospitals run hospital radio services, which are free and available to all patients.

Car parking

Each NHS hospital has its own arrangements for car parking, so there will be different amounts to pay depending on where you are.

Ultimately, it is up to the NHS Trust what it charges. If you are eligible for help with travel costs for healthcare, you can claim back the amount you have paid for car parking as well as any other travel costs. See page 96 for details of help with these costs. If you feel that the costs of car parking are too high, you might want to complain (Chapter 16) or campaign (Chapter 18) about this issue.

If you have to visit regularly (for daily visits for chemotherapy, for example), ask whether there are special rates.

Visitors

Most wards have set times for visitors each day. If you know that someone you would like to visit you cannot come at those times because of other commitments that cannot be changed, ask the nurse in charge of the ward if they can come at another time. This is usually not a problem to arrange but they should check first. For example, some wards prefer not to allow visitors at certain mealtimes so that patients can concentrate on eating and staff can concentrate on helping them.

Remember that it is up to you whether you want to have visitors. If there are some people you don't want to see, tell them but also tell the ward staff. If they come anyway and you don't feel up to seeing them, ask them if they would mind leaving. If there are problems, ask the ward staff for help.

Visitors also play an important role in helping hospital staff to counteract MRSA and other hospital-acquired diseases (see Box 19). This is because MRSA and similar infections can be spread if, for example, visitors:

- do not wash their hands with special spray each time they enter and leave the ward – the special spray is provided by the hospital;
- sit on your bed during the visit.

This is because many people ordinarily carry the bacteria for MRSA and similar infections without showing any symptoms or without knowing they do so; these infections can be passed on by touching bedding, furniture or a patient's skin or clothing.

163

Box 19. MRSA and *Clostridium difficile*

MRSA is a type of bacterial infection that is resistant to the conventional antibiotics that would be the usual treatment for such infections. *Clostridium difficile* (*C difficile*) is a healthcare infection that can cause diarrhoea and sometimes more serious conditions.

Infections such as MRSA are a particular concern for hospital patients because they cause infection in wounds, burns and catheter sites, and in eyes, skin and blood.

Because hospital patients are usually very ill and may be very weak or particularly vulnerable to infection, MRSA and other hospital-acquired infections can have an extremely bad impact on a patient's health. In extreme cases, MRSA may contribute to or even cause a patient's death.

The Government has told the NHS to take extra care to prevent or reduce MRSA-type infections. This includes making sure that doctors, nurses and other clinicians wash their hands in between seeing to each patient, and that wards are kept as clean as possible. Doctors have also been asked to cut back on prescribing antibiotics for bacterial infections, because the bacteria mutate so quickly that many of the antibiotic treatments are now ineffective. Since October 2006, all NHS bodies have been legally required to meet key standards to prevent and control these healthcare infections.

Although problems with dirty hospital wards have attracted much media attention, it is still not clear whether unclean hands or unclean wards are more likely to infect patients.

Hospital environment

Obviously it is extremely important that individual wards, and the hospital overall, maintain high standards of cleanliness. If you or your visitors see any examples of poor hygiene, or areas that have not been cleaned, you should immediately alert hospital staff.

There are other aspects of the hospital's environment that are also important for patients' recovery. There is now good evidence, for example, that patients who can see trees and other greenery from their hospital beds heal faster than those without such a view. In addition, it seems that having interesting art and sculptures to look at, or perhaps soothing music to listen to, also helps patients feel less stressed.

Many hospitals have therefore begun to landscape their outside spaces and to install paintings and other pieces of art to help patients feel better about their surroundings.

Your money in hospital

If you are receiving the state pension and/or Pension Credit, this will still be paid to you throughout your hospital stay. You will also continue to receive Housing Benefit (which helps you pay the rent where you live) and Council Tax Benefit for up to 52 weeks while you are in hospital, provided you intend to return home.

If you are already receiving Attendance Allowance or Disability Living Allowance when you go into hospital, you should notify your local Department for Work and Pensions (social security) office. This is because these benefits must not be paid to you after you have been in hospital continuously for 28 days. The benefits will start to be paid again if you return home, or if you move to a care home for which you will pay the full costs – provided again that you let your local social security office know you have left hospital.

There is more about this in Age Concern's annual book Your Rights to Money Benefits.

Note that being in hospital doesn't affect any private income you have. 'Private income' means any occupational pension (even if this comes from the public sector job you used to do) or private pension or money from investments (such as interest in savings, or dividends on stocks and shares). Any savings you have are not affected.

If you are a private patient and paying for your own hospital care, neither your state benefits nor any other income you receive is affected by your being in hospital (although in practice you may put some of your income towards your bill).

Your pet when you are in hospital

If you don't have someone to look after your pet while you are in hospital, the first thing to think about is whether you could board your cat in a cattery (or dog in kennels). There are also some places that will take rabbits, hamsters and budgerigars – even snakes. You can find these by looking in your local *Yellow Pages* or other telephone directory. You could also ask local animal welfare organisations for suggestions.

If there are problems, or you cannot afford the cost of the boarding arrangement, the charity the Cinnamon Trust might be able to help (contact details on page 274). It has a lot of volunteers working across the country, helping to look after the pets of older people and people with a terminal illness.

Help you were already receiving

If you were already receiving some help before you went into hospital (such as personal care at home), you should tell the people who provide your care what is happening. If any of your support comes from social services, or if they help to organise this for you or pay towards the help you receive, you should also contact that department – or ask someone to do this on your behalf. Make sure that these arrangements are re-started, if needed, when you leave hospital (see Chapter 12).

DAY SURGERY

More surgery and treatment is being carried out during the day, without your needing to stay in hospital overnight. This is because improvements in some treatments make it safe for you to come into hospital in the morning, have an operation and return home later that day. Examples include eye surgery to remove cataracts and hernia repair. Even so, the hospital or clinic that carries out the treatment must be satisfied that you are well enough to leave before you are discharged. There is more about this in Chapter 12.

The booking system for day surgery is part of Choose and Book, described in Box 17 (pages 153–155).

OUT-PATIENT CLINICS

There are many different reasons why you might be asked to attend a hospital out-patient clinic or department. They include:

- to have your illness diagnosed;
- to receive the results of tests, and be told your diagnosis;
- to check whether surgery or a treatment has been successful;
- to monitor your progress;
- for particular help, such as speech and language therapy;
- to complete treatment – for example, by removing stitches from healed surgery wounds.

Depending on your health needs, you may also regularly attend a clinic or service such as one offering day support for people with dementia (see Chapter 8).

Before you are discharged from hospital, either as an in-patient or from an A&E unit, you may be told that you need to make an out-patient appointment (see Chapter 12).

MOVING BETWEEN HOSPITALS

If you have to move between one NHS hospital or clinic and another for medical reasons, the NHS will organise this. This might be in an ambulance, if you need this because of the condition of your health, or it could be in another vehicle that the ambulance service uses as part of its Patient Transport Service (PTS). (See also Chapters 2 and 13.)

LEAVING HOSPITAL

There has been a huge emphasis in recent years on issues about NHS patients needing to leave hospital (being discharged) much more quickly. This emphasis has come from lots of different sources, including various governments, media, health professionals and campaigning charities. This is discussed in Chapter 12.

Coming Out of Hospital

This chapter looks at how your leaving NHS hospital – being discharged – should be handled. It covers the discharge process; discharging yourself; refusing to leave; and getting ongoing care. It also describes the Single Assessment Process (SAP), discusses follow-up care and looks at what rights, if any, extend to private hospital patients.

Chapter 7 explains about intermediate care and the different skills and types of therapists involved in rehabilitation services. Intermediate care and rehabilitation services are intended to provide some time-limited and often intensive support to help promote people's independence when they leave hospital, if this is needed.

PLANNING AHEAD FOR DISCHARGE

All the advice to the NHS is that staff must plan ahead for your eventual discharge from hospital. This includes patients who are admitted following an emergency or accident.

Planning ahead is particularly important for patients who:

- were already receiving some care and support before coming into hospital (eg having help at home or living in a care home);

- are likely to need support for the first time as a result of whatever has happened to bring them into hospital (eg because of a stroke or a fall).

Several steps must be followed before these patients leave hospital, as explained below. If you were already receiving care at home before going into hospital, for example, you should make sure that this will start again on your return home, if it is still needed. If you cannot organise this yourself, ask the ward staff or any social services staff based at the hospital to help you (see page 171).

If you are going back home

Many older patients go into hospital for surgery and treatment, and will not need further support after they have been discharged home. Even so, there may be items you need to take with you that should be ready for you before you are discharged. They include:

- any medication you now need to take (the hospital pharmacy usually issues you with a small amount to tide you over until you can get further supplies on prescription from your GP);
- details of any follow-up or out-patient clinic appointments;
- any advice for once you have left the hospital – such as about not getting any stitches wet.

You may also want to ask staff whom you should contact if you have any concerns about your treatment once you get home.

You may need someone to come and collect you from hospital, if you cannot make your own way home. Failing that, you may need to organise a taxi or find out if there are volunteer car drivers in your area who might take you to your home for a small charge. Or you may need an ambulance or Patient Transport Service (PTS) – for example, if you are leaving hospital with your leg in plaster and would not be able to get into an ordinary car. Ask the ward staff for help in arranging this. Helping you sort out transport should be part of the checklist that staff go through when drawing up a discharge plan for you before you leave hospital.

170

You might need some help when you first get home – for example, food shopping or laundry to be done. If you need help to make these sorts of arrangements before you leave hospital, ask the ward staff how they can help you. You should not be discharged from hospital until all the arrangements identified as needed in your discharge plan are in place.

If you need ongoing care

If any of the NHS staff involved in your care think you may need help to be organised or provided by social services for when you have left hospital, they must tell social services straight away. This involves either contacting the main social services department locally or getting in touch with social workers based at the hospital. Even though they may work in the hospital's building, these social workers are employed by the local authority social services.

However, before they contact social services, the hospital staff must first make sure you would not qualify for fully funded NHS care (sometimes called continuing healthcare). There is more about this in Chapter 13.

If the hospital staff decide you are not eligible for care the NHS would fund in full, but you would still need some support (perhaps from both the NHS and social services), they should tell you that social services is being contacted. You can refuse help from social services – and you can refuse to speak to anyone from social services. Be aware, though, that many older people in need of ongoing support receive at least some of this via their local social services department.

When social services receives the referral, they must visit you in hospital within the next couple of days. They will work with the health staff as well as with you and any carer (for example, a relative or friend) to find out what help you might need.

This 'finding out' has been called the Single Assessment Process (SAP). One of the main ideas behind this Process is that, even though several different professionals may be involved in drawing up a full picture of your current situation and likely future needs, you shouldn't have to keep repeating the same information. Instead, with the Single Assessment Process, each time another professional is involved they should add to the overall picture.

Another major part of the Single Assessment Process is making sure that your views of your needs and circumstances are fully taken into account.

With your permission, information you give as part of the Single Assessment Process will be shared with other professionals who are either already involved in your care or might need to be involved once you leave hospital. If you have a carer, you need to agree to their views being sought.

Once an assessment has been completed, staff will look to see whether your needs will be met by either the NHS or social services. Before you leave hospital the hospital staff must look at whether your needs meet the criteria for different types of continuing NHS healthcare services (see Chapter 13). Help from either the NHS or social services might include:

■ specialist equipment from the NHS such as special mattresses (see page 99);

■ intermediate care (see Chapter 7);

■ help at home arranged by social services;

■ a place in a care home;

■ a move to sheltered housing.

The NHS and social services set eligibility criteria for the support that each provides. These are 'rules' or measures against which your needs are compared. If your needs meet the criteria, you will be eligible for help and receive the relevant support. There is more about this in Chapter 13.

Once it has been agreed that some services will be provided for you, you should be given a care plan setting out what is needed, who will provide it and whether you will have to pay anything. Unlike the

NHS, you will have to pay towards the costs of support from social services. How much you pay depends on the type of service. There are different rules, depending on whether this will be care at home, a place in a care home, or an adaptation to your house or flat (for example, fitting grabrails or a stairlift).

For more information about help from social services, contact Age Concern's Information Line (details on page 271).

Chapter 13 has more information about continuing NHS healthcare. If you are told you are not eligible for continuing NHS healthcare but you believe you meet the criteria, you have the right to ask for this decision to be reviewed. Ideally, you should do this before you are discharged. While the review is being carried out, you should not be discharged from hospital.

For more information, contact Age Concern's Information Line (details on page 271).

BEING DISCHARGED

It is generally accepted that being in a hospital ward for a long time is not very good for you. Wards tend not to be either very stimulating or relaxing places to be. On the other hand, you should be asked to leave hospital only when it is clinically (medically) appropriate for you to do so. This means that the doctor in charge of your care (either the consultant or, sometimes, a GP in a community hospital) has to decide that you can now leave hospital.

You can also choose to discharge yourself, even if this is against the doctors' opinion. You will probably be asked to sign something to say that this is your decision and you understand what the consequences might be.

Every NHS hospital should have a discharge policy, and every ward should have a key discharge person who is able to tell you what will happen before and after you leave hospital. This includes information about any follow-up appointments you might need, perhaps at an out-patient clinic, together with supplies of any medicine you are to

173

take in the immediate future (plus instructions on how to take it) or details of diet or exercise plans you should be following.

If staff can't give you any information about how discharge is handled at the hospital, you can ask the hospital's Patient Advice and Liaison Service (PALS) for help to find this out (see also Chapter 16).

If it has been agreed that you will be provided with care and support after you have left hospital, you should not be discharged until this is ready. It must be safe to discharge you – this means that whatever is needed next must be in place. If it is not, 'transitional' arrangements can be made. They can include:

■ A temporary place in a care home – perhaps because the home you would like to go to has no vacancies at that time; or because adaptation work to your own home is too disruptive for you to be there while it is being carried out.

■ A temporary stay in a sheltered housing scheme.

Or you might want to make your own temporary arrangements while everything is sorted out, perhaps staying with a relative or friend.

For more information, contact Age Concern's Information Line (details on page 271). All options should be considered before a decision to move to a care home is made.

Another option might involve you moving temporarily to a different ward – perhaps from a specialist stroke ward to a general ward. This might also happen if you no longer needed the specialist stroke care but were not quite ready to be discharged from hospital.

Arrangements made by social services for you to receive help at home after being in hospital should be reviewed within two weeks of your returning home (and preferably within the first few days if you live alone). This review is to check that everything is working as it should be and to make sure that what is being provided meets your assessed needs.

If you are eligible for help from social services with the cost of a place in a care home (including a home that offers nursing care), social services should help you find somewhere suitable. However, if you will be paying privately, you (or someone on your behalf) may need to make these arrangements yourself.

> *Contact Age Concern's Information Line (see page 271) or the charity Counsel and Care (address on page 275) for advice and information on finding and paying for a care home.*

You can, of course, refuse any of the help you are offered. There are a few circumstances where you would have to accept care and support – these are described in Chapter 8. But even if you do refuse the help on offer for when you leave hospital, this doesn't mean you can stay in the hospital indefinitely.

If any part of your discharge is handled poorly, you can use the NHS complaints system if your complaint is about the hospital or its staff (see Chapter 16); or if you have a complaint about social services, you can use the local authority's complaints system.

REFUSING TO LEAVE HOSPITAL

Sometimes NHS patients refuse to leave hospital at the point they are told they have been discharged. There is usually one of two reasons for this:

- The patient doesn't agree that they are clinically (medically) fit to leave. They believe that further treatment is needed in hospital.

- The patient refuses to accept the arrangements being proposed for them once they have been discharged. This is often when either: the assessment is for a place in a care home but the person believes they could manage at home (albeit with some support); or they understand they will be moving to a care home but there is nothing suitable with a vacancy.

In the first situation, you should make sure that the ward staff and the consultant in charge of your care understand your concerns. You could ask the hospital's Patient Advice and Liaison Service to get involved and help you sort this out (see page 227). You may want to ask for a second opinion (see page 39). You might also find it helpful to talk to a charity that specialises in the health condition that is being treated at the time (see the Appendix for examples); it may be able to shed further light on whether anything else should or could be done at that hospital at that time.

In the second situation, it's really important for you to know that:

- The hospital should have a policy – a written document – that sets out what action it will take in these situations. You should ask for a copy.

- You cannot be forced to go into a care home except in very extreme circumstances (see Chapter 8). You can ask social services to come up with alternatives – but if you refuse all reasonable options (and you have been asked about these more than once), social services can decide it has met its duty in law to provide support. In that case, everyone may be asking you to make your own arrangements.

Nevertheless, it's equally important that you don't feel pressured or even bullied into doing something that will be wrong for you. Moving into a care home is a major decision. There is a lot of focus (shared by all governments since the early 1990s) on people being supported to stay at home for as long as possible. If you think you could manage at home, ask social services and the NHS what they can do to help support you at home or in a sheltered flat, perhaps on a temporary or short-term basis just for everyone to see what is really possible and whether it will work. Ask about the rehabilitation and intermediate care services that are available in your area. If, in the end, you decide to move into a care home, do bear in mind that many people enjoy living there.

Even if the NHS has bought your care from a private hospital, the NHS remains responsible for handling your discharge from hospital.

PRIVATE PATIENTS

Things are a little different if you are paying privately for your pre-arranged hospital treatment. Most people pay for private healthcare by either:

- a private health insurance policy; or
- paying in full for the cost of each treatment.

If you stay longer than your insurance policy allows, your insurer may ask you to pay for any extra costs. The basic rule of thumb is that, the longer you stay, the bigger your bill is likely to be. If the private hospital doesn't believe you have either the money or the intention to pay for the bill, it may insist that you leave.

If, following your private treatment, you will need ongoing care, you should first talk to the hospital staff and your private healthcare insurer (if you have one) about what might be needed. Even if you are a private patient, you are still eligible for ongoing support from the NHS and social services. Bear in mind that the emphasis on reducing delayed discharges applies to patients who are being discharged from NHS beds. But you should still contact social services and ask them to assess your needs as quickly as possible.

The private hospital might also refer your case to the NHS for ongoing support. It might do this if, for example, you unexpectedly need rehabilitation services that it cannot provide.

177

NHS Care Where You Live

This chapter describes two different types of NHS entitlement. The first part looks at your rights to NHS services depending on the level of your care needs. This considers the rights of people living in care homes (with or without nursing care) or sheltered housing to NHS services. It also looks at the system of continuing NHS healthcare for people with ongoing and often serious health problems and/or high levels of healthcare needs.

The second part of this chapter looks at your rights to the NHS if you are away from where you usually live, including when you are temporarily away from home but still in the UK and if you normally live abroad but are taken ill on a visit to the UK. This also explains the differences for UK citizens who live in EU (European Union) and non-EU countries.

PEOPLE WHO LIVE IN A CARE HOME OR SHELTERED HOUSING

No matter where you live, you may still need the services of a GP and a dentist, among other NHS professionals.

If you live in a care home (a home registered to give you personal care but not nursing care) or in sheltered housing (whether you own or rent this), you have exactly the same rights to the NHS as if you were still living in your own home. This includes:

- being registered with a GP – but you may find that you are taken on by a different practice, if by moving to live in a care home or sheltered flat you leave your previous surgery's area;
- being registered as an NHS patient with a dentist;
- district nursing services;
- free NHS hearing tests;
- access to free NHS hospital treatment.

If you are aged 60 or over and live in any type of care home, you are also still entitled to:

- free NHS prescriptions;
- free NHS eyesight tests.

You may also be eligible for particular types of NHS care called *continuing NHS healthcare*. This is explained below. It includes continence advice and pads, and some transport to and from hospitals and clinics. There are also some reductions in the cost of NHS dentistry and optical services. You may also be able to get some help with equipment (see page 99).

> *The Department of Health's leaflet HC11* Help with health costs *explains about reduced charges for some NHS dentistry and optical services (see pages 93–95).*

If you live in a care home and pay towards this cost (with or without help from social services), you should have a contract with the home that sets out the support the home provides that you have to pay towards. If this includes services you believe should be available from the NHS, you can:

- ask the home to arrange these for you;
- contact your local Patient Advice and Liaison Service for advice (see Chapter 16).

If you believe you are being asked to pay for services that the NHS is either already providing free of charge to the care home or should be providing, you can also share this information with the Commission for Social Care Inspection (CSCI), which inspects and registers care homes (see page 275). You can also complain to your Primary Care Trust (Chapter 16).

PEOPLE LIVING IN NURSING HOMES

There is a major difference between people living in care homes and those living in homes registered to provide nursing services (nursing homes) in England in terms of access to NHS services. This is about how the nursing elements of your care are funded.

Instead of providing you with NHS district nursing services, the NHS makes a payment to the home for the nursing care you need and which the home provides. This system is called *registered nursing care contribution* (RNCC). The payment is made by your Primary Care Trust covering the part of the country where you live in the home. There are other parts of your care that you will have to pay for, though, including food, accommodation and personal care. Although you should not also pay the home for the RNCC, the home can either:

■ charge you for the entire cost of all the care it provides, then give you the money for the RNCC it receives from the NHS for you; or

■ charge you for everything it provides except the amount of the RNCC it receives for you.

However this is paid, you should be told exactly how the RNCC payment affects your fees. The nursing home must give you written information about your fees, including the arrangements for paying for different services.

There are some limits as to what the RNCC covers. The first is that it applies only to care provided direct by a registered nurse or to the time he or she takes to delegate or supervise care carried out by another worker (such as a care assistant). It does not cover the care provided by that delegated worker. Chapter 3 explains how trained nurses are registered.

The second limit is that an RNCC *determination* (or decision) must be carried out before the NHS will make the payment. Just because you live in a nursing home doesn't mean you automatically qualify – a formal determination must be made.

Before an RNCC determination is made, however, your care needs should first be assessed jointly by the NHS and social services. If you have recently moved to a nursing home for the first time, this care assessment should have happened before you moved into the home; but if you have lived in a nursing home for some years and been paying for this yourself, an assessment may not have been carried out recently. The health and social services assessment should also look at whether you are entitled to continuing NHS healthcare (see page 184). Only when this assessment has concluded that you should be living in a nursing home but you are not eligible for continuing NHS healthcare would an RNCC determination be carried out.

If you are not sure what assessments have been carried out, or decisions made, start by asking the manager of the home where you are living. They should tell you if and when a care or needs assessment has been done, and whom to contact in the NHS or social services if this has not happened. Otherwise, you could contact your local Primary Care Trust and ask that both the continuing NHS healthcare assessment and the RNCC determinations be carried out. Once these have been carried out, you should be told that they have been done and about the outcome(s) (result), and how to appeal against the decision if you think this is wrong.

A nurse employed by the Primary Care Trust will carry out the RNCC determination. They will look at your needs as an individual, bearing in mind that care needs can vary over several days or weeks. Once the determination is completed, the Primary Care Trust decides whether the amount and type of nursing care you need to receive in the home falls into one of three 'bands':

- *Low band* – £40 per week. This applies if your nursing care needs can be met with minimal registered nurse input.

- *Medium band* – £87 per week. To fit this band, you will have multiple (several) care needs. A registered nurse will need to provide care to you on at least a daily basis. Although you may need access to a nurse at any time, your condition is stable and predictable and likely to remain so provided that your current treatment and care arrangements continue.

- *High band* – £139 per week. This applies if you have complex needs that require frequent attention by a registered nurse throughout a 24-hour period, and your physical/mental state is unstable and/or unpredictable.

Although the government sets these three bands, your Primary Care Trust can vary the amount it pays in your particular case. It can do this if, for example:

- Your needs are assessed as somewhere between the low and the medium bands.

- Your needs exceed the high band but still do not meet local criteria for fully funded continuing NHS healthcare. In this case you should ask for an explanation, and challenge the decision if you disagree with it – see page 188. You may also want to check whether you qualify for continuing healthcare if you have been placed in either the high or the medium band).

If you pay privately for your nursing home care and don't want the NHS to contribute to the costs of your care, you have the right to refuse this funding.

The system described above applies only to England. There are different arrangements in Scotland, Wales and Northern Ireland. The amounts for each band were last changed on 1 April 2007. Unlike state benefits, however, these amounts may not increase every year. To check if amounts have been increased, you can contact Age Concern's Information Line (see page 271).

Apart from this RNCC system, you have the same entitlements to other NHS services as if you were still living at home. This includes access to NHS ambulance services because of an emergency admission to hospital from the home, or non-emergency transport to and from healthcare facilities. Such transport is part of the arrangements for continuing NHS healthcare services. It is often called Patient Transport Services (PTS) and is part of the service provided by Ambulance Trusts (see Chapter 2).

Continuing NHS healthcare

For many years there have been concerns about what some see as an artificial 'line' between the care from social services and that provided by the NHS. One of the reasons this is important is that people have to pay from their income and savings towards social services' care, whereas most NHS care is provided free.

'Continuing NHS healthcare' is not the same thing as 'continuing care'. This might sound pedantic but it's important to know that these terms mean different things. *Continuing care* simply means you – or someone you know – has an ongoing (or continuing) condition or disability or illness. You, or they, will continue to need some kind of support or treatment. This might come from lots of different sources – some from the NHS, some from social services, perhaps some bought privately or some unpaid because it comes from friends and family. *Continuing NHS healthcare* is quite different. It doesn't describe your situation, it describes particular services that the NHS either pays for or provides itself. Sometimes it is called 'fully funded NHS care'.

Continuing NHS healthcare is one area where investigations by the Health Service Ombudsman (see Chapter 16) and case law (see Chapter 1) have had an important impact. They have helped to ensure that the NHS does provide certain types of support that, over many years, had been reducing. This includes:

- Continuing NHS healthcare in a care home or other setting, which the NHS pays for in full.
- Rehabilitation and recovery services (such as physiotherapy).
- Palliative care (this is for people whose life-threatening disease no longer responds to treatment).

CONTINUING NHS HEALTHCARE

- Respite healthcare (social services can also provide ordinary respite care – but you may be asked to pay towards this).

- Specialist healthcare support and advice (such as advice for diabetic care or stoma care, and specialist medical advice or treatment).

- Specialist healthcare equipment (such as continence pads and equipment to help prevent pressure sores).

- Specialist nursing and medical equipment (such as artificial feeding equipment that is normally available only in hospitals).

- Specialist transport (such as ambulances) to and from specific healthcare treatment (eg in hospital or a hospice) if this transport is required because of your medical condition.

How do I get this?

Your health needs have to be assessed against criteria for different continuing NHS healthcare services. These criteria are a set of 'standards' or 'measures' – people whose health needs 'match' these measures will receive continuing NHS healthcare. So the main question is not are you ill or disabled but what does this mean you need?

The criteria in England are drawn up separately by each of the ten Strategic Health Authorities (StHAs – see page 2). But all the criteria must be based on national guidance. The part of England covered by each Strategic Health Authority is quite large and so includes a number of different local authorities. Strategic Health Authorities have to agree their criteria with the local authorities in their area. This is because there can be overlaps between continuing NHS healthcare and what the local authorities' social services departments provide. They need to agree who pays for what.

Although the Strategic Health Authority agrees the criteria, the services provided to people meeting these criteria are paid for by the Primary Care Trust in which the person lives. The local Primary Care Trust is also responsible for making sure that your health needs are assessed, in order to compare these with the criteria that apply in your area. The Government has been consulting on this issue of criteria, and a national eligibility scheme, announced in June 2007, comes into force in October 2007. It may also cover eligibility for the RNCC for people in nursing homes (see above). Contact Age Concern Information Line (page 271) for details on the current position.

Professionals with skills and knowledge relevant to your medical condition should be involved in your assessment. If you think you may be eligible for any continuing healthcare service because of the state of your health or disability, you can request an assessment. There are also times when an assessment must be carried out, including:

- when you are about to be discharged from hospital;
- when the annual review of your Registered Nursing Care Contribution (RNCC) is carried out (or sooner if your health gets significantly worse and you are already living in a care home registered to provide nursing care);
- if your health gets significantly worse and your current care package, regardless of where you are currently living, seems inadequate;
- if you have a terminal illness.

You might also want to ask for your healthcare needs to be assessed (or reassessed – it can be done more than once) if you live in a care home that isn't registered to provide nursing care but you are receiving intensive support from the district nursing service on a continual basis because you have a complex or unstable medical condition. Even if you are living at home and a relative and/or home care staff from a private agency or social services provide your care, you may be eligible for fully funded continuing NHS healthcare if your health needs are extremely high (psychological as well as physical health). This can be provided to support you to remain living at home.

For more information, contact Age Concern's Information Line (details on page 271).

A report from the Health Service Ombudsman, published in December 2004, drew on details from almost 4,000 complaints made by members of the public on this complex issue.

Fully funded continuing NHS healthcare

In order for all your care to be funded by the NHS, your assessment must conclude that your main need (sometimes called your 'primary need') is for healthcare. Even if you also need other support such as help with accommodation and personal care (such as bathing) these may be secondary to your needs for healthcare. This can include your psychological (or mental) health as well as physical health.

When the NHS agrees to fund all the care you need, this is called 'fully funded continuing NHS healthcare'. This can be provided in your own home, in a nursing home or in a long-stay NHS facility.

In 2003, Strategic Health Authorities and Primary Care Trusts were required to check whether people in care homes (including nursing homes) in their area were wrongly denied access to fully funded NHS care at the time. They have had to review all the cases already brought to their attention and also take steps to identify other cases that might have arisen, going back to 1996.

In some instances the NHS has now found that people were wrongly charged for their care in a home when the NHS should have paid for it. In these cases the NHS is reimbursing the amount those people have spent on their care. This includes people who have since died – it is being paid to their estate. While they were paying this charge themselves, people might have used their state benefits (for example, Attendance Allowance) for it. When the NHS pays for care in full (as it does for people staying in NHS hospitals, for example), state benefits are reduced or withdrawn over time (see page 165). But because people were paying by mistake, the Government has told the Pensions Service (part of the Department for Work and Pensions, DWP) not to ask for these state benefits to be repaid when the person receives the NHS funds.

The Government has also told the NHS that, when someone's health needs are assessed for continuing NHS healthcare services, the decision must be recorded in his or her medical notes. They must also be told how they can ask for the decision to be reviewed. Primary Care Trusts and NHS Trusts also have new responsibilities about how assessments for continuing NHS healthcare services should be handled before patients are discharged from NHS hospital care. But your needs for continuing NHS healthcare can be assessed wherever you are – at home, in a care home, in sheltered housing; you don't have to be in hospital for this to happen. An example of why this assessment might be requested is the worsening of an illness or disability of someone already living in a care home but who does not need to be admitted to hospital.

For more information, contact Age Concern's Information Line (details on page 271). The Alzhiemer's Society (contact details on page 271) also has further information

Appealing against continuing NHS healthcare decisions

If you disagree with the decision about continuing NHS healthcare (including disagreeing with the nursing 'band' allocated to you following a reassessment under the Registered Nursing Care Contribution arrangements), you have the right to an independent review. You need to write to the Strategic Health Authority that issued the eligibility criteria used in your case and request an independent review.

An independent review will be done only if you are unhappy about:

- the procedures followed by the Primary Care Trust in deciding whether you meet the eligibility criteria;
- how the criteria have been applied in practice.

If you are unhappy about the criteria themselves (for example, you think they are more strict than the Government's guidance requires), you should pursue this through the NHS complaints system – see Chapter 16. An independent review cannot be used for this purpose.

Once it has received your request, the Strategic Health Authority decides whether to convene a review panel. It does not have to do this. For example, if your health needs fall well short of the criteria, it is extremely unlikely that the panel will meet. Even so, you should be told why a review panel is not going to be called to look at your appeal. You can use the NHS complaints system to complain about this decision not to convene a panel (see Chapter 16).

If a panel is convened, the aim is to complete the review within two weeks. If you are in hospital or in another facility funded or provided by the NHS, you have the right to stay there until the review is concluded.

Although the review panel's decision is not binding, the expectation is that it will be followed. Once the decision has been made, you should be told this in writing. If you disagree with the panel's decision, you can go on to use the NHS complaints system. This would mean appealing to the Healthcare Commission and ultimately to the Health Service Ombudsman against the review panel's decision (see page 233).

For more information, contact Age Concern's Information Line (details on page 271).

ILLNESSES AND ACCIDENTS WHEN YOU ARE AWAY

Visiting another part of the UK

If you are taken ill or have an accident while visiting another part of the UK, you are of course entitled to NHS services as usual.

There is, however, one difference in situations where you now need permanent care (perhaps in a care home or your own home) because of the illness or accident that occurred during your trip. This is because there are different systems of long-term care support for people who usually live in England, Wales, Northern Ireland or Scotland. If you will be returning to another part of the UK (your home area), you will need to make sure that whoever assesses your care needs understands this.

Sometimes, if you will need care from social services, someone from your local social services department will travel to where you are in hospital and assess your needs there. Or your social services department will ask equivalent staff at the hospital to do this for them (for example, if it is too costly for your local staff to travel to the hospital treating you).

If you need to be moved to another hospital, or to a care home, and your medical condition is such that you can't travel by ordinary transport, the NHS where you are will arrange to transport you to the new facility. Unless you are being moved because of an emergency (for example, if you need to go immediately to a more specialised NHS unit, because of a sudden change in your condition), the local Patient Transport Service (PTS – usually part of the local Ambulance Service) will sometimes provide transport.

For more information, contact Age Concern's Information Line (details on page 271).

UK citizens visiting abroad

The European Health Insurance Card (EHIC) was introduced in December 2005 for UK citizens to prove their entitlement to healthcare services in countries with which the UK government has a reciprocal health agreement. EHICs are provided free of charge. The quickest way to obtain one is online, as this will be sent to you within seven days or you can telephone and receive an EHIC within ten days; or apply by post using an EHIC form and pre-paid envelope available from the post office (contact details are on page 277).

The card contains your date of birth, name and NHS or National Insurance number. It is valid in EEA (European Economic Area) countries and Switzerland. It will also give you entitlements to some healthcare in some non-EU countries such as Norway: the EHIC helpline (0845 606 2030) will be able to advise further.

Note that the EHIC covers only emergency treatment. It is not an alternative to the health cover offered as part of a travel insurance policy.

In addition, if you visit other countries, especially those without a reciprocal healthcare arrangement, you should make sure you have sufficient appropriate private insurance to cover emergencies as well as non-emergency treatment or healthcare.

Non-UK citizens on holiday in the UK

If you are a citizen of an EEA (European Economic Area) country, or of Switzerland, and you are taken ill while on a visit to the UK, you are entitled to reciprocal arrangements made between your government and that of the UK. This means that you are entitled to receive the same NHS care as those who live in the UK. Hospitals and GP surgeries can ask you to provide proof that you are visiting the UK from a country with which the UK government has a Bilateral Healthcare Agreement. It is for you to decide what to supply, but examples include:

- passport or identity card;
- travel documents;
- the European Health Insurance Card.

UK CITIZENS WHO LIVE ABROAD

Many people believe that, because they are UK citizens, they are entitled to all NHS care even though they no longer live in the UK. They may think that, because they paid taxes and National Insurance contributions while they lived in the UK, this has somehow 'bought' them an entitlement for life. This is not the case.

Our rights to receive NHS treatment are limited by where in the world we are living at the time of needing NHS care.

This fact affects some older people who have decided to retire to live abroad. If your move is permanent, you are considered not to live in the UK any more – you now live in your adopted country (for example, France or Spain). You may still visit the UK but, because you don't live here any more, you are regarded as a visitor. This is the case even if you still hold a UK passport. Being a visitor to the

UK gives you fewer rights to NHS services than people who live here permanently.

There are some exemptions to this rule that apply only to people over the age of 60. One exemption allows people who are still permanently living in the UK and spend at least six months out of every twelve here to be able to spend up to six months in an EEA (European Economic Area) country and not lose their full entitlement to NHS services. This exemption does not apply if you spend more than six months away from the UK in an EEA country. If you spend time visiting non-EEA countries (for example, the USA), the six-month period does not apply; instead, you can keep your entitlement to NHS services only if you are out of the UK in non-EEA countries for fewer than three months. These times don't have to be over a calendar year – they are taken as three months or six months out of the twelve months before you needed the NHS treatment.

The NHS can ask you to prove your entitlement to NHS services. You would need to show evidence that you do live in the UK permanently.

Health records if you move abroad
When you leave the UK to move abroad, your GP surgery sends the records they have kept to the local Primary Care Trust for storage. If you have had any hospital treatment, these records remain at the hospital or in a local archive. Hospital records are kept for at least eight years following the end of treatment. GP records are kept for at least ten years. At the end of these times, it is up to the Records Manager at the Primary Care Trust, hospital or archive to decide whether to continue to keep the records or to destroy them.

You cannot take your records with you when you leave the UK but you may apply for copies, which you will have to pay for. You can take these copies with you. (The system of accessing copies of your records is explained in Chapter 17.)

Health treatment if you live overseas

When you move to live abroad, you should make sure you know about that country's health services. The UK has reciprocal arrangements for its citizens with EEA (European Economic Area) countries, as well as Switzerland. This means that you have the same entitlement to that country's health services as do the citizens of that country who also live there permanently. But each country's system may be quite different from what is available through the NHS. For example, if you now live in Spain you will be entitled to the same local Spanish health system as local Spanish citizens; it does not mean that the Spanish system delivers NHS care.

There are many countries, however, that do not have a reciprocal arrangement; the USA, for example. In those countries, you will probably have to pay for that country's healthcare services yourself, whether through relevant private health insurance schemes, from your savings or via other private arrangements.

Treatment on visits back to the UK

If you live abroad but are taken ill on a visit to the UK, there are some NHS services you can receive free of charge. These include:

- Services received in hospital accident and emergency (A&E) departments, walk-in centres and other units providing A&E-type treatments. (It does not, however, include the cost of any in-patient care or out-patient clinics attended following A&E care – surgery, for example.)
- Emergency treatment at a GP surgery.
- Compulsory psychiatric treatment.

There are also exemptions relating to family planning services, and treatment for certain illnesses on public health grounds.

If the care you need goes beyond these categories, the NHS can and will ask you to pay. The NHS can also ask you to pay if you visit the UK with a pre-existing condition (perhaps in the hope of receiving free treatment).

Even if you live abroad, however, you would be able to receive NHS services as usual in England if you are taken ill on a visit to the UK and receive either:

- UK War Disablement Pension; or
- UK War Widows Pension.

You might also be asked for proof that you receive these pensions – for example, a letter from the Ministry of Defence (MoD) or Department for Work and Pensions (DWP) stating that you receive one of these benefits. But you would still have to pay for any of the NHS services for which there is normally a charge (for example, NHS dentistry).

Returning permanently to the UK

If you have lived abroad but are now returning to live in the UK, you will be entitled to the same NHS care as everyone else who lives here, from the moment you arrive back in the UK. But you may well find that the NHS (for example, a GP surgery) will ask for proof that you are now living here permanently. It is up to you what documents you provide in support of this, because ultimately it is up to you to prove you are living here permanently again: it is not up the NHS to do this. Examples of proof include bank statements showing withdrawals of money ending in one country and beginning in the UK, or details of travel documents.

If proposals to introduce a national identity card do eventually go ahead, you may be asked to provide this to prove your entitlement to NHS services. This could apply to everyone in the UK.

NON-UK CITIZENS WHO LIVE IN THE UK

Although the rules for non-UK citizens vary, depending on whether or not you are here working or studying for example, the same broad rule of thumb about living here permanently applies. If you are entitled to live in the UK and you have made this your permanent home, you have the same rights to NHS services as everyone else who lives here.

Information on the entitlement of overseas visitors to free NHS treatment is available from the Department of Health (contact details on page 275).

14

Organ and Blood Donation

This chapter looks at different ways of donating, including being a blood donor, and donating tissue, organs and bone marrow. It discusses being a 'living donor' as well as donating tissues and organs after death, including donating your body to medical science. It also looks at your rights to be a donor, to receive a donation and to refuse donations.

Sometimes organs and tissues might be retained after a post-mortem examination after you have died – this is not the same thing as organ donation. There is more about this in Chapter 15.

BLOOD DONORS

The National Blood Service (NBS) runs the blood donor system for the NHS across the UK. Sessions are often run in doctors' surgeries or from mobile clinics put up for a few days in town hall car parks or other locations.

There are some restrictions as to who can give blood. Many of these relate to particular health issues, so check with the NBS first before arriving to donate, to make sure you are eligible. There is an upper age limit for people who give blood. This is 60 if you have never given blood before, but if you are already a regular donor you can continue to give blood up to the age of 70. This is not the only part of the system of donation where there is an upper age limit. Bone marrow donors can do so only up to the age of 44.

There are no age restrictions on who can receive blood, however – although you can refuse to receive blood (see page 202). No one receives payment for the blood they give to the NHS but, if you give blood, it will be tested and you will be told your blood type. If you are fit and healthy, you can give blood every six months. It is up to you whether you do this – no one can force you to give blood. To find out more, and to register to become a donor, get in touch with the National Blood Service (contact details on page 282).

Platelet donation

As well as donations of blood and bone marrow, the NBS also accepts donations of platelets. These are tiny fragments of cells made in the bone marrow, and help repair damage. They are given to patients who cannot make sufficient platelets in their own marrow – for example, some patients with leukaemia or other cancers are affected, as can be those who have a significant loss of blood as a result of major injury.

Not everyone who gives blood is also suitable for platelet donation; but if you are suitable and wish to donate, you can do so up to the age of 60, or 65 if you are an existing donor. This slightly lower age limit is in place because of the extra strain put on the circulation compared with donations of whole blood. Platelet donors are asked to donate between eight and ten times each year.

TISSUE AND ORGAN DONATION

When we think about 'donors', we tend to think about blood donors and about donating organs such as heart, kidney and liver. But it is also possible to donate human tissue such as skin, bone and heart valves. The National Blood Service also runs a tissue donation programme, through NBS Tissue Services.

Some of these can be donated while you are still alive. For example, if you are having a hip replaced, you may be asked whether you would agree to donate any of the hip bone to other patients – perhaps someone who needs a bone graft because of disease or accident. You don't have to wait to be asked – you can offer this. Speak to the doctor or nurse in charge of your care at the time but make sure this is arranged before the operation takes place. It is also possible to donate some organs while you are alive. A good example of this is kidney donation. But the risk to you must be low, and you should not be pressured into doing this in any way – it must be voluntary on your part. You don't have to be related to someone for a transplant to work.

If you are a 'live' donor, the NHS can (but does not have to) reimburse you for any expenses relating to the operation such as travel, or loss of earnings if you are still working. Ask the NHS hospital where the transplant is to take place whether they might be able to help you with any expenses.

Tissue donation may also take place after a donor has died. Tissues can be successfully donated up to 24 hours after someone's heart has stopped beating. Some tissues, such as heart valves and corneas, can be successfully donated up to 72 hours after death.

As with blood and organs, you have to agree to donate tissue. You can do this either by carrying a donor card or by registering with the organ donor scheme (Box 20). It is worth telling your spouse or partner, and other family and friends, that you want to donate tissues and organs (and which ones – you can choose to donate some organs or tissues but not others) so that they can alert doctors to this fact at the time of your death.

Some doctors are understandably reluctant to ask families about donation when someone dies. But the nature of donation means that these questions have to be asked at this difficult time. If you are asked about donating the organs of someone you love who has just died or is dying, try to remember that the person asking isn't doing this to upset you. They are asking because of the patients who might be helped as a result of the donation.

But you should also not feel bad about saying no. If the person who has died didn't want to donate organs or tissues, everyone will understand the refusal. Just occasionally a family will refuse organ donation even though the person had an organ donor card and had already told them they wanted to donate organs in the event of their death. At present, although there is nothing in the law that requires doctors and the transplant service to find out what friends and family want, this is felt to be good practice. In the event that your family wanted to override your wishes to donate, it is likely that the NHS would accept the family's view.

Box 20. The Organ Donor Scheme

Most people are familiar with the organ donor card and many people carry one with them in their purse or wallet. You can also register with the National Organ Donor Register scheme. Hospitals can search the Register to see whether you had decided to donate organs, so they can let your family know about your wishes. Not everyone is comfortable talking about this in advance, especially if it is known that you are very ill and perhaps near death. People often prefer not to have to think about what might come next – this might be just as true for you as it is for your family or your friends.

You can contact the NHS Organ Donor Register or the British Organ Donor Society (BODY); their addresses are on pages 282 and 273.

You have the right to choose whether to be an organ or tissue donor. Indeed, if you are not registered with the organ donor scheme, and your family refuse permission, organs will not be taken. If you are not capable of deciding, or to say what your choice would be (perhaps you are in a coma), someone else can decide that your organs should not be donated. See also Chapter 8 for more information about people who lack the mental capacity to make decisions.

Your age doesn't affect whether your organs would be accepted. The important factor is their condition – age doesn't always affect this, especially in terms of organs such as corneas (from your eyes). If you die in hospital, it is possible that all your organs could be removed and used provided they are sufficiently healthy and you have given permission. If you die at home, though, usually only the corneas can be used.

If you are a donor, you cannot attach conditions to your donation, although people sometimes try. If you try to say you want your organs or blood or tissues to go to a woman or a child, or to specify age or religion or anything else, your donation may be refused. The NHS is quite within its rights to refuse such donations. So if you agree to donate, you must understand that you have no say over who receives this.

Receiving a donation

Everyone who is entitled to receive NHS care has the same rights to receive a donated organ, tissue or blood. This right is irrespective of whether they are being treated in NHS facilities at the time. Even if you are a private hospital patient, if you are entitled to NHS treatment, you could be offered a donated organ through the NHS service, which is run by a UK-wide part of the NHS called United Kingdom Transplant.

Note that seeking private treatment in the UK does not help you receive a transplant any faster. All transplants in the UK are handled through the NHS. This is because it is illegal to pay anyone to donate an organ or to receive payment for making a donation.

The details of everyone who is entitled to NHS treatment and needs a transplant are held on a database. This means that, as soon as an organ becomes available, the best possible clinical 'match' can be found as quickly as possible. There is also an agreed formula that decides which patient is top of the list at any one time. This varies according to the type of organ involved. For example, for kidney transplants there is a points system that takes into account the patient's tissue type, their time on the waiting list and any previous transplants as well as how far they are geographically from the donor.

If someone who is not entitled to NHS treatment needs a transplant in the UK, they will be offered the organ or tissue only if there is no one listed on the UK database who provides a 'match'.

If they wish, your family can be given some details such as the age, gender and family circumstances of the person or people who have benefited from the donation. The patient(s) who receive the organs can also receive similar details about the donor. Families can choose to exchange letters of thanks or good wishes through the transplant co-ordinator but these are anonymous. Sometimes it is possible for the donor's family to meet the person who has received an organ but both sides must agree; this, too, would be arranged through the transplant co-ordinator. You do not have the right to be told the name or address or other identifying facts about the people who receive donations from someone close to you.

REFUSING TRANSPLANTS AND BLOOD TRANSFUSIONS

Just as with any medical treatments, you may refuse a transplant and/or a blood transfusion. There are many reasons why someone might want to refuse, although perhaps the best known is refusing on the grounds of religious beliefs. Although most of the major world religions find the donating and receiving of organs, tissues and blood acceptable within their belief systems, Jehovah's Witnesses hold a strong belief against accepting blood transfusions if this involves blood from another person. However, some Jehovah's Witnesses will accept what is called auto-transfusion. This takes place during surgery, and involves any blood you lose during the operation being returned to you immediately.

If you would want to refuse a transplant or blood transfusion, you might find it helpful to carry a personal advance directive card or Living Will that says this (see also Chapter 8). Some hospitals also have forms that you can fill in to record your refusal of blood.

If you are involved in an accident and are brought to the hospital unconscious, staff will do their best to find out if you would refuse blood or other treatments. If you do not have anything on you that says so, and if staff can't get hold of someone quickly enough who would know your views and beliefs, they may go ahead with such treatments. This is because their overriding responsibility is to preserve life where possible. Unless they know differently about you, they may administer blood products if these are needed. In these circumstances, it would be difficult for you to succeed in any claim of assault or injury you wanted to bring.

DONATING YOUR BODY TO MEDICAL SCIENCE

Some people would like their body to be used for research or teaching purposes after their death. There are some circumstances where your body would not be accepted. These include if it has undergone a post-mortem examination or if organs (excluding corneas) have been donated.

You are advised to make your arrangements about this before your death, rather than leaving it to the person who will administer your estate (the Executor of your Will). Not all medical schools are looking for cadavers (corpses) at any one time, and if you've not already made an agreement, your Executors may find that no one will accept the body.

Arrangements in England, Wales and Scotland to donate the whole body for research, or for anatomical examination, can be made through the Human Tissue Authority. People in Northern Ireland who want to find out about donating their bodies to medical science should contact the Senior Medical Officer, Department of Health, Social Services and Public Safety. (Contact details for these are on pages 275 and 280.)

Death and Dying

This chapter looks at the many difficult issues that may arise when someone is dying, or has recently died. Much of it looks at the roles of government departments and state bodies other than the NHS. For example, the role of coroners and of register offices (to register deaths).

DIAGNOSIS

A diagnosis of a life-threatening illness can be very shocking to receive. You may find you have not been able to take in everything you have been told by the doctor or consultant about the illness and what may happen next. If you have any questions, you should talk to your GP or the consultant. Ask about any local support groups, and whether there is someone you can talk to in private about aspects of the illness. When you do speak to someone, you might find it helpful to take notes, or have someone come with you who could make a note of what is discussed. This way, you have a brief record you can refer to later.

If you're not able to take notes, ask if there are any leaflets you can be given that describe your condition or treatment. Do also ask if there are any support groups or charities you can contact for further advice and information.

PALLIATIVE CARE

Palliative care describes a particular approach to the care of people facing life-threatening illness. It aims to provide relief from pain and to offer support to patients so they can have as active a life as possible until their death. It also supports the families of, and others close to, someone with such an illness. This includes support once the person has died.

There is nothing in the palliative care approach that aims either to speed up or to postpone death. Instead, it accepts that dying is a normal process and tries to support the patient as much as possible during this time.

Many people think that palliative care, which can be provided in hospices as well as in your own home, is only for people who are terminally ill with cancer. Whilst it is true that many services have been aimed at people with cancer, there is a much greater understanding now of the range of life-threatening illnesses and of the need for end-of-life care for everyone.

Since 2001, more than 15,000 district and community nurses have been trained in end-of-life care approaches and techniques. The Government has also set up an Advisory Board to develop an end-of-life care strategy. Due to report at the end of 2007, the Board is expected to build on this training programme, invest in hospice-at-home care and improve the quality of end-of-life care provided to hospital patients and care home residents. It is in addition to other work being carried out by the Government to improve end-of-life care. One aim of the approach will be to support patients so that they can live and die in the place of their choice. For older people, for example, this means reducing the numbers who are transferred from their care home to an NHS hospital in the last week of their life if they would rather remain in the care home. It also means that end-of-life care issues apply not just to NHS hospital staff but also to staff working in care homes run by private individuals and companies and by charities, as well as to GPs. There are also plans to make sure that, where there are Specialist Palliative Teams in the NHS, the patients referred are not just those with cancer.

A publication for care home managers, *Introductory Guide to End of Life Care in Care Homes,* is available from the Department of Health (address on page 275).

There is more about palliative care, and about continuing NHS healthcare for people who it is thought are likely to die soon, in Chapter 13. If you, or someone you know, have been told that you have a life-threatening illness, start by asking your GP about what help and support is available locally.

HOSPICES AND OTHER SERVICES

Hospices were first set up as charities, and most are still run by voluntary organisations. They may receive some NHS funding but often rely on donations from members of the public.

Although most people think of hospice care as somewhere you go and stay, some hospices also provide support to you at home, or offer other daytime support. Two charities, Help the Hospices and St Christopher's Hospice, have joined forces to provide Hospice Information, which can tell you about hospice services in your area and about other palliative care services (their addresses are on pages 279 and 285).

Other services include specialist nursing services, such as Macmillan and Marie Curie nurses (addresses on page 280), named after the two cancer charities. These specially trained nurses are often part of NHS specialist palliative care teams.

END-OF-LIFE ISSUES

This section of the chapter looks at some of the more controversial issues about the end of someone's life. You may find some of these sections upsetting, especially if someone close to you has recently died. But the reason for including the information is to explain what might happen in these very difficult situations.

Do-not-resuscitate (DNR) decisions

'Resuscitation' means cardiopulmonary resuscitation (CPR), carried out when a patient's cardiac (heart) or respiratory (breathing) function stops. The Department of Health has issued guidance to the NHS, setting out the four circumstances when a 'Do Not Resuscitate' (DNR) decision can be made:

- If a patient's condition is such that resuscitation is unlikely to succeed.

- If a patient who has the capacity to understand and make this decision has consistently stated or recorded the fact that he or she does not want to be resuscitated.

- If there is an advance directive or a Living Will that the patient has drawn up, stating that he or she does not want to be resuscitated.

- If successful resuscitation would not be in the patient's best interests because it would lead to an intolerable quality of life.

Each NHS hospital consultant is responsible for the resuscitation policy used. The responsibility for the decision not to resuscitate a patient also lies with the consultant in charge of that patient's care.

This does not mean that the consultant makes the decision on his or her own. It should be discussed with other members of the medical and nursing team. Although this is a very sensitive issue, doctors should also talk about DNR issues and decisions with patients whenever possible, as well as with their families (but see Chapter 17 about sharing medical information with people other than the patient). This may be especially helpful with decisions affecting quality of life. The doctor in charge of the patient's care should record in their medical notes any decision taken; this should also be copied by nursing staff into nurses' notes.

There is more about advance directives and Living Wills in Chapter 8.

If you (or someone close to you) feel that doctors are making the wrong judgement about your quality of life because of your serious illnesses and disabilities, and this is adversely affecting their views about DNR in your case, the Disability Rights Commission (page 276) may be able to advise.

Euthanasia and assisted suicide

Many people find the idea of euthanasia and assisted suicide completely unacceptable. Others firmly believe that these are the better options given the inevitable, and often terrible, circumstances they are facing. This book does not tell you what beliefs you should hold about life and death nor how you should behave in this respect. It is, rightly, a matter entirely for you. However, it is important that you know that both euthanasia and assisted suicide are illegal in the UK.

The difference between the two relates to who causes the death. In euthanasia, someone else causes the death of the person (for example, by injecting a drug); in assisted suicide, it is the person who causes his or her own death but is helped to do this (for example, the person injects him- or herself – but someone else gets the drug for them). In both, you are able to understand that you are asking for help to end your own life. (Assisted suicide is illegal, under the Suicide Act 1961. The law surrounding euthanasia is slightly more complex but, if someone is believed actively to have caused the death of another person, they may be charged with murder or attempted murder.)

There is some important case law about the issue of assisted suicide, particularly the case of Diane Pretty. Mrs Pretty had a degenerative neurological condition. This meant that she was gradually losing control over her body: losing the ability to walk or to use her arms or to speak. Eventually the condition can lead to being unable to swallow. If other internal organ failure followed, the lungs would fill with fluid, leading to death. There is currently no cure for the condition: the question was when, not if, Mrs Pretty might die.

If things became too intolerable for her but she wasn't then physically able to take her own life, she wanted to know that if her husband helped her to die he would not face a prison sentence. However, the UK's law would not allow for this and her case was not successful.

There have been some other high-profile cases where people have chosen to end their lives in overseas clinics set up for this purpose. But where someone else has helped them make the arrangements, and perhaps gone with them, in some cases this person has been investigated by the police on their return to the UK.

WITHHOLDING OR WITHDRAWING TREATMENT

The first important point is that you can always refuse treatment. Provided that you have the mental capacity to make this decision for yourself, you are perfectly within your rights to decide not to have a particular treatment even though you know that, as a result, you might die sooner than if you had the treatment (see Chapter 8 for more information about mental capacity). If you refuse a treatment, and this goes against what your doctor or other clinician believes to be the right thing to do, they may arrange for another doctor who does not find your decision difficult to follow to be responsible for your care.

You are equally entitled to ask doctors to do everything they can for you. This does not mean, however, that you have the right to receive all the services you ask for from the NHS. It's important not to confuse the two. Asking doctors to do everything they can means in part what is possible for them to do, and what they believe is in your best interests. This may vary according to your current health circumstances.

For example, to perform a particular procedure you may need to have a usable artery, and you may no longer have one. It will also vary according to what the NHS provides over all. There may be an operation that is available in only one hospital in the USA: the fact that the operation exists doesn't mean the NHS will pay for you to travel to the USA to have the treatment. You will probably have read lots of stories in your local newspaper, or heard appeals on local radio, from people trying to raise funds to fly someone – often a child – for an operation overseas (usually the USA) that is not available in the UK or on the NHS.

Both rights are very important. It is also important that you understand it is your right to choose between the two. You might be happy to accept some treatments but want to refuse others. The treatments you could refuse or ask for range from having a tooth extracted to treatment that will prolong your life.

The biggest difficulties arise when the treatment you want, or are refusing, might prolong your life.

Life-prolonging treatments

The withholding or withdrawing of life-prolonging treatments is a very difficult issue for everyone concerned, including doctors. They have to follow guidance from the General Medical Council (GMC).

Some aspects of this guidance have been challenged in the law courts in recent years. The initial challenge was brought by Mr Burke, who has a degenerative brain condition. It was about whether the guidance was in line with the European Convention on Human Rights, which is now part of UK law in the form of the Human Rights Act 1998. It looked at who could make decisions about artificial hydration and nutrition (Box 21).

Box 21. Artificial hydration and nutrition

Sometimes people are not able to take in any nutrition or hydration (food or liquid) by mouth for some reason, such as being in a coma. Instead, help is provided artificially; for example, by putting a feeding tube into the person's stomach.

The case involving the Hillsborough survivor Tony Bland decided that artificial nutrition and hydration is a medical procedure.

Mr Burke wanted to make sure that, in the event that he wasn't able to make his own decision at the time, his wishes that he should always be provided with artificial hydration and nutrition would be respected.

The Court of Appeal's ruling in Mr Burke's case is particularly important, as this appears to mean that any doctor who disregards the wish of a patient with mental capacity to receive artificial hydration and nutrition would be guilty of murder. However, patients cannot demand treatment(s) that a doctor considers to be futile or detrimental. Although individual doctors must take account of any distress caused by overriding a patient's wishes, a doctor cannot be compelled to provide treatment that he or she considers to be adverse to the patient's clinical needs.

If someone lacks mental capacity but has made an 'advance decision' that they want to be provided with artificial nutrition and hydration, doctors must follow this, in line with the judgement above. There is more about advance decisions in Chapter 8.

Some people have been seriously worried about this issue because of their disabilities or illnesses. They are very concerned that they, not doctors, should decide whether the quality of life they have is 'good enough' to mean that everything is done to help them remain alive. The Disability Rights Commission (see page 276) may be able to advise if this affects you or someone you know.

If there are disagreements – for example, the doctor treating a patient and the patient's family disagree about what should happen next – these should be taken to the courts to decide. While a court ruling is being sought, life-prolonging treatment can be provided.

Making your own decisions and having these followed doesn't always mean prolonging your life. In the case involving Miss B, she was able to express her views and could understand the decisions she was making. Following a major accident, she decided she wanted treatment and support machinery to be removed, knowing that this would lead to her death. The courts agreed she was able to make that decision for herself and her wishes were respected. The doctors and nurses who had been caring for her, however, asked not to be involved in this final stage. This request was respected and another team of staff was involved.

Much of the case law referred to here is about very particular individual circumstances. They help us to understand what the law means in those circumstances, but new situations will always need to be looked at as and when they arise.

Under the Mental Capacity Act 2005, from October 2007 a Welfare Lasting Power of Attorney (LPA) can be drawn up. This can specifically authorise the giving or refusing of life-sustaining treatment. It involves appointing someone to make decisions on your behalf on health and welfare matters if, at a later stage, you cannot make those decisions yourself because at the time you lack mental capacity. The Act also formally recognises 'advance decisions' (sometimes called Living Wills), in which someone may have stated the circumstances under which no treatment, or a particular treatment, should be given. There is more about mental capacity, LPAs and advance decisions in Chapter 8.

Sometimes, there really is nothing more that can be done for someone. The person might be on a life-support machine and only this is keeping their internal organs working. Hospital staff may ask you, as their next of kin, to decide when to turn off the machine. You may well want to talk to someone for support before and after the decision. Ask NHS hospital staff whom you can talk to there. (See also page 219.)

WHEN SOMEONE DIES

Certifying and registering a death
When someone dies, the first official item that will be needed is a medical certificate that states the cause of the person's death. You will need to take this certificate with you when you go to the local register office. Deaths in England or Wales must be registered within five days. The register office is usually called 'Births, Marriages and Deaths'. The offices are generally in council buildings such as the Town Hall (in county areas, the register office is usually in the

County Council's main office or county hall). You should ideally register the death in the district where the person has died but you can register the death in an office elsewhere. If you do register it elsewhere, it may take a day or two longer for all the paperwork to be completed.

You will probably need to make an appointment at the register office to register the death; your local office will be able to tell you when they are open, if an appointment is needed and how long it will take. They should also explain what documents you need to bring with you. When you are there, they will fill in all the forms needed and issue you with the death certificate, showing the details of the person who has died. You will need this in order to arrange the burial or cremation. Although you will be given one copy of the death certificate, you can buy additional copies from the registrar. It is worth doing this at the time, as you will need extra copies in order to do things such as close bank accounts and notify insurance companies.

If the person died in hospital or in their own home (including in a care home in which they have been living), their death can be registered by any one of the following:

- a relative;
- someone present when they died;
- someone else who lives in the person's house, or a member of staff from the hospital if this is where the person died;
- the person making the arrangements with the funeral director.

If someone dies elsewhere (i.e. not at home or in hospital), the person who found the body can also register the death.

The registrar will also issue a certificate for the burial or cremation of the body. This is usually passed to the funeral director, who cannot go ahead with funeral arrangements without it.

There will also be a certificate to be filled in and sent to the local Pensions Service office. This tells the Department for Work and

Pensions that the person has died, because their state retirement pension and other state benefits stop being paid once they have died.

Sometimes, registrars will report a death to the coroner. They must do this if:

- there is no doctor who can issue a medical certificate stating the cause of death;

- the person had never been seen by the doctor who is issuing the medical certificate giving cause of death; or had been seen by that doctor in the past but not in the last 14 days of their life;

- the cause of death is unknown;

- the cause of death is believed to be unnatural or suspicious;

- the death happened during an operation or before the person had recovered from an anaesthetic;

- the death is due to industrial disease or industrial poisoning.

The death certificate cannot be issued, and the funeral arrangements cannot go ahead, while the coroner is looking into the matter.

The Coroner's Section of the Ministry of Justice has a leaflet, When Sudden Death Occurs, *which is available in several languages and formats and may be helpful (contact details on page 281).*

Coroner's inquests and post-mortems

It is up to the coroner to decide whether to investigate the deaths referred to them. The coroner can decide whether a post-mortem is needed: this involves examining the body, including looking at internal organs, to see if the cause of death can be established.

Once the coroner has decided not to investigate, or has completed the investigations, they will tell the registrar. The registrar can then register the death and issue the relevant certificates.

If the coroner needs to investigate, this may cause some delays to funeral arrangements. In some religious beliefs, it is very important that the person be buried or cremated as soon as possible after they have died. If the person who has died held these beliefs, make sure you let the coroner's office know about this and ask them to do everything possible to speed up the process.

Some people may object strongly to a post-mortem being carried out, whether for religious, cultural or personal reasons. If you feel this way, you can put your objections in writing to the coroner. If the coroner still believes that a post-mortem is essential, you can appeal to the Divisional Court. Be aware that doing this will, inevitably, mean a further delay.

The results of any post-mortem should be shared as soon as possible with the relatives of the person who has died. The person's GP and/or consultant will also be told the results. The coroner's office may also decide to inform the police, if there are suspicions of foul play; but the coroner should tell you what, if anything, is going to happen next.

Box 22. Retaining organs

Serious concerns were raised that internal organs and other human tissues were kept (retained) by the NHS after the post-mortem of babies and young children at Alder Hey Hospital (the Royal Liverpool Children's Hospital) but without the knowledge or permission of their parents or legal guardians. This led to an inquiry, which made a number of recommendations.

Consent must be obtained to use human tissues after the person has died. Once the coroner's enquiries have been completed, the organs and tissues taken during a post-mortem must be returned to the body, unless relatives have given specific permission for these to be kept and used in research, for example.

The Human Tissues Act 2004 sets out many of these requirements.

When the results of a post-mortem are known, the coroner may decide to hold an inquest into what led to the person's death. This is not the same thing as a criminal trial. The coroner's office will explain what might be involved if an inquest is to be held.

Sometimes the NHS hospital in which the person died will ask for a post-mortem to be carried out, to help them understand more about a particular disease or condition. But they have to get permission from the patient's relatives to do so.

Dealing with the body

Every NHS hospital should have a procedure for handling the death of patients. This can include written instructions for staff, reminding them of the importance of finding out the wishes of the dying patient, relatives and close friends on matters such as whether they want to be present during the time leading up to death, about being told about the death, and about any religious and cultural practices.

Some religious beliefs require the mouth and eyes of someone who has died to be closed, or for their feet to face a door, or for their heads to be covered.

You have the right to expect that NHS staff will respect the religious and cultural beliefs of the person who has died. You may need to tell staff what this involves. If you are unhappy about any aspect of the person's death, you can complain using the NHS complaints process (see Chapter 16).

Although people are often understandably distressed when someone dies, and making a complaint may be the last thing you want to have to think about, if the behaviour or attitude of either particular staff or the hospital as a whole changes for the better, you will be helping other families in the future. Do bear in mind, though, that even if you are extremely upset because of how the person's body or their death has been handled, violence and abusive behaviour towards NHS staff will not be tolerated.

The person's body can be moved within England and Wales for burial or cremation purposes. If the body is in England or Wales and you want it moved to somewhere in Scotland, Northern Ireland, the Isle of Man, the Channel Islands or overseas, you will need the permission of the coroner's office in the area where the body is now. You will be asked to complete Form 104 (available from either the coroner or the registrar) and to give this to the coroner together with any certificate for burial or cremation that has already been issued. The coroner will then tell you when the body can be moved. This is usually four complete working days after your application was received. If you want the body moved abroad, you need to ask the airline or other transport company what requirements they have (for example, airlines require that the body be embalmed).

You should note that, if the person has died in hospital but you want their body to be moved to another part of the country, the NHS does not have to pay the costs of transport. You will probably have to pay for this yourself.

Funeral arrangements

If someone dies in hospital and relatives cannot be traced, or relatives cannot afford to pay for a funeral and do not qualify for a funeral payment from the Social Fund, the hospital has a duty to arrange and pay for burial or cremation. The hospital should try to find out if the patient had any views on whether they wanted to be buried or cremated. This might involve asking staff, if the patient had been in hospital for a long time, as well as asking any relatives or friends. The hospital should also try to find out whether the patient held any particular religious views. If so, a minister from that religion should be present to conduct the ceremony. If it is not possible to find out the patient's beliefs or views, the hospital should arrange for cremation.

If the hospital believes that relatives could afford to arrange and pay for the funeral themselves although the relatives say otherwise, the hospital can ask the local authority in whose area the body lies to arrange for burial or cremation. This comes under the Public Health (Control of Disease) Act 1984. Note, though, that if you make the arrangements and pay for a funeral, the local authority cannot reimburse you.

If a care home resident dies and there is no one who can pay for the funeral, this will be organised by the relevant social services department.

When the NHS or social services pays for funerals, these tend to be fairly basic affairs. They often have an agreement with a local firm of funeral directors who will carry this out on their behalf.

Dealing with bereavement

One of the many recommendations of the Alder Hey inquiry (see Box 22) was to remind the NHS that it has to provide bereavement counselling to the families and friends of patients who have died, as well as to staff. This is usually offered immediately after the person has died. But it is up to you whether to take up the offer of counselling, which typically involves you talking to a trained bereavement counsellor about what has happened and about your feelings. The counsellor may offer suggestions on what you could do next, whom else to talk to, and other advice.

Some people who would rather not talk to someone straight away decide that they would like to see someone later on. Ask your GP if this is something they can help organise for you, or for other suggestions. Many people who have been bereaved find it helpful to talk at least once to someone who has an understanding of how they may be feeling. (See also page 106.)

You may also want to talk to someone at a voluntary organisation such as Cruse Bereavement Care. It offers counselling and advice throughout the UK (contact details on page 275).

For more information, contact Age Concern's Information Line (details on page 271).

Death-bed marriages

Someone who wants to marry and is not expected to recover but who is too ill to be moved to a place registered for marriage ceremonies can get a special licence to marry where they are. Their fiancé (or fiancée) would have to arrange this with the superintendent registrar at the register office that covers the part of the country where they will get married. This also applies to gay couples wishing to create a civil partnership.

The registrar will need a certificate from a medical practitioner (such as the person's GP or the hospital consultant) to confirm that the person cannot be married in a licensed venue because they are too ill to move and will not recover.

It is also possible to arrange a Church of England marriage for the reasons above. In this case, the best thing to do is speak to the hospital chaplain or the vicar or rector of the parish where you live.

Equipment, property and possessions

If the person who has died has been using equipment provided by the NHS or social services departments (perhaps by the Joint Equipment Store run by both), you should contact them as soon as you can to let them know the person has died. They may want to collect the equipment but they will tell you what needs to be arranged.

You might also want to speak to the person's GP about cancelling any NHS appointments that are pending. There may be lots of people you need to let know, such as the person's dentist and optometrist. You don't have to tell these professionals – but if you don't, reminders about check-ups and other appointments might still arrive addressed to the person who has died and you could find this very upsetting.

The safekeeping of the possessions of someone who has died in an NHS hospital is not the responsibility of the hospital. They should, however, hand these over to anyone responsible for administering the person's estate (usually called an Executor and named in the person's Will).

If the person was living in a care home when they died, you should check what their contract with the home says. Some care homes charge for the room for a certain period of time after the person has died – for example, for 28 days. During this time, you should be able to collect the person's belongings from the room. But the home will expect the room to have been cleared by the end of the time specified in the contract.

For more information, contact Age Concern's Information Line (details on page 271).

16

Making Complaints

This chapter explains the ways you can make a complaint about different issues. It highlights support to which you are entitled in making your complaint, explores how the NHS considers cases of negligence and compensation, and explains the role of the National Patient Safety Agency. It also looks briefly at complaints about healthcare bought privately.

COMPLAINING ABOUT THE NHS

Some things cannot be dealt with under the NHS complaints procedure; for example:

- Complaints about healthcare treatment you have paid for privately (see pages 241–242).

- Events about which you are already taking legal action (although if you are taking legal action about one issue and there are other matters you want to raise, you can use the NHS complaints process for these other matters).

The NHS complaints system can refer parts of complaints that are about your social services department to the local authority in question. This is particularly helpful if your complaint 'straddles' both NHS and social services issues. For example, if someone is being discharged from an NHS hospital and they think this was done badly, and there were also problems because the care that social services was going to provide for them on their return home wasn't ready.

For more information, contact Age Concern's Information Line (details on page 271).

MAKING A COMPLAINT

As well as using the NHS complaints procedure described below, you can also complain about an individual NHS professional to their registering body (discussed later, under 'Making complaints about individual professionals'). You can also raise concerns about treatment with the National Patient Safety Agency (see page 10).

The NHS complaints procedure is set out in Parliamentary Regulations. It applies to all NHS Trusts in England. It also applies to Special Health Authorities that work across the UK – for example, the National Blood Service.

Who can complain?

You have the right to complain about the treatment and care (or its lack) that you have received. Your complaint might be about any number of things. For example, you may believe you have been discriminated against because of your age; or your complaint might be about lack of privacy or of single-sex wards; about the poor behaviour of staff; or about inappropriate care. You can also complain about decisions your local Primary Care Trust makes about commissioning (funding) or planning NHS services. Chapter 18 looks at other ways you can be involved in influencing local and national NHS decisions. If a mistake was made in your care, you may have grounds for seeking financial compensation for any injuries that resulted, for example (see page 240).

Sometimes people are worried about making complaints. They are anxious that it might get them (or staff) into trouble – for example, if it is about a particular NHS professional or service that they know they will still need to call on after the complaint has been dealt with. But, unless complaints are made, NHS staff and organisations may not know whether mistakes are being made or inadequate care provided. They need to be told about this so that they can take steps to improve healthcare experiences for other NHS patients. Many of the charities that offer advice and information will be able to give you details of the various complaints systems and what to do. For example, Elderly Accommodation Counsel (contact details on page 277) has an information sheet that will help guide you as you go about making a complaint.

You also have the right to complain about the care someone else received if he or she:

- has died;
- is a child (and you are the child's parent or legal guardian);
- cannot make the request him- or herself because of physical or mental incapacity;
- has asked you to act on his or her behalf.

If you are acting on someone else's behalf, the person responsible for dealing with NHS complaints will need to be sure that the person has given their consent. So you should not be surprised if you are asked to produce a letter or some other proof from the person saying you have their permission. Even if this upsets you, think how much more upsetting it would be if someone claimed to represent you without your agreement.

If you are acting for someone who has died or who lacks the capacity to bring their own complaint, the NHS complaints manager is within their rights to expect that you are either a relative or you have (or had) sufficient interest in their welfare to take on this role now – for example, you were the person's spouse or partner, or perhaps held a Lasting Power of Attorney for the person. (See also Chapter 8.)

If the complaints manager does not accept that you are a suitable person to take this forward, they must write to you and explain why. (You could challenge this decision but you would need to set out the reasons why you are suitable.) One reason the complaints manager might give is that the patient has previously said they do not wish their health information to be discussed with a third party (see Chapter 17): you would count as a third party because you are neither the patient (the first party) nor the NHS body (the second party). If your main aim is simply to make sure the complaint is looked at, you could then ask how the complaint will be taken forward if you are not involved. There is no absolute right for you to be able to pursue a complaint on behalf of anybody and everybody, but it would be unusual for a complaint not to be considered at all just because of your lack of suitability.

You can complain verbally (in person or on the telephone), in writing or by email. Make sure that your complaint reaches the right person. There are time limits within which the NHS must consider your complaint, so it will be recorded as starting on the date the complaint was received. In the case of written complaints, this would be when the letter reached the relevant organisation.

There are also time limits that apply to you. You must make your complaint:

- within six months of the event; or
- within six months of your realising there was something to complain about, as long as it is not more than twelve months after the event itself took place.

These time limits can be waived if there are good reasons why you could not complain sooner. You will probably be asked to explain what these reasons are.

The first stage of making (and dealing with) a complaint is sometimes called 'local resolution'. There are slightly different arrangements, depending on whether your complaint is about a primary care provider (such as your GP or an optometrist), about a Primary Care Trust or NHS Trust, or about an NHS Foundation Trust. These are all described below.

Do remember that, if your complaint is about treatment that you have paid for privately, these NHS arrangements will not apply.

Complaints about a Primary Care Trust or NHS Trust

Each Primary Care Trust and NHS Trust must appoint someone to act as a complaints manager. The person with this role may have a different job title but it should be obvious that they handle complaints. The complaints manager deals with complaints made by members of the public as well as by NHS staff.

Box 23. The Patient Advice and Liaison Service and the Independent Complaints Advocacy Service

Every Primary Care Trust and NHS Trust must have a Patient Advice and Liaison Service (PALS). Your local PALS will be able to explain what making a complaint involves, but it will probably start by seeing if it can help to sort out any issues or concerns you have. It can also provide information on local services and support groups. This includes details of your local Independent Complaints Advocacy Service (ICAS).

There is an ICAS covering every Primary Care Trust area. They provide advocacy services for people making formal complaints about NHS services.

You can find contact details for your local PALS and ICAS services by:

- contacting NHS Direct;
- contacting your local Primary Care Trust;
- looking in the telephone directory.

Trusts must also make sure that a senior person in the organisation (for example, a member of the Board of Directors) has overall responsibility for making sure that each Trust meets the requirements of the complaints system. Each Trust must also have a Patient Advice and Liaison Service to help support patients in raising issues and complaints (Box 23).

You should receive an acknowledgement of your complaint within two days of its being received. This will probably be a short letter saying that your complaint has been received and is being looked into. You may also be sent details of the complaints procedure, including the role of the Healthcare Commission. It should also be explained to you that, in investigating your complaint, it may be necessary to share information about you. This should involve only information relevant to your complaint (for example, details of your operation and why this was needed), and should be shared only with the people the Trust needs to speak to for the investigation. (See also Chapter 17.)

At this stage, you should also be told about your right to assistance from the Independent Complaints Advocacy Service (Box 23).

When looking into your complaint, the NHS complaints manager can decide to arrange mediation or conciliation services in order to try to resolve the complaint. This would involve your meeting with someone working as a mediator (probably from an organisation specialising in this kind of support), who is not involved in this complaint in any way. The mediator would also work with those you are complaining about. Both you and the others involved in the complaint have to agree to take part in mediation, however.

You can also request a mediator. Trusts must offer this service. Mediation can be a good way of resolving disputes – for example, ones that are based on misunderstandings on both sides. Sometimes people feel this is a 'soft option' and want to continue with the formal complaints route but it can be an effective way of helping staff understand how they come across to patients, and changing their behaviour as a result. But it is up to you whether you want to try this. If the mediation is unsuccessful, you can tell the complaints manager that you want to continue with the formal complaint.

You should be told the outcome of your complaint within 25 working days of your complaint being made (or 10 working days if your complaint is about any aspect of a GP practice). A 'working day' is Monday through Friday (ie weekdays). This means you have to ignore weekends and Bank holidays when working out the date by when you should hear the outcome.

Sometimes it can take the complaints manager longer than 25 working days to reach their conclusion (or 10 days in the case of complaints about a GP practice). This might be because it is a very complicated issue or because a key member of staff they need to talk to is away. In this case, they must reply as quickly as possible after the 25 days. In the meantime they must write to you and explain why there is a delay. The complaints manager should contact you to discuss this delay so that you can both agree the new date by which you will hear.

When you receive the response to your complaint, you should also be given information about taking the complaint to the next stage, if you want to. The next stage is to ask for an independent review by the Healthcare Commission. You can do this if you are not satisfied with how the complaint has been handled or you are unhappy about the outcome (see page 230).

One of the outcomes from this stage may be an apology for what has happened. It is important that you know that the NHS has been told that an apology is not an admission of liability. In the past, people have often asked for an apology but did not receive one because it was believed that saying sorry meant the NHS was accepting it was at fault in legal terms. This issue had become very mixed up with concerns about legal claims for negligence and compensation (see page 240). It is perfectly possible to be sorry that someone has had an experience that was terrible for them without this automatically meaning the NHS was legally responsible.

Complaints to NHS Foundation Trusts

One of the 'freedoms' that NHS Foundation Trusts have is that they can draw up and use their own complaints procedure. However, if they do not have a procedure and you have a complaint about a Foundation Trust, or if you use their procedure and are unhappy with the outcome, you can take your complaint to the Healthcare Commission.

The Healthcare Commission can consider complaints about NHS Foundation Trusts only if they are made by patients and are about the provision by the Trust of healthcare or other services to patients (or care delivered on behalf of the Trust). If your complaint is about something else, or you are not the patient, the Healthcare Commission must refer your complaint to the Independent Regulator (Box 24). Even if the complaint is something the Healthcare Commission can investigate, and provided it has your agreement, it will in any case seek the views of the Independent Regulator. It will share your complaint with the Independent Regulator in order to do so.

Unless you clearly say otherwise, the Healthcare Commission will assume it has your permission to share your complaint with the Independent Regulator.

Box 24. The Independent Regulator

The Independent Regulator is the formal title of the organisation responsible for authorising, monitoring and regulating NHS Foundation Trusts. Its everyday name (or working name) is Monitor. It is independent from the Department of Health but its members are appointed by the Secretary of State for Health.

Contact details of Monitor (the Independent Regulator for NHS Foundation Trusts) are on page 281.

The Healthcare Commission

The Healthcare Commission is responsible for carrying out independent reviews of complaints.

You must contact the Healthcare Commission within six months of your receiving the outcome of your original complaint. The Healthcare Commission can also consider complaints that have been with the healthcare provider for six months but have not yet been resolved.

You will need to complete a Healthcare Commission complaints form. Your local Primary Care Trust or Independent Complaints Advocacy Service should have copies they can give you; or you can contact the Healthcare Commission and ask for one to be posted to you; or you can download and print a copy from its website (see page 278 for contact details).

If you don't want to complete the form, you can write to the Healthcare Commission with your request, but do make sure you send the copy of the report (the response, or outcome) that you were sent at the end of the local complaints stage, as discussed above. This first stage is sometimes called 'local resolution'.

The Healthcare Commission can also look at some complaints about healthcare services you have bought privately. This is because it also regulates private and voluntary sector healthcare providers (see page 10).

There are some circumstances in which the Healthcare Commission cannot carry out independent reviews:

- You have stated in writing that you are taking legal proceedings.

- The NHS Foundation Trust concerned is taking (or is proposing to take) disciplinary action against their member of staff who is the subject of your complaint.

- The complaint arises out of an NHS Foundation Trust's (alleged) failure to comply with a request for data under the Data Protection Act 1998 or a request for information under the Freedom of Information Act 2000.

- The complaint is being or has been investigated by the Health Service Ombudsman (see page 232).

Once it has received your complaint, and provided this is something it can review, the Healthcare Commission must tell you what it has decided to do next as soon as is 'reasonably practicable' – hopefully within ten working days. Its decision may be:

- not to take any further action; or

- to recommend the action that the organisation concerned should take; or
- to investigate the complaint further; or
- to consider the subject of the complaint as part of any other investigation or review that it is carrying out (or proposing to carry out) as part of its overall role (see page 10), or
- to refer the complaint to the relevant professional body (see page 236); or
- to refer the complaint to the Health Service Ombudsman.

Whatever the decision, the Healthcare Commission must give reasons. It must also send a copy of its decision to the person or the organisation that you are complaining about. It can choose to send the decision to any other organisation that the Healthcare Commission believes has an interest in the matter. If it is to investigate further, you should ask how quickly it expects to be able to complete this and let you know its findings.

If the Healthcare Commission recommends action to the local organisation involved and you are still dissatisfied, you can ask the Healthcare Commission to look at the complaint again.

If an investigation is needed, you have the right to request a panel of three members of the public to hear your complaint. The panel will hear evidence from you, the organisation you are complaining against, any witnesses involved and the Healthcare Commission's report. The panel will make recommendations about how to resolve your case and, when necessary, suggest service improvements.

If you are unhappy with the Healthcare Commission's decision, or if it investigates and you do not agree with the findings, you can take the matter to the Health Service Ombudsman.

The Health Service Ombudsman
The Health Service Ombudsman investigates complaints made by or on behalf of someone who has suffered because of unsatisfactory treatment or service from the NHS. This could include the NHS

not providing a service or a failure in service or maladministration. The Ombudsman also looks into complaints against private health providers, provided that the NHS funded the treatment. She can also investigate complaints about other services provided on behalf of the NHS, and can look at complaints about continuing NHS healthcare – including review panel decisions (see page 188). Contact details are on page 278.

Her office publishes a range of leaflets (in several languages and formats) explaining what she (and her staff, on her behalf) can and cannot investigate. They also explain how to make the complaint. You do not need to use a lawyer to bring a complaint to the Ombudsman but the usual expectation is that you have already taken the matter through local resolution and independent review stages. If you have not done this, and the Ombudsman thinks you should do so first, her office will write to you to let you know what steps you should take.

Unlike other parts of the complaints process, the Ombudsman does not accept complaints made by email. You will need to put your complaint in writing, and you may be asked to provide other documents to help back up your concerns.

It is up to the Ombudsman whether to investigate. If your complaint is not to be investigated, you will be sent a letter explaining why. If you disagree with this decision, and you have significant new (or fresh) evidence that was not available when you made your complaint, you can send this to the Ombudsman and ask for the decision not to investigate to be reconsidered. A member of staff who is more senior than the person who decided not to investigate will look at your new evidence and your original complaint. You should receive their decision within 18 days of your letter and new evidence reaching the Ombudsman's office.

If you don't have any significant new evidence but still disagree with the decision not to investigate, you can still write to the Ombudsman and explain why you think it should be looked into. You will receive a reply within 14 days, but this might still be a refusal to investigate.

The Ombudsman does not have to investigate just because you have written.

If the Ombudsman decides to look into the matter on your behalf, you will receive a letter explaining what the next steps will be. Investigations can take a long time: the Ombudsman's office takes great pains to make sure it sees all the relevant material and may decide to interview all the people involved, including you. But the Ombudsman's office should keep you up to date about their progress.

Many (but not all) of the Ombudsman's investigations are published. You can either buy copies from The Stationery Office (page 285) or you can download copies from the Ombudsman's website (page 278). But everyone whose complaint is investigated receives a copy of this, even if the report is not published. Everyone mentioned in the report, including your relative or friend (if this matter is about someone else) has their details made anonymous (for example, you might be referred to as 'Mrs W' when your name is actually Mrs Brown), so you will not be identified. In recent years, some of these investigations have highlighted matters of national concern regarding continuing NHS healthcare (see Chapter 13).

Although you can't appeal against the Ombudsman's decision, you can challenge it in the law courts through a judicial review. You would need legal advice on doing this, and advice on how you would pay for such legal action, as it can be very costly. Your local law centre or Citizens Advice Bureau may be able to point you in the right direction.

You can, however, complain further if you are concerned about how the Ombudsman dealt with your complaint. For example, under the Freedom of Information Act 2000 the Ombudsman has to give you reasons why some information might have been withheld from you. If you disagree with these reasons, you could raise the matter with the organisation that is responsible for the Freedom of Information issues – the Information Commissioner (see Chapter 17). But if you have other concerns about how your case was handled, you should write to the Ombudsman and let her know what these are.

The outcome of the Ombudsman's investigation can be to tell the NHS to refund you for treatment you have had to buy privately, because, for example, the Ombudsman has ruled that it should have been funded by the NHS. It can also require the NHS organisation involved to make a payment to you in recognition that you have had to bring this action. But the Ombudsman cannot provide funds for compensation, nor insist that compensation for physical or mental injury (for example) is paid. These types of compensation claims are handled through a different route, as discussed later.

MAKING COMPLAINTS ABOUT INDIVIDUAL PROFESSIONALS

The starting point is to tell someone – for example, a dental assistant, the GP, a receptionist – about your complaint. Often it can be sorted out there and then.

If you prefer, you can take a more formal route. You might want to do this if talking doesn't resolve the problem, or because you would rather not talk about this with the person who provides your care. All GPs, dentists, optometrists and pharmacies offering NHS services must have a complaints procedure and a senior member of staff who oversees this. The surgery or clinic concerned should be able to give you this information; if you are unsure, contact your local Primary Care Trust and ask whom you should complain to.

Once you have made a formal complaint, you should hear the outcome within ten working days of its being received. A 'working day' is a weekday, so ignore Saturdays, Sundays and Bank holidays when working out the date by which you should have the response.

If you are not happy with the decision or response, you can take your complaint to the Healthcare Commission (see page 231).

If the person you are complaining about works for the NHS, you can also make a complaint using the NHS's procedure. This is explained on page 223.

But if the person only works for themselves (for example, they run a private dental clinic) you won't be able to use this NHS route.

Most healthcare professionals must be registered with a particular body relevant to their profession. For example, doctors must be registered with the General Medical Council. Sometimes this registration is called being licensed to practise.

If your concern is a case of serious misconduct, you may want to go straight to the body that registers that person and make your complaint. Serious misconduct includes fraud, abuse (whether physical, financial, emotional or sexual), unnecessary treatment or treatment resulting in injury. These are not the only examples.

If you believe a crime has been committed, you can also go to the police.

Many concerns are, however, not so serious as to need the involvement of the police or a formal complaint to the registering body. In such cases, in the first instance you should make your concerns known to the professional concerned. This can be hard to do, so you may want someone to help you do it. If you don't have a close friend or relative you would like to involve, you could ask your local Age Concern if they can help or if they can suggest someone you might approach.

Most clinics and individual professionals offer some arrangement for patients to make a complaint. Ask for details and then follow what is suggested. If you are still unhappy, or if you feel that how you are being asked to complain is a problem, approach the relevant registration body and raise your concerns with them.

Complaints about doctors

All doctors must be registered to practise (sometimes known as 'being licensed to practise') with the General Medical Council (GMC). This applies to hospital doctors, GPs and those working in private clinics as well as for the NHS. It is illegal to work as a doctor unless you are registered.

If you have concerns about the actions or behaviour of a doctor, you can raise them with the General Medical Council. It has a guide for patients about how to make a complaint.

The General Medical Council can investigate and, if necessary, withdraw (strike off) or suspend the person's registration, which would make it unlawful for the person to work as a doctor in the UK. Examples of why someone might be 'struck off' include if they hit or otherwise abused a patient or stole from a patient. The role of the General Medical Council is being reviewed by the Government during 2007 as part of a wider look at patient safety issues and regulation of health professionals.

If a doctor commits a crime, you or the General Medical Council can also involve the police.

If the doctor you are complaining about works for the NHS, you can also make a complaint using the NHS's procedure.

Complaints about nurses, health visitors or midwives
All nurses, health visitors and midwives must be registered with the Nursing and Midwifery Council (NMC).

The Nursing and Midwifery Council can investigate and, if necessary, withdraw (strike off) or suspend the person's registration. This would make it unlawful for that person to work as a nurse (or health visitor or midwife) in the UK. Examples of why someone might be 'struck off' include if they hit or otherwise abused a patient or stole from a patient.

If a nurse, health visitor or midwife commits a crime, you or the Nursing and Midwifery Council can also involve the police.

If the person you are complaining about works for the NHS, you can also make a complaint using the NHS's procedure.

Complaints about dentists
All dentists, whether they offer NHS or private treatments, are registered by the General Dental Council (GDC). The General

Dental Council also registers dental hygienists and dental therapists (sometimes these are collectively called dental auxiliaries), and, in 2006, also began to register dental nurses and dental technicians.

The General Dental Council can remove a dental professional's registration, and without registration the person cannot lawfully work as a dentist. As with registration of doctors and nurses, removing an individual from the professional register is often reserved for the most serious of complaints. Different routes may be needed for other types of complaint. Anyone dissatisfied with the NHS dental treatment they have received can make a complaint using the NHS complaints procedure outlined earlier.

In May 2006, the General Dental Council introduced a new system for handling complaints about private dentists and private dental treatment. Private patients should first use their dentist's own complaints procedure. If a complaint cannot be sorted out this way, the patient should contact the Dental Complaints Service (see under General Dental Council, page 277). An adviser will then discuss the complaint with the patient and the dentist. If this is unsuccessful, the complaint will be considered by a regional panel. The panel will be made up of two members of the public (lay volunteers) and one dental professional volunteer, who will advise the lay panel members on clinical issues. The panel will meet with the dentist and the person making the complaint, and recommend some common-sense solutions.

Any serious complaints (for example, about patient safety or whether a practitioner should be allowed to continue) will be dealt with by the General Dental Council.

Complaints about optometrists

Dispensing opticians and optometrists are registered by the General Optical Council (GOC). As well as regulating individuals, the General Optical Council regulates organisations carrying on business as optometrists or dispensing opticians – for example, the larger chains such as SpecSaver or Dollond & Aitchison.

Complaints about therapists

Each of the therapies (for example, occupational therapy, physiotherapy, arts therapy) has its own professional association or college: the College of Occupational Therapists, the Royal College of Speech and Language Therapists, the British Association of Arts Therapists, the British Association of Dramatherapists, the Association of Professional Music Therapists and the Chartered Society of Physiotherapy (contact details in the Appendix).

If you have a complaint about someone in one of these professions, you can contact the relevant association. If the individual is registered with the Health Professions Council (HPC), your complaint can also be made to that organisation. This can be done whether the person works for the NHS or runs their own private clinic. If there is anyone calling themselves an occupational therapist, a speech and language therapist, an art, drama or music therapist, or a physiotherapist, and is not registered with the Health Professions Council, tell the Council immediately so that it can take action. This could involve the person being prosecuted.

Complaints about pharmacists/prescriptions

If your complaint is about a pharmacist, or about the owner of a pharmacy business, you can raise this with the Royal Pharmaceutical Society (contact details on page 284).

If your complaint is about an NHS prescription, you can also use the NHS complaints process as outlined earlier in this chapter.

If your complaint is about prescriptions by a doctor, nurse or dentist, you can complain about this to the professional organisation they have to register with. If they are providing services to you as an NHS patient, you can also follow the NHS complaints route.

Complaints about chiropodists/podiatrists

If you think the chiropodist has behaved badly or the standard of care has not been good, you can contact the Health Professions Council. This applies both to private chiropodists and to those who work in the NHS. If you are concerned about the NHS treatment you have received, you can also use the NHS complaints procedure.

CLAIMING COMPENSATION FROM THE NHS

The Government has set up and runs two specific compensation schemes for patients with particular illnesses. The first – the Skipton Fund, a UK-wide body – is for people who have contracted hepatitis C through NHS blood or blood-related products. Information is also available on the condition from the charity Hepatitis C Trust. (Contact details on pages 285 and 279.)

The second compensation scheme is for the small number of people who have so far developed variant Creutzfeldt–Jakob disease (vCJD). Compensation for people, and their families, with vCJD is administered by the vCJD Trust (contact details on page 286). The charity the CJD Support Network (contact details on page 274) may also be helpful. To make a claim resulting from vCJD, you should contact either Edwina Rawson or Jonathan Zimmern, at Charles Russell Solicitors (address on page 273).

Most other compensation claims arise out of issues of clinical negligence. This is where doctors and other clinicians have been remiss in their treatment of you. In other words, they have failed in their 'duty of care'. As a result you have sustained some form of injury, suffered pain or been disadvantaged in some other way. In the worst cases, someone might have died as a result of the negligent action. Negligence can include not taking action as well as doing something wrong such as giving someone the incorrect dose of medicine.

The NHS has a UK-wide compensation scheme for people who have been affected in this way. It is run by the NHS Litigation Authority (NHSLA). The NHS Litigation Authority is a Special Health Authority that covers the whole of the UK.

In order to gain financial compensation arising from clinical negligence, you will probably need legal advice. Depending on your income and capital, and the details of your case, you may be eligible for some Legal Aid to help with those costs. Your local law centre will be able to advise about this. You can also contact Community Legal Service for information on the Legal Aid system and advice on other legal matters (see page 275 for contact details).

A good starting point, if you want to pursue this legal route, is to contact the charity Action for Victims of Medical Accidents (AvMA; address on page 271). AvMA has a team of legally trained caseworkers who can provide free and confidential advice after a medical accident. They can also suggest experienced solicitors, advise about legal challenges (such as seeking a judicial review, including how to pay for this), and give you a list of questions to ask if you want to find your own legal representative.

COMPLAINTS ABOUT PRIVATE HEALTHCARE SERVICES

Sometimes the NHS buys (or commissions) healthcare services from the private sector, on behalf of NHS patients. As far as patients are concerned, this still counts as NHS care because the NHS funds it even if a private organisation provides it. If your complaint is about the care the NHS has funded for you, you can use the NHS complaints procedure. You would need to complain to the NHS Trust that paid for the healthcare you received. Or you could choose to complain direct to the organisation that provided the service. Private healthcare providers must have a complaints procedure you can use, and they must give you details of this on request. Whichever way you complain, if you are not happy with the response you receive, you can ask the Healthcare Commission for an independent review.

If you yourself have paid for your healthcare from a private healthcare organisation, you can make a complaint using its complaints procedure. You can also complain about individual professionals to the relevant organisation with which they must be registered – such as the General Medical Council or the Health Professions Council. (See also Chapters 3, 4, 5 and 7.)

Some NHS hospitals offer private 'pay beds'. Under this arrangement, you are treated as a private patient even though you may be on NHS premises. If you have a complaint about private pay bed treatment, you can use the NHS complaints procedure but only about issues to do with the facilities (such as the ward or room you were in, or the food) and non-medical staff (for example, the porters or the nursing staff – basically anyone who is not a doctor) provided by the NHS hospital in question. If you have a complaint about the medical input to your care from, say, the consultant, you have to complain about this to the General Medical Council (see page 237).

Even if the consultant also works for that NHS hospital as an NHS doctor, the NHS employer is not responsible for the consultant's private practice.

Complaints about private doctors

If you are unhappy with a doctor's behaviour or treatment, you can complain to the General Medical Council. You may also be able to make a complaint to the Healthcare Commission, as some private clinics have to be regulated by them under the Care Standards Act 2000.

The NHS complaints procedure does not apply in the case of private treatment for which you have paid.

OTHER INVESTIGATIONS

The complaints and compensation systems outlined above are not the only way the NHS finds out about issues. Nor are they the only actions the NHS might take.

Coroner's inquest and post-mortems

The coroner holds inquests into unexpected or suspicious deaths. The NHS is expected to liaise with the coroner's office, especially if such deaths might have involved NHS staff.

Criminal offences

There is nothing to stop you, or the NHS, from calling the police if you believe that a criminal offence has taken place. This could include indecent assault, physical assault, harm or injury, or even death. The police should tell you whether this is something they can investigate.

National Patient Safety Agency

The National Patient Safety Agency (NPSA) is a Special Health Authority that co-ordinates the system of reporting errors and 'incidents' (whether deliberate or accidental) across the country. It is believed that, if NHS staff are encouraged to report mistakes when they make them, lessons can be learned quickly and patient safety improved across the UK.

Both patients and carers can report any unexpected suffering or harm they have experienced as a result of contact with NHS services.

You should note, however, that you might still need to bring a complaint against the organisation involved, as outlined above. This is because the National Patient Safety Agency can't investigate individual complaints.

Information and Communication

There is a great deal of healthcare information you should be given. You have a right to receive:

- Copies of letters that NHS doctors write to each other about your health (eg copies of letters about your care from your GP to a hospital consultant).
- A copy of your dental treatment plan (Chapter 4).
- A copy of any assessment of your health and care needs (Chapters 12 and 13) and a copy of any care plan, if services will be provided.

If you need this information in a particular form, such as large print, Braille, recorded on a cassette tape or in a language other than English, the NHS should provide this for you. Other information, such as the decision whether or not to provide you with NHS fully funded continuing healthcare (Chapter 13), may be recorded in your medical notes (see page 248 for details of how to access these).

If the NHS care you need is provided only if you meet local criteria, copies of these criteria should be available to you. If you are in hospital, you should have information about how your discharge will be handled; there may also be leaflets about what to expect while you are in hospital. Your GP surgery should have leaflets explaining what it provides, when it is open and what to do if you are taken ill when it is closed.

Under the Freedom of Information Act 2000, public bodies (such as the Department of Health, local councils or the NHS) must say what information they publish, how the information is made available, and whether it is free or if there is a charge.

There may also be other information that you receive when you ask for treatment. For example, some hospital Accident and Emergency (A&E) units have a digital display showing approximate waiting times.

If English is not your first language

One of the basic principles on which the NHS works is that everyone who is entitled to NHS care should have equal access to this.

If English is not your first language, or you have no spoken or written English at all, you may need some help with translations so that you can understand what is happening. Nurses, doctors and others also need to be able to talk to you.

All A&E units in England have copies of *The Emergency Multilingual Phrasebook*. This is funded by the Department of Health but produced by the British Red Cross. It covers, in 36 languages (from Albanian to Welsh), the most common medical questions and terms. Other organisations can buy copies from the British Red Cross (page 273), or it can be accessed on the Department of Health's website.

The aim of the *Phrasebook* is to help staff communicate with patients who do not speak English at this first, emergency, stage. It can also be helpful where the shock of accident or injury means that someone who, in ordinary circumstances would speak English, has reverted to their mother tongue. After using the *Phrasebook* to begin with, though, staff are likely to need to ask an interpreter to come into the hospital.

Some NHS Trusts employ their own interpreters; others use interpreters from other organisations. If no one who speaks a particular language can be found, the hospital or clinic may contact a telephone interpreter service such as Language Line.

If you need an interpreter, you will not be asked to pay for this. In non-emergency settings your language needs may be noted in your health records. People may take a relative or friend with them who can speak English to translate for them but this is not always ideal. Some people feel that certain medical matters are very private and they do not want their family or friends to know all the details. In these cases, ask the surgery or healthcare professional how they can help you to have a more private consultation or treatment.

INFORMATION BEFORE MAKING DECISIONS

Before you make decisions about certain treatments, you will need information about the benefits and risks to you of either agreeing to or refusing a treatment. You should be told about alternative treatments, drugs or approaches. Depending on your particular health problem, you may also want to know about side effects (for example, the side effects of chemotherapy) or about any longer-term problems that could arise.

The information should be given to you in a format that you can understand. If this means it needs to be in another language, for example, this should be made available. If you have a disability and need information in another format because of this, the NHS must provide it for you under the Disability Discrimination Act 1995.

You can ask for a second opinion about your condition or any proposed treatment – although this does not have to be provided (see page 39). You might also want more information about your condition or its treatment from NHS Direct (see page 24) or from a self-help group or charity that specialises in particular health issues, such as the Alzheimer's Society or the National Osteoporosis Society.

ACCESS TO YOUR HEALTH RECORDS

Access to your health records comes under the Data Protection Act 1998. This applies to records held by the NHS as well as by private or voluntary healthcare providers. A health record means information about your physical or mental health (or about the condition of any identified living person) made by or on behalf of a health professional who is connected with your care. This includes your GP, a hospital physiotherapist or a district nurse, for example.

The Data Protection Act gives everyone the right to ask to see health information kept about them. This might be written records or information stored on a computer. It includes X-rays, photographs or printouts from monitoring equipment. You can ask to see records no matter how long ago they were compiled (but see page 251, about how long these are kept after someone dies). However, your right is only to ask to see your records – there is no law that says that whoever holds the records must agree to your request. Nevertheless, the NHS's current policy is always to agree to your seeing your records unless whoever holds the records thinks that something in them might:

- cause serious harm to your physical or mental health or condition or that of any other person; or
- where giving you access would reveal information about (or provided by) someone else who has not agreed to this being shared.

In such a situation, the person holding the records could either:

- keep back some information, but let you see the rest; or
- keep back the whole record and refuse any access.

The record holder (such as your GP surgery or hospital records office) doesn't have to explain why it is withholding access but, if this happens, you can complain about it. Approach the record holder in the first instance. Because this area comes under the Data Protection Act, if there is a dispute you can also contact the

Information Commissioner (address on page 280) whose role it is to oversee matters that come under that Act.

If you want to see your health records, put your request in writing and send it to the organisation or professional holding your records.

There is a charge for you to see your NHS health records. The most you can be asked to pay is £10 for manual (written) records, and £50 for computer records (or where there is a mix of computer and manual records). You will have to pay this before a copy of your records will be made available. The amount you are asked to pay will depend on the cost to the NHS of making a copy and posting it to you. The charge has to cover these costs; some records (such as X-rays) are particularly expensive to copy. But you should not be asked to pay more than these maximum sums.

Once the organisation that holds your records has received this amount, and satisfied itself you are who you say you are, it should provide the copy to you between 21 and 40 days later. The 21-day target is something the NHS should try to achieve but it is not a legal requirement; however, the 40-day limit is a requirement under the Data Protection Act 1998.

Electronic records

The Government is planning to put into place a national system for storing and updating patients' medical records, to be accessed by NHS staff across the country if needed. The electronic system is called NHS Care Records.

The idea behind this is to link all GP surgeries, NHS hospitals, ambulances, and nursing and other staff so that details about patients' medical conditions can be accessed immediately in the event of an emergency, for example. There are plans for pharmacists also to have access to this information.

There are some concerns, however, about the number of people who will have legitimate access to information about you and your health that you would prefer is not shared.

The Department of Health has said that you will be able to opt out of having a summary of the medical notes your GP holds added to this national NHS computer system. You would need to write to your GP to say you wished to opt out of having this summary shared. You can always opt in later, if you change your mind.

A taskforce set up in 2006 to advise the Government has said that you should be able to 'seal-off' any information that you consider sensitive, so that access to this is much more restricted. There are also some concerns that you might want to opt out of having details such as your name, address, date of birth and telephone number (which would include ex-directory numbers) included if, for example, it is important to restrict the number of people who know either your 'real name' (if you have changed this as part of a witness protection programme, for example), or because you have left an abusive relationship and it is important that your new details are kept as private as possible.

It is expected that this new system will be piloted in some parts of the country during 2007, and applied across the country by the end of 2008. Contact Age Concern's Information Line (page 271) for further details. If you wanted to make sure now that the details about yourself that are included in the national scheme will be limited, you can contact the campaigning organisation NHS Confidentiality (page 282) or your GP to opt out of having your summary notes included. You can always opt back in, later.

If you have other concerns about this proposed new system, you may want also to take these up with your Member of Parliament (MP).

Amending your records

If, when you receive the copy of your health records, you think some information is missing or incorrect, you should first contact the organisation or individual holding the records and ask for this to be put right. If this is unsuccessful, and these are NHS records, you can make a complaint using the NHS complaints procedure explained in Chapter 16. You can also complain to the Information Commissioner, because the records come under the Data Protection Act (see page 248).

APPLYING TO SEE THE RECORDS OF SOMEONE WHO HAS DIED

You can apply to see the health records of someone who has died. You have to do this in writing to the organisation holding the records, and provide enough information to make sure that the correct records can be identified. When someone dies, their records either are sent to the local Primary Care Trust (the primary care records) and held for ten years or are held for at least eight years by the hospital (or in the hospital's archive) where the person was treated. You may be asked about your connection with the person and about your right to access their records. You will need a reason why you want to look – such as a claim arising from the way someone died.

If anything in the person's records shows that they did not want these shared, those wishes will be respected and you will not be allowed to see their records. The organisation holding the records can also decide not to share their records if to do so might cause serious harm to you or another person, or would mean that information about another person would be shared without their consent. Otherwise, you will need to pay a fee and wait to receive a copy as outlined above.

AGREEING FOR OTHERS TO SEE YOUR RECORDS

There is a Code of Practice about confidentiality that the NHS must follow. This means that you have to agree (give your consent) to any part of your health records being shared even if this is with another healthcare professional involved in your care. Giving consent doesn't have to be particularly formal but you should be asked. For some people, healthcare professionals will also want to share details with social care staff. Again, you should be asked if this is all right with you. If you're not sure, ask the staff involved to explain why this needs to happen, how it will benefit you and what might happen if you don't agree.

But there are some circumstances where your consent is not needed. For example:

- If you make a complaint on behalf of a patient who has died, any organisation with statutory powers to investigate complaints (such as the Healthcare Commission or the Health Service Ombudsman) can gain access to that patient's medical records if these are needed to pursue their investigation.

- The courts, including coroner's courts (and some tribunals and people appointed to hold inquiries) have legal powers to require that relevant information be disclosed; in this case, although the person's consent is not needed, they should be told that this is happening.

The key principle of the duty to keep information confidential is that information given should be shared only with the permission of the person who gave it. The Human Rights Act gives us all a right to a private life but there are some circumstances when NHS staff might well break this confidence. These are generally to do with the prevention, exposure or investigation of serious crimes such as:

- murder or manslaughter;
- rape;
- treason;
- kidnapping;
- the abuse of someone (child or adult);
- any other cases where individuals have suffered serious harm;
- serious harm to the security of the state or to public order;
- crime involving substantial financial gain or loss.

Sometimes Members of Parliament (MPs) are asked by patients to raise matters with the NHS organisation relating to their concerns. If the MP writes to the NHS about your situation, the NHS will take this to mean that you agree to details of what has happened in your care being shared with the MP if this is needed in order to answer the points made in the MP's letter.

There are plans to allow individual patients to opt out of having a summary of their NHS medical records placed on and shared across a planned national NHS computing system (see pages 249–250).

If you cannot consent

If you cannot give your consent, either because you are unconscious or because your disability or illness means you cannot understand what you are being asked to agree to or are unable to express your views, doctors and other clinicians may need to decide about medical treatments on your behalf.

Any decision must be in your best interests as the individual patient concerned. This is not about what is in the best interests of any of your relatives or the doctors or the hospital or anyone else.

To find out what decision might be in your best interests, doctors may want to talk to people who know you, especially to find out if you have ever indicated anything to suggest what decision you might make now. To do so could involve doctors sharing some information about your current medical situation, in order for your family and friends (for example) to reflect on what your views might have been. The information that is shared should only be that needed to find out what your best interests might be.

If you have already recorded what you would want to happen if such a situation arises (for example, in an advance decision – see page 127), or you have set up and named the person you want to make health and welfare decisions on your behalf, through a Lasting Power of Attorney (see page 130), this should be respected and followed by the doctors involved in your care. You might want to place a copy of your wishes with your health records – perhaps with your GP if the surgery agrees.

There is more about consent in these situations in Chapter 8.

18

Getting Involved in the NHS

There are many ways in which you can be involved in, and influence, different parts of the NHS. Most NHS organisations want (and ask) members of the public to take part in some way. For example, the National Institute for Health and Clinical Excellence (NICE) has a Citizen's Council, drawn from different members of the public. To help with its overall policy approach, NICE asks its Citizens Council to debate some of the ethical issues about access to different healthcare services and treatments from the NHS.

Other NHS bodies, such as the National Patient Safety Agency, also look for lay members – people who aren't involved in this work professionally – to join committees looking at issues such as (for example) the information needed by patients and carers.

Most of these positions are unpaid, although you will receive expenses such as travel costs. These opportunities are usually advertised in national newspapers, such as *The Guardian*. There are other ways you can also become more involved, outlined below.

PATIENT AND PUBLIC INVOLVEMENT FORUMS

Each Primary Care Trust and NHS Trust must have a Patient and Public Involvement (PPI) Forum, which consists of members of the public. There are over 400 Forums in England. There must be at least seven members in each Forum but many involve 15–25 people. Members receive training to help them carry out their roles:

- to find out the views of their local communities about health services, and make recommendations and reports based on these views;

- to make reports and recommendations on the range and day-to-day delivery of health services;

- to influence the design of and access to NHS services;

- to provide advice and information to patients and their carers about services;

- to monitor the effectiveness of local Patient Advice and Liaison Services (see Chapter 16).

Forums also hold public meetings that you can go to and share your views and experiences of the NHS locally. The Commission for Patient and Public Involvement in Health (CPPIH) is an independent body that currently has the overall responsibility for all the forums across England, although this function is expected to pass to the Appointments Commission in due course. Local not-for-profit organisations (voluntary organisations or charities) provide support to local Forums, under contract to the CPPIH. To find out about getting involved or for details of your local Forum, you can contact Make Time for Health (address on page 280).

In the summer of 2006, the Government announced plans to replace Patient and Public Involvement Forums with new Local Involvement Networks (LINks). It is expected that LINks will work with existing voluntary and community sector groups, as well as interested individuals, to promote public and community influence in health and, importantly, also in social care. Further details are expected to be announced during 2007. Contact Age Concern's Information Line (page 271) for further information.

EXPERT PATIENTS PROGRAMME

The Government has told the NHS to actively involve people with chronic (long-term) health conditions in managing their illnesses. These include:

- arthritis
- epilepsy
- schizophrenia.

Over the last few years, the Department of Health has been developing the Expert Patients Programme for people with chronic conditions. It's based on studies that have found that it is often the person with the condition or illness who has the greatest expertise into what affects this and their overall health.

The Expert Patients Programme offers training sessions to people with chronic conditions, to help them learn about their condition and its symptoms in order to improve their confidence in dealing with it the best possible way. This might be about managing pain, reducing anxiety or finding ways to feel less tired. The sessions also look at diet, exercise and the best ways to talk to healthcare professionals. The courses take place over a six-week period, each session lasting two and a half hours. There are currently 12,000 places on courses each year; the Department of Health plans to increase this to 100,000 by 2012.

The training sessions are run by other people who have long-term conditions. But they are not about replacing help from the NHS. You will still see your GP and hospital consultant, physiotherapist or dietitian as needed. Many people who have taken part have found that it helps them to have much more control, and a better say, over what happens.

Each Strategic Health Authority has to draw up plans to introduce the Programme in its area. This will be run by Primary Care Trusts, who have been told that the scheme must be available across England by 2008. To find out about taking part, you can contact the Expert Patients Programme at the address on page 277.

NHS Patient Surveys

Every year a survey of NHS patients takes place. Some years it looks at particular types of services that only some people receive, such as cancer services; other years it looks at services that everyone receives, such as GPs. The Healthcare Commission carries out these national NHS patient surveys.

Individual surgeries, clinics, hospitals and other NHS services often run their own local surveys. Or there may be a 'comment card' available for you to complete. If you use a particular service, you might be asked to take part in a review. This will look at what is good about the service as it is at the moment as well as what might need to change for the future. Most research about NHS services involves seeking the views of patients and carers. An NHS Ethics Committee in each area looks at each research proposal before the go-ahead is given to talk with patients.

Clinical trials

Many drug trials are carried out among patients. These trials can be run either by the NHS or by private drug (pharmaceutical) companies. The trials are usually the final stages in testing drugs before it is finally agreed that they should be made more widely available. Or they may look at the effects of taking certain treatments, already available on prescription, over a period of time.

Typically the people taking part are divided into two groups: those who are given the drug or treatment to take, and those given a placebo. A *placebo* is something that looks the same as the drug but is made up of something else that is quite harmless. You will not know until the end of the trial whether you were taking the drug being tested or a placebo.

Some clinical trials might involve your attending a clinic or hospital for tests. For example, the trial could involve regular scans to see any changes in your brain (this is often carried out among people with a particular health condition, such as depression or a stroke).

Your GP surgery may ask you to take part. Or you may see advertisements in national or local newspapers asking for volunteers. Either way it is up to you whether you take part – you are free to say no. Some trials offer you a payment, others do not; or you may be reimbursed for any expenses involved in taking part (such as the cost of travel to a clinic).

In the spring of 2006, it was reported that a small number of male volunteers taking part in a clinical trial of a drug for a private company had experienced severe reactions to the drug they were given. Such clinical trials in the UK are subject to statutory guidance and regulations, overseen by the Medicine and Healthcare products Regulatory Agency (MHRA). The events of those particular trials have been reviewed. The Department of Health has stressed that it is rare for such serious outcomes to occur.

OTHER INVOLVEMENT

Many people have been involved with the NHS in other ways, by volunteering or by raising money. Most NHS hospitals have benefited at some point from fundraising involving the help of former patients (and their families and friends) to buy specialist equipment or perhaps refurbish parts of the hospital (such as waiting areas) or to raise funds to buy art and sculpture to display in the hospital.

Some hospitals have a 'Friends' organisation that you can join. They arrange events to raise money or to help support the hospital in other ways. The charities the British Red Cross and the Women's Royal Voluntary Service have traditionally been very involved with NHS hospitals. Volunteers for both organisations often run extra services for hospital patients, such as:

- café for patients and visitors;
- hospital shop;

■ lending library.

Sometimes volunteers visit particular wards and, if patients are interested, will help with putting on make-up, styling hair or painting their fingernails. For more information about volunteering, contact your local hospital, the British Red Cross or the Women's Royal Voluntary Service (addresses on pages 273 and 286).

CAMPAIGNING

Many individuals, charities and support groups campaign for local and national changes to health services. For example, Age Concern England's recent campaigns include: raising the age up to which women are invited for breast screening from 65 to 70 (page 17); changing how 'Do Not Resuscitate' decisions are made (page 208); and challenging age discrimination (page 224). Campaigns often begin with someone who is unhappy about a healthcare experience contacting their MP or a national or local charity or support group to see if these concerns are shared. Some people decide to contact the media: if you do so, say clearly whether you agree to their reporting your story using your real name and details.

Not all stories are reported in the media, nor do charities or local support groups take up every issue. This may be because they have different priorities; not enough time or money to take it up; or they don't share your view that this is an important issue. If this happens, you may want to rethink your approach. Successful campaigning – both national and local – tends to take more than your simply believing you have a good case. You need to be able to persuade others that change is needed. Although it can take time to achieve, though, it is worth persevering.

Keeping Up to Date with Change

As this book may already have made clear to you, changes to how and what the NHS does can happen at any time. In recent years there have been lots of changes to the NHS, particularly in terms of:

- new organisations;
- different responsibilities;
- quality and monitoring of services;
- where you can go for help from the NHS;
- how quickly you are seen.

There is no doubt that more change will follow – and keep on coming. The NHS has been changing since it began in 1948. There is no reason to think it will stop now.

In some organisations, keeping up to date with change in the NHS and with healthcare services in general is a full-time job. For the rest of us, it can be difficult to know where to go and how to find out what the NHS does now. But there are lots of ways we can keep up to date – at least with the parts of the NHS that affect us the most.

Some people who are part of campaigning groups may be involved in local or national networks that keep them up to date with the latest developments by email, telephone or letter. Others may want to look at specialist health journals, such as the *British Medical Journal* (*BMJ*) or the *Health Service Journal* (*HSJ*). If you don't want to buy these, you may be able to read them at your local library if it has a subscription to them.

There is a lot of information available on the Internet. The Department of Health has its own website, as does NHS Direct (see pages 275 and 282) and many of the other organisations listed in the Appendix. There are also many local websites – for example, your local Primary Care Trust will have a website. (See also page 25.)

Sometimes, newspapers and other media (TV or radio) report changes in the NHS. Although this may alert you to change, you may find that these reports don't give you enough information about what the changes mean for you as a patient. You may need to go elsewhere to find out more.

Having access to accurate and detailed information is an incredibly important part of understanding what the NHS is doing, should do, won't do and can't do. Charities such as Age Concern England help explain these changes as they are happening by producing information leaflets and policy papers. You can also contact them by telephone with other queries (see page 271).

If you belong to an organisation that specialises in a particular health condition or disability, such as Arthritis Care, Cancer BACUP or the Alzheimer's Society, you will probably receive regular newsletters and other information from them. This will also help keep you up to date with the things affecting people with those illnesses and disabilities.

Of course, none of this may interest you. The last thing you might want to do is try to keep tabs on the NHS. So perhaps the most important lesson is not to be surprised that something has changed when you next come to use any of the huge range of NHS services. Your last experience of the NHS may be quite different from your next one.

Keeping Healthy

You may think it a little strange to end a book about older people's rights to healthcare with a chapter about keeping healthy, but many people would prefer to stay away from hospitals and doctors - for example – for as much of the time as possible. This is because most of us would rather be healthy and not need NHS services, or at least not very often.

It is really important, however, that you seek medical advice as soon as you realise you may have a health problem. This might involve contacting NHS Direct, your GP or a walk-in centre, for example. Chapter 2 has more information about these services.

This chapter looks at different aspects of keeping well and healthy, including physical fitness, diet and weight, sexual health, and mental or emotional well-being.

Age Concern's leaflet Heathy Living *may be helpful, too.*

CHECK-UPS AND PREVENTATIVE MEASURES

Chapters throughout this book highlight the different options available to check on health, and to take steps to prevent becoming ill. These include:

- vaccinations against flu and pneumonia (Chapter 1);
- dental check-ups (Chapter 4);
- eyesight tests (Chapter 5);
- over-75s annual health check (Chapter 1);
- screening for bowel cancer, in some parts of the country (see Chapter 1).

Health services such as continence advice and falls prevention services can also help people to improve their health (Chapter 7). In addition, older women should make sure they are still having regular breast cancer checks (Chapter 1).

PHYSICAL EXERCISE

Keeping physically active is a very important aspect of keeping healthy. It can help to reduce the risk of stroke, heart attack or diabetes; can help people's sense of balance and so help prevent falls; whilst weight-bearing exercises can also help reduce the chances of osteoporosis.

Sometimes people are put off the idea of 'exercise', either because they think it means going to a class (which they don't want to do) or a gym (which they think is too expensive) or because they would rather be active in ordinary daily life.

There are lots of ordinary ways people can be physically active on a regular basis; for example:

- walking to the shops;
- walking up the stairs (at home, and using the stairs instead of lifts or escalators when out and about);
- gardening (especially mowing the lawn, pruning hedges, or digging);
- cleaning the house (especially vigorous vacuuming or turning bed mattresses over);
- carrying shopping;
- going for a bike ride.

There are other 'ordinary' physical things you might want to do, either on your own or with other people. For example, you may know someone who would enjoy dancing, swimming or playing golf or bowls with you. Or, if not, you might enjoy taking classes or lessons in similar activities, or perhaps in:

- yoga, t'ai chi or Pilates
- tennis
- line dancing.

Many parts of the country now offer 'Healthy Walking' groups. These are sometimes organised locally through the NHS (your GP surgery should have details). There are 350 local walking schemes run by the British Heart Foundation and Natural England as part of their joint 'Walking the way to Health Initiative' (WHI); there are also many local walking groups who are part of the Ramblers' Association (contact details on pages 286 and 283).

You might be interested in other ways of keeping fit, such as the practical outdoors work run by the British Trust for Conservation Volunteers (BTCV) in their Green Gyms. There are other local 'outdoors' interest groups where an element of taking part includes physical exercise; for example, bird watchers and archaeologists may do a lot of walking to get to the sites they are visiting, whilst canal restoration – or helping to run restored steam trains – may include a lot of very physical tasks!

It can be helpful to think about different types of physical activity that would interest you, and try to incorporate these into your daily life. If you can join a group, you might also find that you make new friends: active interests and good friendships will also help you to enjoy life more because your mental (or emotional) health is also being looked after.

The aim is to carry out up to 30 minutes of physical exercise on at least five days each week. You might be surprised, if you add up what you are already doing, at the totals. Some people may do far more than 30 minutes – but perhaps need to spend more time on a different type of exercise: for example, building stamina, weight-bearing exercises, maintaining balance or flexibility. Some people may do a lot less than the 30 minutes – in which case, they might gain most health benefits from doing something extra. You don't have to do 30 minutes continuously. You could do three separate 'sessions' of 10 minutes a day instead. Or you could divide the sessions differently, to suit you. The important thing is that you do something.

Remember: whatever exercise you choose, take time to warm up beforehand, and wind down afterwards. Don't strain any muscles and, if you have an existing injury or weakness, seek advice from a GP or physiotherapist before starting anything or changing what you have already been doing.

Activities for people with disabilities

It can be easy to think that there is nothing suitable for you, if you have an illness or disability that makes moving, carrying or lifting (for example) difficult or painful for you.

Your particular disability or illness might not be as much of a barrier to taking part as you might think at first. It is a good idea, though, to ask your GP or your physiotherapist (if you are seeing one), for example, what sorts of activities you should avoid because they might make your symptoms worse.

There will always be physical activities that you can enjoy. These might include gardening groups, such as those run by the charity Thrive (contact details on page 285); or 'carpet bowls' often offered by local Age Concerns as one of many different day services; and 'chair' exercises, which are based on dance movements and are carried out to music, involve techniques that can be done sitting down. Or you might find that the large exercise balls that physiotherapists sometimes use would suit you.

Some people with disabilities are extremely talented at sport, as can be seen every four years in the Paralympics and in other local, national and international competitions. Not everyone will reach paralympian standards, but its growing popularity as a spectator event means there should be more opportunities to try out sports activities in local leisure centres.

Further information about 'chair' exercises is available from Help the Aged.

A GOOD DIET

Most people know what a 'good diet' involves but are not necessarily very good at following it. A good diet really means eating a balance of different food types, especially making sure to eat:

- at least five portions of fruit and vegetables a day;
- less fat, and fewer fried foods;
- less salt;
- less sugar (including the 'hidden sugar' in fizzy drinks and canned food).

Some people must pay special attention to what they eat if they have allergies (such as to peanuts or shellfish), if they have coeliac disease and cannot digest gluten, or if they have diabetes.

There are also concerns in the UK that people are becoming much heavier because we are over-eating, as well as eating too many of the 'wrong' foods. At the same time, there are people whose eating disorders mean they do not eat enough. Sometimes these issues can be helped by some of the 'talking therapies' techniques described in Chapter 8. Or you could start by asking your GP for advice, or by finding a dietitian (Chapter 7).

There are a large number of diet books and aids that you can buy. It's not advisable to start making huge changes to your diet, however, without first seeking some medical advice, especially if you have any underlying health problems.

If you think you need to lose weight, it's best to do this slowly over a long period of time. That way, the weight should stay off. You might find that joining a local group such as WeightWatchers might help.

In terms of drinking, most of the advice is to make sure you take in between 1.5 and 2 litres of non-alcoholic liquids each day. This can be a mix of water, cups of herbal tea, fruit juice, or ordinary tea or coffee. You may find you feel better if you drink more water out of this total than other types of drink.

STOPPING SMOKING, DRINKING OR DRUG-TAKING

There is a great deal of support available from the NHS to help you stop smoking. This includes nicotine replacement patches and other treatments that are available on NHS prescription for which, if you are aged 60 or more, you will not have to pay. You can also telephone the NHS Gosmokefree Helpline (number on page 282) for free advice and information.

Since 1 July 2007, it is against the law to smoke in the workplace or in enclosed public spaces such as shops, pubs, bars, restaurants, membership clubs and public transport.

If you have been a smoker for a long time, you may have already caused some damage to your long-term health. But this does not mean that your health would not improve if you stopped smoking now. You are likely to find that your sense of smell and taste improves within only a few weeks, whilst you may find it becomes easier to breathe more deeply and take physical exercise. Perhaps more importantly, your circulation will start to improve, and your risk of serious disease will begin to fall.

If you are dependent on any kind of drug or medication – whether taking an illegal, recreational or prescribed drug – you may be harming your health. This book cannot advise you on the law regarding illegal drugs. If you think there is a problem, or you know someone for whom this may be a problem, the first thing to do is to contact your GP. He or she can give you advice and support and refer you for specialist treatment. Or you could contact the National Drugs Helpline (telephone number on page 282): this is a free and confidential telephone helpline, offering information about drugs and drug abuse, which is open at all times.

In men over 40 and women over menopausal age, there is evidence to suggest that moderate drinking of alcohol can be beneficial to health. But the emphasis here is on the word 'moderate'. The Department of Health recommends that women drink no more than 14 units of alcohol each week, and men no more than 21. If you or someone you know is regularly drinking more than this, and you think it is a problem, you could talk to your GP. Or you could contact Drinkline (the National Alcohol Helpline, number on page 276) for free, confidential information and advice on alcohol.

LOOKING AFTER YOUR SEXUAL HEALTH

No matter what your age, if you are sexually active you must look after this aspect of your health. Increasing numbers of older people are forming relationships with new partners. It does not follow that, because you are older, you are 'immune' from such sexually transmitted diseases as HIV and syphilis. The best protection, if you are having penetrative sex, is usually to insist on using a condom.

If you already have a sexually contracted disease, you must tell your sexual partner(s) so that he or she may make sure they are protected against infection. If you have concerns about any aspect of your sexual health – including any difficulties you may be having – you can talk to your GP or to the practice nurse; or you could contact NHS Direct for advice.

EMOTIONAL HEALTH

'Emotional health' is a term increasingly being used to describe the part of life that makes us feel happier, more relaxed and fulfilled.

There are many different aspects to this. What works will vary from individual to individual, but there are some common themes that affect us all. These aspects include having a meaning or purpose to our lives and having good relationships.

Some people find that creative and spiritual aspects to their lives are also important. Often these give us meaning to life as well as the companionship of like-minded people.

If you find that these aspects of your life are not so positive, there are steps you could take to improve matters. But you may find this takes some time to achieve, and that you need to take small steps – at least to begin with.

If you need to find meaning and a purpose in your life, and you are not seeking a religious answer, you might want to think about playing a role in someone else's life. Volunteering is an ideal way of doing this. It doesn't necessarily mean a large commitment, and if you are nervous about joining a group, or find it difficult to leave your home, there may be things you could do from home, such as telephoning someone regularly or becoming a 'pen pal' (or 'email pal'). Taking part in something like volunteering may also give you contacts with new people, and a chance to form new friendships, if this has been lacking in your life.

The key is to think what you *can* do, rather than all the reasons you cannot take part. But sometimes this is easier said than done. Some local Age Concerns offer a 'buddies' scheme – someone who will introduce you to a new group and a new activity, and stay with you while you get used to going. Many people who become buddies were themselves given a buddy when they first began to get involved. You might already know someone who would go along to things with you – or would at least encourage you to try, and be interested in how you got on.

Contact Age Concern's Information Line (page 271) for details of your nearest Age Concern.

Appendix
Useful addresses

Only a few self-help or support organisations are listed in this Appendix. For information about the many others that exist, ask at your local library for a directory such as *Charity Choice* (published by Waterlow Professional Publishing) or *Voluntary Agencies Directory* (published by the National Council for Voluntary Organisations).

Note Telephone codes/charges are: 01, area code/national rate; 02, area code/national rate; 07, mobile rate; 080, free; 084, local rate; 087 national rate; 09, premium rate.

Action Against Medical Accidents (avma)
44 High Street
Croydon CR0 1YB
Tel: 020 8688 9555
Helpline: 0845 123 2352
www.avma.org.uk
For advice after a medical accident.

Age Concern England
Astral House
1268 London Road
London SW16 4ER
Tel: 020 8765 7200
www.ageconcern.org.uk
Use the online search to find the Age Concern nearest to you.

Age Concern Information Line
Information Line: 0800 00 99 66
(8am–7pm, 7 days a week)

Alliance of Private Sector Chiropody and Podiatry Practitioners
3 Pendorlan Avenue
Colwyn Bay
Conwy LL29 8EA
Tel: 01492 535795
     07703 576553
www.thealliancepsp.com
For information about the training and registration of their chiropodist and podiatrist members.

Alzheimer's Society
Gordon House
10 Greencoat Place
London SW1P 1PH
Tel: 020 7306 0606
www.alzheimers.org.uk
For information about Alzheimer's disease and other dementias.

271

Associated Chiropodists and Podiatrists Union (formerly **Association of Chiropodists and Podiatrists**)
Suite 14
Anglesey Business Centre
Anglesey Road
Burton on Trent
Staffordshire DE14 3NT
Tel/Fax: 01283 741174
For information about the training and registration of their chiropodist and podiatrist members.

Association of Professional Music Therapists
61 Church Hill Road
East Barnet
Herts EN4 8SY
Tel: 020 8440 4153
www.apmt.org
The professional organisation of music therapists.

British Association of Arts Therapists
24–27 White Lion Street
London N1 9PD
Tel: 020 7686 4216
www.baat.org
The professional organisation of arts therapists.

British Association for Counselling and Psychotherapy
BACP House
15 St John's Business Park

Lutterworth LE17 4HB
Tel: 0870 443 5252
www.bacp.co.uk
To find a trained counsellor near you.

British Association of Dramatherapists
Waverley
Battledown Approach
Cheltenham
Gloucestershire GL52 6RE
Tel: 01242 235515
www.badth.org.uk
The professional association of dramatherapists.

British Chiropody & Podiatry Association
New Hall
149 Bath Road
Maidenhead
Berkshire SL6 4LA
Tel: 01628 632440
www.bcha-uk.org
For information about the training and registration of chiropodists and podiatrists.

British Deaf Association
see Sign Community

British Lung Foundation
73–75 Goswell Road
London EC1V 7ER
Tel: 0845 850 5020
www.lunguk.org
For information about lung diseases.

British Organ Donor Society (BODY)
Balsham
Cambridge CB1 6DL
Tel: 01223 893636
www.argonet.co.uk/body
For information about donating organ(s).

British Red Cross
UK Office
44 Moorfields
London EC2Y 9AL
Tel: 0870 170 7000
www.redcross.org.uk
For the hire/loan of equipment; it also publishes The Emergency Multilingual Phrasebook of Medical Terms.

British Tinnitus Association
Ground Floor, Unit 5
Acorn Business Park
Woodseats Close
Sheffield S8 0TB
Tel (voice):0800 018 0527
0845 4500 321
0114 250 9922
Textphone: 0114 258 5694
www.tinnitus.org.uk
For information about tinnitus.

British Trust for Conservation Volunteers (BTCV)
Sedum House
Mallard Way
Potteric Carr
Doncaster DN4 8DB
Tel: 01302 388 888
www.btcv.org.uk
For information about volunteering.

Charles Russell Solicitors
fao Edwina Rawson/Jonathan Zimmern
8–10 New Fetter Lane
London EC4A 1RS
Tel: 020 7203 5000
020 7203 5335 (direct line
– Edwina Rawson)
020 7203 0207 (direct line
– Jonathan Zimmern)
www.cjdtrust.co.uk
For obtaining compensation regarding Creutzfeldt–Jakob disease.
See also CJD Support Network *and* vCJD Trust

Chartered Society of Physiotherapy
14 Bedford Row
London WC1R 4ED
Tel: 020 7306 6666
www.csp.org.uk
The professional organisation of physiotherapists.

Child Poverty Action Group (CPAG)
94 White Lion Street
London N1 9PE
Tel: 020 7837 7979
www.cpag.org.uk
For a copy of its publication The Welfare Rights Handbook.

Choose and Book
www.chooseandbook.nhs.uk
For information about the new system of booking a hospital appointment yourself.

Cinnamon Trust (The National Charity for the Elderly and their Pets)
10 Market Square
Hayle
Cornwall TR27 4HE
Tel: 01736 757900
www.cinnamon.org.uk
Helps with looking after pets of people in hospital.

CJD Support Network
PO Box 346
Market Drayton
Shropshire TF9 4WN
Helpline: 01630 673973
Tel: 01630 673973
www.cjdsupport.net
For obtaining compensation regarding Creutzfeldt–Jakob disease.

Coeliac UK
Suites A–D
Octagon Court
High Wycombe
Bucks HP11 2HS
Helpline: 0870 444 8804
Tel: 01494 437 278
www.coeliac.org.uk
Charity/support group for people allergic to gluten.

College of Occupational Therapists
106–114 Borough High Street
London SE1 1LB
Tel: 020 7357 6480
www.cot.co.uk
The professional organisation of occupational therapists.

Commission for Patient and Public Involvement in Health (CPPIH)
Help Desk, 7th Floor
120 Edmund Street
Birmingham B3 2ES
Tel: 0845 120 7111
Textphone: 0845 120 7113
www.cppih.org
For information about Patient Forums.

Commission for Social Care Inspection
33 Greycoat Street
London SW1P 2QF
Customer services helpline: 0845 015 0120
www.csci.org.uk
The official body regulating care homes and agencies that provide nurses or care workers who carry out personal tasks.

Community Legal Service
Tel: 0845 345 4345
www.clsdirect.org.uk
An organisation set up by the Legal Services Commission to help people find the right legal information and advice.

Counsel and Care
Twyman House
16 Bonny Street
London NW1 9PG
Advice line: 0845 300 7585 (Mon–Fri, 9am–1pm)
www.counselandcare.org.uk
For information on finding and paying for a care home.

Cruse Bereavement Care
PO Box 800
Richmond
Surrey TW9 1RG
Helpline: 0844 477 9400
Tel: 020 8939 9530
www. crusebereavementcare.org. uk
For bereavement counselling and advice.

Dementia Services Development Centre
Iris Murdoch Building
University of Stirling
Stirling FK9 4LA
Tel: 01786 467740
www.dementia.stir.ac.uk
Researches into ways to help support people with dementia.

Department of Health
Richmond House
79 Whitehall
London SW1A 2NS
Tel: 020 7210 4850 (Mon–Fri, 9am–5pm)
Textphone: 020 7210 5025
www.dh.gov.uk
For up-to date information about NHS services and health issues, go to the Department of Health website where you will find information that can be downloaded or ordered online. There is also a link to a publications library.

Department of Health, Social Services and Public Safety
Senior Medical Officer
Castle Buildings
Stormont Estate
Belfast BT4 3SQ
Tel: 028 9052 0500 (Mon–Fri, 9am–5pm)
www.dhsspsni.gov.uk
For donating one's body for medical research in Northern Ireland.

Depression Alliance
212 Spitfire Studios
63–71 Collier Street
London N1 9BE
Tel: 0845 123 2320
www.depressionalliance.org
*Go to the website to find contact
details of over 60 self-help
groups throughout the UK.*

Diabetes UK
Macleod House
10 Parkway
London NW1 7AA
Tel: 020 7424 1000 (Mon–Fri,
9am–5pm)
www.diabetes.org.uk
*For information and advice
about diabetes.*

**Disability Rights Commission
(DRC)**
FREEPOST MID02164
Stratford upon Avon
Warwickshire CV37 9BR
Helpline: 0845 762 2633
Textphone: 0845 762 2644
www.drc-gb.org
*Government-sponsored
centre with publications and
information on the Disability
Discrimination Act.*

Disabled Living Foundation
380–384 Harrow Road
London W9 2HU
Helpline: 0845 130 9177 (Mon–
Fri, 10am–1pm)

Tel: 020 7289 6111 (Mon–Fri,
10am–1pm)
Textphone: 020 7432 8009
www.dlf.org.uk
*Information for disabled and
older people on all kinds of
equipment that will promote
their independence and quality
of life.*

Drinkline (the **National Alcohol
Helpline**)
Tel: 0800 917 8282 (Mon–Fri,
9am–11 pm)
*Drinkline offers a confidential
information and advice service
on alcohol and where to go
for help. Callers to the above
number have the option of
listening to recorded information
about alcohol or talking to an
adviser.*

**Driver and Vehicle Licensing
Agency (DVLA)**
Swansea SA6 7JL
Tel: 0870 240 0010
Textphone: 01792 782756
www.dvla.gov.uk
*Available on the DVLA website
is an at-a-glance guide to the
current medical standards of
fitness to drive. There are also
directions on how to tell DVLA
about a medical condition.*

Elderly Accommodation Counsel
3rd Floor
89 Albert Embankment
London SE1 7TP
Tel: 020 7820 1343
www.eac.org.uk
For their information about services to help you adapt or improve your home, or provide care or help at home.

European Health Insurance Card (EHIC) Applications
PO Box 1115
Newcastle-upon-Tyne NE99 1SW
www.ehic.org.uk/Internet/home.do
To obtain a card: use the website; or call 0845 606 2030; or pick up an application form from the Post Office.

Expert Patients Programme
Central Support
Room 47
Burnhill Business Centre
Burrell Road
Beckenham
Kent BR3 1AT
Tel: 020 8249 6464
www.expertpatients.co.uk
Go to the website to find contact details for branches throughout the UK

General Chiropractic Council
44 Wicklow Street
London WC1X 9HL
Tel: 020 7713 5155
www.gcc-uk.org
The official regulating body of chiropractors.

General Dental Council
37 Wimpole Street
London W1G 8DQ
Tel: 020 7887 3800
www.gdc-uk.org
The official regulating body of dentists.

General Medical Council
Regent's Place
350 Euston Road
London NW1 3JN
Tel: 0845 357 3456
        0845 357 8001
www.gmc-uk.org
The official regulating body of doctors.

Doctors' fitness to practise
Tel: 0845 357 0022

The GMC's Manchester office also deals with some fitness to practise issues:
St James Building
79 Oxford Street
Manchester M1 6FQ
Tel: 0845 357 8001

General Optical Council
41 Harley Street
London W1G 8DJ
Tel: 020 7580 3898
www.optical.org
The official regulating body of optometrists and dispensing opticians, both individuals and organisations.

General Osteopathic Council
176 Tower Bridge Road
London SE1 3LU
Tel: 020 7357 6655
www.osteopathy.org.uk
The regulating body for osteopaths.

Guide Dogs for the Blind Association
Burghfield Common
Reading RG7 3YG
Tel: 0118 983 5555
www.guidedogs.org.uk
For information about guide dogs.

Health Professions Council
Park House
184 Kennington Park Road
London SE11 4BU
Tel: 020 7582 0866
www.hpc-uk.org
The body for registering therapists such as occupational therapists and speech and language therapists.

Health Protection Agency Central Office
7th Floor
Holborn Gate
330 High Holborn
London WC1V 7PP
Tel: 020 7759 2700/2701
www.hpa.org.uk
Responsible for public health threats to the UK.

Health Service Ombudsman
Millbank Tower
Millbank
London SW1P 4QP
Tel: 0845 015 4033
www.ombudsman.org.uk
To make a complaint about or appeal against a decision made by the NHS.

Healthcare Commission
Finsbury Tower
103–105 Bunhill Row
London EC1Y 8TG
Tel: 020 7448 9200
www.healthcarecommission.org.uk
Inspects NHS services in England and Wales, and regulates private and voluntary healthcare services in England.

HealthSpace
www.healthspace.nhs.uk
An online service provided by the NHS for people aged 16 or over in England. If you want, you can

use this secure website to keep a record of your health details.

Hearing Concern
95 Gray's Inn Road
London WC1X 8TX
HelpDesk: 0845 0744 600 (voice and text)
Tel: 020 7440 9871
www.hearingconcern.org.uk
Volunteer-led charity offering advice, information, training and support groups for people who are deaf or hard of hearing.

Hearing Dogs for Deaf People
The Grange
Wycombe Road
Saunderton
Princes Risborough
Buckinghamshire HP27 9NS
Tel: 01844 348100 (voice and text)
www.hearing-dogs.co.uk
For information about Hearing Dogs.

Help the Aged
207–221 Pentonville Road
London N1 9UZ
Tel: 0808 800 6565 (Helpline Mon–Fri, 9am–4pm)
www.helptheaged.org.uk
For information and leaflets about preventing falls, as well as a wide range of other information for older people.

Help the Hospices
Hospice House
34–44 Britannia Street
London WC1X 9JG
Tel: 020 7520 8200
www.helpthehospices.org.uk/
For information about the hospice movement.

Hepatitis C Trust
27 Crosby Row
London SE1 3YD
Tel: 020 7089 6220
www.hepctrust.org.uk
For information about hepatitis C.

Home Office – Drugs Branch
Licensing Department
2 Marsham Street
London SW1P 4DF
Tel: 020 7035 4848
Textphone: 020 7035 4745
www.homeoffice.gov.uk
For information about medicines that may not be taken out of the UK.

Hospice Information
Tel: 0870 903 3903
www.hospiceinformation.info
For information about help available from hospices

Human Tissue Authority
Finlaison House
15–17 Furnival Street
London EC4A 1AB
Tel 020 7211 3400
www.hta.gov.uk
Regulates the removal, storage, use and disposal of human bodies, organs and tissue from the living and deceased.

Information Commissioner
Wycliffe House, Water Lane
Wilmslow
Cheshire SK9 5AF
Helpline: 0845 630 6060
01625 545745
Tel: 01625 545700
www.ico.gov.uk
The organisation responsible for Freedom of Information Act issues.

Institute of Chiropodists & Podiatrists
27 Wright Street
Southport
Merseyside PR9 0TL
Tel: 08700 110 305
www.inst-chiropodist.org.uk
For information about the training and registration of chiropodists and podiatrists.

Limbless Association
Queen Mary's Hospital
Roehampton Lane
London SW15 5PN

Tel: 020 8788 1777
www.limbless-association.org
For information about obtaining/ using a wheelchair.

Macmillan Cancer Support
89 Albert Embankment
London SE1 7UQ
Macmillan CancerLine: 0808 808 2020 (Mon–Fri, 9am–6pm)
Tel: 020 7840 7840
www.macmillan.org.uk
For specialist nursing services.

Make Time for Health
Commission for Patient and Public Involvement in Health (CPPIH),
7th Floor
120 Edmund Street
Birmingham B3 2ES
Tel: 0845 120 7111
Textphone: 0845 120 7113
www.cppih.org/
For enquiries about Patient and Public Involvement Forums.

Marie Curie Cancer Care
89 Albert Embankment
London SE1 7TP
Tel 020 7599 7777
www.mariecurie.org.uk
For specialist nursing services.

Medicine and Healthcare products Regulatory Agency (MHRA)
10-2 Market Towers

1 Nine Elms Lane
London SW8 5NQ
Tel: 020 7084 2000
www.mhra.gov.uk
To obtain a Yellow Card to report side effects from a medication you are taking.

Mental Health Foundation
9th Floor
Sea Containers House
20 Upper Ground
London SE1 9QB
Tel: 020 7803 1101
www.mentalhealth.org.uk
For information about mental illnesses.

Scotland office
Merchants House
30 George Square
Glasgow G2 1EG

MIND
15–19 Broadway
London E15 4BQ
Information helpline: 0845 766 0163 (Mon–Fri, 9.15am–5.15pm)
Tel: 020 8519 2122
www.mind.org.uk
For information on solicitors specialising in mental health law, and about financial help with these costs; and advocacy support

Mind Cymru
3rd Floor, Quebec House
Castlebridge
5–19 Cowbridge Road East
Cardiff CF11 9AB
Tel: 029 2039 5123

Ministry of Justice – Coroner's Section
Selborne House
54 Victoria Street
London SW1E 6QW
Tel: 020 7210 8500
For the information leaflet When Sudden Death Occurs.

If you require further information, contact the Coroners' Society of England and Wales

HM Coroner's Court
The Cotton Exchange
Old Hall Street
Liverpool L3 9UF
Tel: 0151 233 4708

Monitor
4 Matthew Parker Street
London SW1H 9NL
Tel: 020 7340 2400
www.monitor-nhsft.gov.uk
The Independent Regulator for NHS foundation trusts, making sure they are well managed and financially strong so that they can deliver excellent healthcare for patients.

NHS Confidentiality

Tel: 01494 882458 (Mon–Fri, 9am–5pm)
Email: admin@thebigoptout.com
Website: www.thebigoptout.com
An organisation campaigning about the planned electronic health records. The NHS Confidentiality campaign was set up to protect patient confidentiality and to provide a focus for patient-led opposition to the government's NHS Care Records System.

NHS Direct

7th Floor
207 Old Street
London EC1V 9NR
Helpline: 0845 4647 (24 hours, every day)
Textphone: 0845 606 4647
Tel: 0845 464 7647
Website: www.nhsdirect.nhs.uk
24-hour helpline offering confidential healthcare advice, information and referral service 365 days of the year.

Scotland office
Delta House
50 West Nile Street
Glasgow G1 2NP
Helpline: 08454 242424 (24 hours, every day)
Textphone: 18001 08454 242424
Tel: 0141 225 0099
www.nhs24.com

NHS Gosmokefree Helpline

Tel: 0800 169 0169
www.gosmokefree.co.uk/
For free advice and information about stopping smoking. Helps you get into a confident and determined state of mind and gets you thinking about everything you have to gain by going smoke-free.

NHS Organ Donor Register

Tel: 0845 6060 4000
www.uktransplant.org.uk
For information about donating organ(s).

National Blood Service

Tel: 0845 771 1711
www.blood.co.uk
To find out about becoming a blood donor.

National Cochlear Implant Users Association (NCIUA)

PO Box 260
High Wycombe
Bucks HP11 1FA
www.nciua.demon.co.uk
For information about cochlear implants and local help groups.

National Drugs Helpline (also called Talk to Frank)

Helpline: 0800 77 66 00 (operates 24 hours)
Textphone: 0800 917 8765
www.talktofrank.com

Free and confidential, 24 hours a day 365 days a year, 'Frank' can give you information on drugs.

National Federation of Shopmobility UK (NFSUK)
PO Box 6641
Christchurch BH23 9DQ
Tel: 0845 644 2446
www.justmobility.co.uk/shop
For the loan of wheelchairs/ powered scooters to use when shopping.

National Osteoporosis Society
Camerton
Bath BA2 0PJ
Helpline: 0845 450 0230 (Mon–Fri, 10am–3pm)
Tel: 0845 130 3076 (Mon–Fri, 10am–4pm)
www.nos.org.uk
For information and advice about osteoporosis.

National Patient Safety Agency (NPSA)
4–8 Maple Street
London W1T 5HD
Tel: 020 7927 9500 (general enquiries)
Freephone: 0800 015 2536
Textphone: 020 7631 4661
www.npsa.nhs.uk
Patients and carers can report any unexpected suffering or harm they have experienced resulting from contact with NHS services.

Nursing and Midwifery Council
23 Portland Place
London W1B 1PZ
Tel: 020 7637 7281
www.nmc-uk.org
The official/registering body of nurses and midwives.

Ramblers' Association
2nd Floor, Camelford House
87–90 Albert Embankment
London SE1 7TW
Tel: 0207 339 8500
www.ramblers.org.uk
For details of local Ramblers walking groups.

Royal College of Speech and Language Therapists
2 White Hart Yard
London SE1 1NX
Tel: 020 7378 3012
www.rcslt.org
The professional organisation of speech and language therapists.

Northern Ireland
Merrion Business Centre
58 Howard Street
Belfast BT1 6PJ
Tel: 028 9050 1802

Scotland
21 Queen Street
Edinburgh EH2 1JX
Tel: 0131 226 5250/4940

Wales
Llanyravon House

Llanfrechfa Grange Hospital
Cwmbran NP44 8YN
Tel: 07976 905346

Royal National Institute of the Blind (RNIB)
105 Judd Street
London WC1H 9NE
Helpline: 0845 766 9999
www.rnib.org.uk
For a range of information and services for people who are blind or partially sighted.

Royal National Institute for Deaf People (RNID)
19–23 Featherstone Street
London EC1Y 8SL
Freephone: 0808 808 0123
(Mon–Fri, 9am–5pm; answerphone at other times)
Textphone: 0808 808 9000
www.rnid.org.uk
For a range of information and services for people who are deaf or hard of hearing, including:

RNID Tinnitus helpline
19–23 Featherstone Street
London EC1Y 8SL
Helpline: 0808 808 6666
(Mon–Fri, 9am–5pm; answerphone at other times)
Textphone helpline: 0808 808 0007
www.rnid.org.uk
For general queries and information about tinnitus, information on tinnitus clinics in your area.

RNID Typetalk
Tel: 18001 0151 709 9494
(24 hours a day, 365 days a year)
18001 0800 500 888 (service team)
0800 7311 888 (customer service team)
0870 240 51 52 (relay assist)
Textphone: 0800 500 888
www.typetalk.org
A service for speech-impaired and deafblind people in the UK.

Royal Pharmaceutical Society of Great Britain
1 Lambeth High Street
London SE1 7JN
Tel: 020 7735 9141
www.rpsgb.org.uk
The official body of pharmacists in the UK.

Samaritans
Tel: 08457 909090 (24 hours a day, all year round)
www.samaritans.org.uk
24-hour helpline for people needing to talk. Also available by personal visit, an email or by letter. By letter: to Chris, PO Box 9090, Stirling FK8 2SA (remember to give your address if you want a reply). For a personal visit, see the phone book for your local branch.

SANE/SANELINE
1st Floor, Cityside House
40 Adler Street

284

London E1 1EE
Tel: 020 7375 1002
Saneline: 0845 767 8000 (1pm–
11pm weekdays; 12pm–6pm
weekends)
www.sane.org.uk
*For information about
schizophrenia.*

Shopmobility
see National Federation of
Shopmobility UK

Sign Community (British Deaf
Association)
69 Wilson Street
London EC2A 2BB
Tel: 020 7588 3520
Videophone: IP: 81 138 165 105
Textphone: 020 7588 3529
www.signcommunity.org.uk
*Local branches located across
the UK.*

Skills for Health
2nd Floor, Goldsmiths House
Broad Plain
Bristol BS2 0JP
Tel: 0117 922 1155
www.skillsforhealth.org.uk
*For information about
developing skills across the
health workforce.*

Skipton Fund
PO Box 50107
London SW1H 0YF
Tel: 020 7808 1160
www.skiptonfund.org
For obtaining compensation for

*contracting hepatitis C through
NHS blood and blood-related
products.*

**Society of Chiropodists and
Podiatrists**
1 Fellmonger's Path
Tower Bridge Road
London SE1 3LY
Tel: 0845 450 3720 (Mon–Fri,
9am–5pm)
www.scpod.org
*For information about the
training and registration of
chiropodists and podiatrists.*

St Christopher's Hospice
51–59 Lawrie Park Road
London SE26 6DZ
Tel: 020 8768 4500
www.stchristophers.org.uk
*For information about the
hospice movement.*

The Stationery Office (TSO)
St Crispins
Duke Street
Norwich NR3 1PD
Tel: 01603 622211
www.tso.gov.uk
*To order government
publications, including
reports by the Health Service
Ombudsman.*

Thrive
Geoffrey Udall Centre
Beech Hill
Reading RG7 2AT
Tel: 0118 988 5688

www.thrive.org.uk
*For information about
therapeutic gardening for people
with disabilities.*

Time Banks UK
City Works
Alfred Street
Gloucester GL1 4DF
Tel: 01452 541439
www.timebanks.co.uk
*To find out about the Time Bank
schemes locally.*

**United Kingdom Home Care
Association (UKHCA)**
Group House
52 Sutton Court Road
Sutton
Surrey SM1 4SL
Tel: 020 8288 5291
www.ukhca.co.uk
*An organisation whose member
organisations provide care at
home.*

UK Transplant
Communications Directorate
Fox Den Road
Stoke Gifford
Bristol BS34 8RR
Tel: 0117 975 7575
Organ donor line: 0845 6060 400
(7am–11pm; closed Christmas
Day and New Year's Day)
www.uktransplant.org.uk
*For information about donating
blood, organs and tissues.*

vCJD Trust
www.vcjdtrust.co.uk/
*For obtaining compensation
regarding Creutzfeldt–Jakob
disease*; *see* Charles Russell
Solicitors

**Walking the way to Health
Initiative (WHI)**
WHI Team Countryside Agency
John Gower House
Crescent Place
Cheltenham GL50 3RA
Tel: 01242 533258
www.whi.org.uk
*For everyone with an interest in
walking for health, particularly
those who take little exercise or
who live in areas of poor health.*

**Women's Royal Voluntary
Service (WRVS)**
Garden House, Milton Hill
Steventon
Abingdon
Oxfordshire OX13 6AD
Tel: 01235 442900
www.wrvs.org.uk
*Volunteer services such as
hospital shop and lending
library.*

About Age Concern

Age Concern is the UK's largest organisation working for and with older people to enable them to make more of life. We are a federation of over 400 independent charities who share the same name, values and standards and believe that later life should be fulfilling, enjoyable and productive.

Age Concern Books

Age Concern publishes a wide range of bestselling books that help thousands of people each year. They provide practical, trusted advice on subjects ranging from pensions and planning for retirement, to using a computer and surfing the internet. Whether you are caring for someone with a health problem or want to know more about your rights to healthcare, we have something for everyone.

Ordering is easy To order any of our books or request our free catalogue simply choose one of the following options:

 Call us on 0870 44 22 120

 Visit our website at www.ageconcern.org.uk/bookshop

 Email us at sales@ageconcernbooks.co.uk

You can also buy our books from all good bookshops.

Age Concern England
1268 London Road
London SW16 4ER
SW16 4ER
Tel: 020 8765 7200
www.ageconcern.org.uk

Age Concern Cymru
Ty John Pathy
Units 13 and 14 Neptune Court
Vanguard Way, Cardiff CF24 5PJ
Tel: 029 2043 1555
www.accymru.org.uk

Age Concern Scotland
Causewayside House
160 Causewayside
Edinburgh EH9 1PP
Tel: 0845 833 0200
www.ageconcernscotland.org.uk

Age Concern Northern Ireland
3 Lower Crescent
Belfast BT7 1NR
Tel: 028 9024 5729
www.ageconcernni.org

FREE Information Guides We have launched a range of comprehensive and **free** information guides designed to answer many of the questions that older people – or those advising them – may have. The guides cover many issues from pensions and benefits to health and education however *Your health services* and *Healthy living* may be of particular interest to readers of *Your Rights to Healthcare*.

Order your guides by calling our free information line on **0800 00 99 66** or by downloading them from **www.ageconcern.org.uk/ information**

Another great book from Age Concern...
How to be a silver surfer, 3rd Edition
A beginner's guide to the internet   *Emma Aldridge*

'Wonderful ... this book was so easy to understand researching my family tree was a doddle' Tom Hawkins, London

This bestselling guide is perfect for people who are new to the internet and apprehensive about what to do. User-friendly with its clear format, full colour illustrations and simple step-by-step explanations, this guide 'hand-holds' readers through the initial stages of getting to grips with the internet. Learn how to:

Search the web	Take up new hobbies
Send an email	Track down the best deals
Use chat rooms to meet new	and last-minute bargains
friends or chat with existing ones	Research your family tree

£7.99 • **Paperback** • **978-0-86242-421-3**

Ordering is easy

To order any of our books or request our free catalogue simply choose one of the following options:

☎ **Call us on 0870 44 22 120**
✍ **Visit our website at www.ageconcern.org.uk/bookshop**
📠 **Email us at sales@ageconcernbooks.co.uk**

You can also buy our books from all good bookshops.

Index

abroad, living 191–4
abusive behaviour (patients) 20–21, 36–7, 217
accidents
 medical 10, 241, 243
 road 160, 189–90
Acts of Parliament 3, 4–7, 42
acupuncture 41, 42, 84–5
adaptations, to home 79–80, 81, 99, 100, 173
'advance decisions'/'advance directives'/'Living Wills' 117, 127–8, 158, 202, 208, 213, 253
advance statements 128–9
advocacy services 120, 227
age discrimination 12, 14, 224, 260
agitation 110
aids see equipment and aids
alcohol consumption 269
Alder Hey inquiry 216, 219
Alzheimer's disease 110, 111–12
 see also dementia
ambulance services 3, 28–30, 113, 170, 184
angina 16
antidepressants 106
appointments 21, 35–6, 52
 see also Choose and Book
Aricept (donepezil) 111
art(s) therapists/therapy 77, 78, 82, 239
arthritis 44, 257
artificial feeding 43, 128, 185, 211
assessments of needs 14, 65–6, 171–2, 185–6
asthma, people with 44, 86
astigmatism 59
Attendance Allowance 165, 187
audiograms 72
audiology tests 71

back pain 83, 85
bathing services 43, 44
benefits, state 38, 93, 130, 165–6, 187

 see also Pension Credit
bereavement counselling 77, 219
'best practice' 4, 10
biomedical scientists 78
Bland, Tony 7–8, 211
blindness see sight problems
Blood, Diane 8
blood donation 197–8, 201, 202, 203
blood pressure monitoring 43
blood transfusions 202–3, 240
Blue Badge parking scheme 66, 130
bone marrow donation 197, 198
Bournewood case, the 123–4
bowel cancer screening 20, 264
brain injuries 16, 125
bras, surgical 91
breast cancer screening 17, 260, 264
British Red Cross 30, 101, 246, 259
British Sign Language 75, 76
British Trust for Conservation Volunteers 108, 265
'buddies' schemes 270
Burke, Mr 128–9, 211–12

campaigning groups 260, 261
cancers 5, 16–17, 52, 82, 153, 198
 screening for 17, 20, 260, 264
 see also palliative care
cannabis 116
care homes 169, 172, 176
 charges 9, 175, 187
 and death of residents 219, 220–21
 dental care 51
 equipment and aids 100
 and NHS care 38, 41, 43, 179–81, 184–9
 temporary stays in 89, 174
 see also nursing homes
case law 4, 7–9
cataracts 59–60, 62, 68, 152, 153, 166
cats, boarding 166
check-ups 19, 263–4
 see also screening

chemists *see* pharmacies/pharmacists
'Child B' 8
chiropodists/podiatrists 39, 42, 78, 87,
    131–2, 134–5, 139, 145, 146
  complaints about 132, 239–40
  private 138–9
chiropractic 84, 85
Choose and Book 26, 153–5
Cinnamon Trust
clinical errors *see* accidents, medical
clinical negligence claims 240–41
clinical scientists 78
clinical trials 258–9
Clostridium difficile 18, 164
cochlear implants 76
cognitive behavioural therapy 106
Commission for Patient and Public
    Involvement in Health 256
Commission for Social Care Inspection
    (CSCI) 180–81
commodes 40, 99
community health services, NHS 39
community matrons 44
community mental health nurses 108,
    114
community nurses 43–4, 206
compensation schemes 240–41
complaints, making
  on another's behalf 225–6, 252
  about individual professionals 132,
    224, 235–40, 242
  about NHS Foundation Trusts 226,
    229–30
  about Primary Care Trusts or NHS
    Trusts 224, 226, 227–9
  about social services 223–4
  NHS procedures 12, 91, 175, 189,
    217, 223–7
  see also Healthcare Commission;
    Ombudsman, Health Service
complementary therapies 41–2, 77, 84–6
confidentiality 17, 18, 19
  and access to medical records 251–3
consent 18, 120, 122–3, 157–60, 251–2,
    253
  see also 'mental capacity'
consultants 17, 39
contact lenses 20, 59, 60, 64–5, 94–5

continence services 14, 40, 100, 180,
    185
'continuing NHS healthcare' 184–9
cornea donation 199, 201
coroners 215, 216, 218, 242, 252
corsets 20
cosmetic dentistry 51
Coughlan, Pamela 8–9
counselling services 77, 78, 219
Court of Protection 130
Creutzfeldt–Jakob disease 240
criminal offences 242–3, 252
'crisis cards' 117
cultural issues 17, 217

Data Protection Act (1998) 248, 249
day care services 113–14, 137
day surgery 151, 166–7
deafness *see* hearing impairment/
    deafness
death-bed marriages 219–20
deaths 207
  certifying and registering 213–15
  and dealing with bodies 217–18
  and medical records 251
decision-making 124–5, 126–7, 247
delusions 104, 116
dementia, people with 82, 103, 130
  communicating with 115
  and depression 109–10
  getting a diagnosis 110–11
  treatment and support 111–15
dentists 2, 12, 20, 47–9, 57–8, 145
  anaesthetics 57
  charges 48, 53–5, 93–4, 98, 99
  check-ups/examinations 49, 51, 264
  complaints about 235, 237–8
  cosmetic treatments 51
  dentures 53, 54
  emergency care 50
  home visits 48, 50–51
  hospital 50, 56–7
  information provided 51–2
  missed appointments 21, 52
  nurses and assistants 53
  and oral health 49, 51, 52
  private 47, 55–6
  referrals 52–3

'salaried' 48
treatment plans 51, 52
depression, people with 83, 103, 104–5
and dementia 109–10
getting a diagnosis 105
help and support 105–6, 108–9
private therapy 107–8
treatments 106
'deputies' 130
diabetes, people with 17, 44, 135
eye screening and tests 62, 63, 67
and foot care 133, 135–6
diabetic retinopathy 60, 68
diet(s), healthy 267
dietitians 77, 78, 84
dignity, respect for 15, 17, 18
Directions, government 4, 5, 9–10
Disability Discrimination Act (1995)
66–7, 69, 74, 144, 247
Disability Living Allowance 165
Disability Rights Commission 212
Disabled Living Foundation 133, 144
discrimination 12, 14, 66, 69, 224, 260
district nurses 23, 39, 43, 100, 206
'do-not-resuscitate' decisions 208–9,
260
doctors, NHS see general practitioners
doctors, private 45, 242
dogs, boarding 166
see also guide dogs; 'hearing' dogs
donation
blood 197–8, 201, 202, 203
bodies for research 203
organs and tissues 197, 198–202
donepezil (Aricept) 111
drama therapists 78, 82, 239
drinking 83, 268, 269
driving 66, 130
drugs see medication/drugs
drugs, recreational 19, 116, 268

ears
syringing 70
see also hearing impairment/deafness
eating disorders 267
electro-convulsive therapy 121
emergencies 28
dental 50
treatment and consent 158

emergency departments, hospital 23,
28–9, 152, 203, 246
Emergency Multilingual Phrasebook
246
emotional health 269
emphysema 92
Enduring Powers of Attorney 130
'enough treatment' 5
epilepsy 16, 257
equipment and aids 14, 40, 80, 99, 100,
220
European Health Insurance Card (EHIC)
190
euthanasia 129, 209, 210
Exelon (rivastigmine) 111
exercise, physical 264–5
and depression 106
for people with disabilities 266–7
Expert Patients Programme 257–8
eye problems see sight problems
eye tests see sight tests

fabric supports see support items
Falls Prevention Services 15, 77, 87–9
and nail-cutting services 136, 137
flu vaccinations 15, 19
fluid intake 268
foot care 131, 133–6
see also chiropodists/podiatrists;
nail-cutting services
footwear 131, 133
Foundation Trusts 3
frames, walking 80, 101
Friends organisations 259
funeral arrangements 214, 215, 218–19

galantamine (Reminyl) 111
gay couples 159
General Medical Council 236, 237, 242
general practitioners (GPs) 2, 10, 12,
33–4, 37–8
appointments 35–6
changing 36
complaints about 228, 229, 235,
236–7
and complementary therapies 41–2
home visits 41
out-of-hours services 42
referrals 17, 38–40

registering with 34–5
removal from list 36–7
second opinions 39, 247
services charged for 41
temporary patients 36, 191, 193–4
with Special Interests (GPwSI) 38–9
geriatricians 109
glasses *see* spectacles
glaucoma 60, 62
government policy decisions 4, 11–12
GPs *see* general practitioners
Guidance, government 4, 5, 9–10
guide dogs 67

hallucinations 115
handrails 81, 99
head injuries 16, 125
health checks, annual 19, 264
Health Professions Council 78–9, 82,
    83, 84, 132, 239
Health Protection Agency 10–11
health visitors 43, 237
healthcare assistants 43
Healthcare Commission 10, 68, 157,
    189, 228, 230–32, 235, 242
HealthSpace 26
hearing aids 69, 71–3
'hearing' dogs 69, 74
hearing impairment/deafness, people
    with 69, 70
    and cochlear implants 76
    sign language courses 75
    support services 75–6
    telephones 75, 99
    tests 69, 70–71, 72, 83
    tinnitus 73–4
heart disease 16, 264, 265
heart valve donation 199
hepatitis C 240
hernia operations 166–7
hip, fractured 87, 88
hip protectors 88
hip replacements 198–9
home adaptations 79–80, 81, 100, 173
home care 166
home visits
    dentists 48, 50–51
    general practitioners 41
    optometrists 63

for people with dementia 114
homeopathy 41, 84, 86
hospices 206, 207
hospitals 2, 15, 165
    accident and emergency (A&E) 23,
        28–9, 152, 203, 246
    admission 152
    car parking 162–3
    Choose and Book system 26, 153–5
    cleanliness 10, 17, 18, 164
    consent forms 157–8
    day patients 151
    day surgery 151, 166–7
    and deaths 213, 214, 215, 217, 218,
        219, 220
    dental services 50, 56–7
    detention in 119–22
    discharge from 168, 169–75, 245
    ear, nose and throat (ENT)
        departments 71
    eye services 63, 68
    food 10, 160–61
    Friends/volunteers 259–60
    infections 18, 163, 164
    in-patients 151
    intermediate care beds 89
    and life-prolonging treatments
        211–13
    minor injuries units 23, 30–31
    mixed wards 160
    moving between 167, 190
    occupational therapists 81
    orthopaedics departments 133
    out-patients 151, 167, 170
    'pay beds' 241–2
    performance ratings 154
    pharmacies 170
    private 166, 176, 177
    psychiatric 109
    records 192
    refusal to leave 175–6
    and religious and spiritual needs
        161–2
    and state benefits 165–6
    telephones 162
    televisions 162
    travel to and from 93, 96–7, 170
    treatment targets 153
    visitors 163

Human Rights Act (1998) 12, 161, 211, 252

incontinence 40
    see also continence services
Independent Complaints Advocacy Service 227, 228
Independent Regulator *see* Monitor
infectious diseases 10–11, 18, 163, 164
information 245–6, 247, 261–2
    for non-English speakers 246–7
Information Commissioner 249
insurance, health 45, 86, 160, 177, 190–91
'integrated' services xii, 14
intermediate care services 14, 39, 77, 83, 89–90, 169, 176
Internet access 25–6
    see also NHS Direct Online
interpreters 155, 246–7

Jehovah's Witnesses 202
Jobseekers' Allowance 93
'joint' services *see* 'integrated' services

kidney donation 199

labels, large-print 145
laser eye surgery 68
Lasting Powers of Attorney 127, 130, 158, 213, 253
laundry services 40
Legal Aid 241
legislation *see* Acts of Parliament; case law
lesbian couples 159
Lewy body dementia 110
    see also dementia
life-prolonging treatments 211–13
'Living Wills' *see* 'advance decisions'
lobotomies 121
lung diseases 92

Macmillan nurses 39, 207
macular degeneration 60
Marie Curie nurses 207
marriages, death-bed 219–20
mattresses, special 99, 172
mediators 228

Medical Eye Centres 62
medical records *see* records, medical
medical reports 41
medication/drugs 143–4
    advice on 27
    brand and generic names 143
    checks on 20
    clinical trials 258–9
    collecting 145
    dosage pill boxes 144
    'over-the-counter' 142
    psychiatric 121
    side effects 40, 104, 109–10, 112, 125, 148
    taking abroad 148
    and visually impaired people 145
    see also prescriptions
Medicentres 23
Medicine and Healthcare products Regulatory Agency (MHRA) 148, 259
medicines use review 147
memory loss 110
'mental capacity' 124–5
Mental Capacity Act (2005) 124, 125, 126, 127, 130, 159, 213
Mental Health Act (1983) 117, 119
Mental Health Act Commission 121–2
Mental Health Bill (2006 draft) 122
Mental Health Foundation 106
Mental Health Review Tribunal 120, 121
mental health services 2, 15, 39, 78
Mental Health Trusts 3
mental illness 103–4
    and benefits 130
    and 'sectioning' 119–22
    see also dementia; schizophrenia
midwives, complaints about 237
MIND 120, 122
Mini Mental State Examination 111
'Miss B' 8, 129, 212–13
Monitor (Independent Regulator) 230
motor neurone disease 8, 16, 82
MRSA 17, 18, 163, 164
multiple sclerosis 16, 82
music therapists/therapy 78, 82, 115, 239

nail-cutting services 131, 132, 136–8
National Health Service (NHS) 1–3
  core principles 13
  core standards 11, 14–15, 18–19
  patient involvement 255–60
  patients' rights 3–7, 12–13, 17,
    19–20
  services charged for 41–2, 98–9,
    193, 194
  staff rights 20–21
  targets 11, 12
  see also NHS Direct *etc. below*
National Institute for Health and
  Clinical Excellence (NICE) 4, 6,
  10, 49, 106, 111, 142
  Citizens' Council 255
National Patient Safety Agency 10, 224,
  243, 255
National Service Frameworks (NSFs)
  13–17, 19, 44, 161
negligence, clinical 240–41
neuroleptic drugs 112
neurological conditions 16
neurologists 109
next-of-kin 158, 159
NHS Direct 23, 24–5, 29, 36, 42, 48,
  51, 136
NHS Direct Interactive 23, 27
NHS Direct Online 23, 25–6, 48
NHS Litigation Authority 240
NHS Low Income Scheme 53, 94, 97–8
NHS Plan, The 13, 161
NHS Trusts 2–3
NICE *see* National Institute for Health
  and Clinical Excellence
nicotine replacement patches 142
999 calls 23, 29
noise generators 73
NSFs *see* National Service Frameworks
nurses 145, 146
  agency/private 44
  community mental health 108
  complaints about 237
  dental 53
  district 23, 39, 43, 100, 206
  hospice at home or Macmillan 39
  practice 37, 38
nursing homes: and NHS services
  181–4, 186

obesity 19, 267
occupational therapists/therapy 77, 78,
  79–82, 83, 90, 100, 239
Office of the Public Guardian 130
Ombudsman, Health Service 184, 187,
  189, 231, 232–5
operating department practitioners 78
ophthalmic opticians *see* optometrists/
  ophthalmic opticians
ophthalmologists 61–2, 65
opticians 61, 235, 238
  see also sight tests
optometrists/ophthalmic opticians 2, 61,
  62, 63, 145, 146
organ donation 197, 198–202
organs, retention of 216
orthodontic therapists 53
orthoptists 62, 78
orthotics/orthosis/orthotists 78, 132, 133
osteopathy 41, 84, 85
osteoporosis 83, 89, 264
out-of-hours services 23, 27, 42, 50, 150
'outreach' services 114
'over-the-counter' treatments 142
overseas, NHS healthcare 156–7
overseas visitors 10, 191, 194–5
oxygen supplies, home 92, 142

palliative care 184, 206–7
PALS *see* Patient Advice and Liaison
  Service
paramedics 78
Parkinson's disease 16, 82
Patient Advice and Liaison Service
  (PALS) 36, 37, 48, 88, 101, 136,
  174, 175–6, 180, 227
Patient Power (telephone and TV
  facilities) 162
Patient and Public Involvement Forums
  255–6
Patient Transport Service (PTS) 30, 113,
  167, 170, 184, 190
'pay beds' 241–2
pedicures/pedicurists 132, 134
Pension Credit 93, 94, 95, 165
Personal Medical Service 34
pets 166
pharmacies/pharmacists 2, 23, 27–8,
  141, 146, 149–50, 170, 235, 239

physiotherapists/physiotherapy 39, 42,
    78, 83–4, 90, 100, 101, 145, 146,
    184, 266
  private 84, 86
placebos 258
platelet donation 198
pneumonia vaccination 19, 264
podiatrists see chiropodists/podiatrists
post-mortems 215, 216–17
powers of attorney 127, 130, 158, 213,
    253
Practitioners with Special Interests
    (PwSI) 38
prescriptions 20, 21, 45, 53, 141, 142
  complaints about 239
  private 141, 145
  professionals allowed to prescribe
    145–6
  repeat 146–7
  when going abroad 148
pressure sores 43, 185
Pretty, Diane 8, 209–10
primary care 33
Primary Care Trusts 2, 3, 6, 40, 41, 42,
    43
  complaints about 226, 227–9
  contracts with diagnostic and
    treatment centres 68
  and dental care 48, 50, 57–8
  drugs bills 142–3
  Expert Patients Programme 257–8
  and general practitioners 33, 34, 35
privacy 17, 19
private healthcare xii, 11, 44, 45, 68,
    155, 157
  complaints about 241–2
  dentists 47, 55–6
  occupational therapists 81–2
  physiotherapy 84, 86
  psychotherapy 107–8
  speech and language therapists 83
  see also prescriptions, private
prosthetics 78, 132, 133
psychiatric drugs 121
psychiatric services, NHS 109
psychiatrists 109, 110
psychogeriatricians 109, 110
psychosurgery 121
psychotherapy 107–8

'psychotic' illnesses 116–17

radiographers 78, 146
records, medical 25
  access to 248–9
  amending 250–51
  and confidentiality 251–3
  electronic 249–50, 253
  and moving abroad 192
  of someone who has died 251
referrals, GP 17, 38–40
reflexology 41, 84, 85–6
refunds of NHS charges 98–9
refusal of treatments 202–3, 210
registered nursing care contribution
    (RNCC) 181–4, 186, 188
Regulations, government 4, 9–10
rehabilitation services 169, 176, 177,
    184
religious issues 17, 161–2, 215–16, 217,
    270
Reminyl (galantamine) 111
respite care 185
rivastigmine (Exelon) 111
RNCC see registered nursing care
    contribution
Royal National Institute of the Blind
    (RNIB) 67, 145
Royal National Institute for Deaf People
    (RNID) 71, 73, 74, 75, 76

St Christopher's Hospice 207
Samaritans 105
SANELINE 106
schizophrenia 103, 115–16, 257
  and 'sectioning' 119–22
  treatment and support 116–18
scooters, powered 101
screening 2, 17, 20, 68
second opinions 39, 247
secondary care 33
'sectioning' 119–22
sexually transmitted infections 19, 269
sheltered housing 38, 43, 172
  and healthcare services 51, 179–80
  temporary stays in 89, 174
shoes see footwear
Shopmobility schemes 101
shower chairs 99

showers, walk-in/wheel-in 100
sight problems 59–60, 65–7
    and large-print labels 145
    private treatments 68
sight tests 11–12, 20, 21, 59, 60–63, 64,
    98, 99, 264
sign language 75, 76
SignTalk 75–6
Single Assessment Process 14, 171–2
Skipton Fund 240
smoking 16, 19, 28, 142, 143, 268
social services xii, 14, 38, 43, 44
    and care home costs 175
    and continuing care 184
    and discharge from hospital 170,
        171–3, 174
    eligibility criteria 172–3
    funerals 219
    occupational therapists 79–80
    respite care 185
    and sight loss 65–6
    sign language classes 75
social workers 38
sound generators 73
Special Health Authorities 2
spectacles 20, 59, 60, 63, 64–5, 93, 94–5
speech and language therapists/therapy
    77, 78, 82–3, 90, 239
spinal injuries 16
spiritual needs 161–2, 269
Standards for Better Health 11, 18–19
'state registered' 79
stockings, support see support items
Strategic Health Authorities 2, 29, 185,
    187, 189, 257
stroke services 15, 77, 83, 90–91
suicidal feelings 105
suicide, assisted 129, 209–10
support items 20, 91, 93, 95
surgeries, GP 23, 27, 33–4, 37–8
surgery, day 152, 166–7
surveys, NHS patient 258

taxis 96, 170
    and guide and 'hearing' dogs 67, 74

teeth, care of see dentists
temporary residents 36, 191, 193–4
terminal illnesses 205
    see also palliative care
textphones 75
therapies/therapists 41–2, 77–86
Time Banks 108
tinnitus 73–4
tissue donation 197, 198–201
toenail-cutting services 131, 132, 136–8
toilet seats, raised 99
transient ischaemic attacks 91
transplants see organ donation; tissue
    donation
transport 2, 30, 48, 93, 96–7, 170, 185,
    190
    of bodies 217–18
Typetalk 75

vaccinations
    flu 15, 19, 264
    holiday and travel 41
    pneumonia 19, 264
vascular dementia 110
    see also dementia
visual impairment see sight problems
voluntary organisations xii, 11
    see also British Red Cross
volunteering 108, 259–60, 265, 270

walk-in centres, NHS 2, 23, 27
walking/walking groups 106, 143, 264,
    265
walking frames and sticks 80, 101
'wandering' 112
war pensioners 92, 94, 95, 194
Welfare Lasting Powers of Attorney
    127, 130, 213
Welfare Rights Handbook 7
wheelchairs 77, 80, 100–1
wigs 20, 77, 91–2, 93, 95–6
wills 220
Women's Royal Voluntary Service
    (WRVS) 259–60

The Big Brother

STEPHANIE DAGG

• Pictures by Alan Clarke •

THE O'BRIEN PRESS
DUBLIN

First published 2003 by The O'Brien Press Ltd,
12 Terenure Road East, Rathgar, Dublin 6, Ireland.
Tel: +353 1 4923333; Fax: +353 1 4922777
E-mail: books@obrien.ie
Website: www.obrien.ie
Reprinted 2005, 2009.

ISBN: 978-0-86278-779-0

British Library Cataloguing-in-Publication Data
Dagg, Stephanie
The big brother. - (O'Brien pandas ; 24)
1.Brothers and sisters - juvenile fiction
2.Children's stories
I.Title
823.9'14[J]

3 4 5 6 7 8 9 10
09 10 11 12

The O'Brien Press receives assistance from

Typesetting, layout, editing, design: The O'Brien Press Ltd
Printing: CPI Cox and Wyman

Can YOU spot the panda
hidden in the story?

Dara's Mum was going
to have a baby.
'A new baby brother or sister,'
Mum told him.
'Soon you will be a
big brother.'

Dara smiled.

That sounded cool!

Dara, the Big Brother.

Some of his friends
had big brothers.

Big brothers
know everything and
tell everyone what to do.

They help look after
their little brothers and sisters.

Suddenly Dara
stopped smiling.

He didn't know
how to look after
a brother or sister.
He didn't know
how to care for a baby.

He needed to practise
being a big brother.
But how? And who on?
He tossed and turned in bed
for ages that night.

But just as night came
and the owl began to hoot,
he had an idea.

'Mum, will you get me
a doll, please?'
he asked at breakfast next day.
'I need to practise being
a big brother.'

But Mum wasn't
really listening.
So when she went to the shops
she bought Dara
a dinosaur instead.

It was a great dinosaur.
Its eyes lit up and
it made **growly noises**.

If Dara hadn't wanted
a doll so much
he would have been thrilled.

GRRRRRRRRRRRRRRRRRRRRRRR

But a dinosaur is
not like a baby.
He couldn't practise
being a Big Brother
with a dinosaur.

'Thanks, Mum,' he said,
pretending to be pleased.
But inside he was very sad.

He went to the bathroom
and opened the bag of nappies
Mum had already bought
for the baby.
He took a nappy
back to his room.
He spread it out and laid
the dinosaur on it.

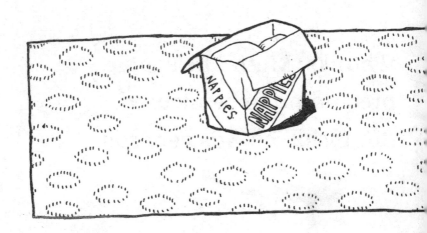

21

JF/2238722

GRRRR

22

The nappy was far too big
for the dinosaur.
And when Dara tried
to do it up he scratched
his finger on the
dinosaur's **spiky** tail.

RRRRR RRRRR

When he tried to
rock the dinosaur to sleep,
its claws dug into him.

A dinosaur would **not do**.
It would not do at all.

Dara needed a **doll**.

'Dad, can I have a doll, please?'
he asked at teatime.

'I need to practise being
a big brother.'

But Dad wasn't really listening.
He was watching the news
on television.

Next morning he came
back from town with
a doll for Dara,
only it was
the wrong sort of doll.

It was a Super Spaceman doll.
It wasn't a bit like a baby.
It had a spacesuit and
big white boots.

It came with its own
moon buggy which had
flashing lights and
made engine noises.

It was fantastic.

If Dara hadn't wanted
a doll so much
he would have been delighted.

'Thank you,' he said,
pretending to be pleased.
But inside he was very sad.

He didn't even bother trying
to put a nappy on
Super Spaceman.
And everyone knows
you can't rock
a spaceman to sleep.

Next day was Sunday.
Dara went to Grandad's
for dinner.
After dinner,
Grandad took him
to his shed.

'Look!' he said.

In his shed was a doll's pram.
It was blue with
big shiny wheels.
It had a wire tray underneath
to put things in.

'My neighbour gave me this,'
said Grandad.
'She knows I like
making things.
I am going to turn it into
a go-kart for you.'

'Oh, please don't!' cried Dara.
'I like it just the way it is.
I can practise pushing
the baby's pram.'

But Grandad wasn't
really listening.
He was already planning
how to make a go-kart.

After Dara had gone,
he began to take
the pram apart.

On Tuesday Dara's
Auntie Pat came to visit.
Dara's cousin Penny
came too.

Penny had a new doll.
It was a lifesize
Bouncy Baby doll.
It looked just like a new baby.

Dara thought it was
the most beautiful doll
he'd ever seen.

But Penny hated it.
She dragged it around
by its feet so its head went
bump bump bump
on the floor.

42

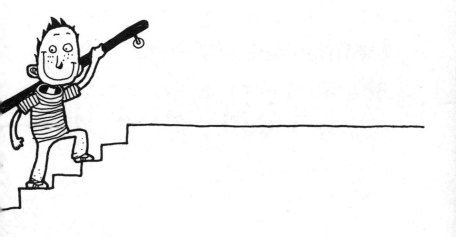

Mum sent Penny and Dara
to play in his room
while she chatted to Auntie Pat.

'Wow!' said Penny
when they went in.
'You've got a Super Spaceman!
I wanted one of those.
But Mum got me
this **silly doll** instead!'

'And I wanted
a doll like yours.
But my Dad got me
this stupid Spaceman,'
moaned Dara.

They both felt sorry
for themselves for a moment.

Then they looked at each other.

Then they grinned.

'Let's swap,' they said together.

Dara handed over
his Super Spaceman and
the moon buggy.
Penny handed over
her Bouncy Baby doll.

They hugged their new dolls
happily.

'Don't tell your mum,'
begged Dara.
'And don't tell yours,'
begged Penny.
(Mums don't like it
when you swap things.)

Dara cared for
his baby doll in secret.

He put a fresh nappy
on her every day.

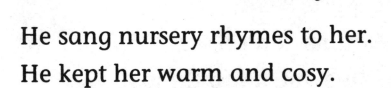

He sang nursery rhymes to her.
He kept her warm and cosy.

He practised being a
big brother
till he nearly burst.

One morning,
when Dara was at school,
Mum found Bouncy Baby
hidden in Dara's bed.

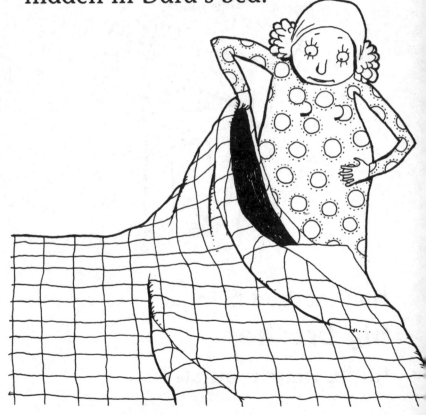

Bouncy Baby was
wrapped up in a towel.
She had Dara's
woolly hat on.

There was a tiny teddy bear
tucked in next to her.

Mum smiled.
Now she knew why
Dara had wanted a doll.

She went to make
a few phone calls.

That night at teatime
Dara had some surprises.

First, Dad came home
with a present.

'Here's something for
that doll of yours,' Dad said.
Oh no! thought Dara.
Penny has the Super Spaceman.
What will I say?

He was about to
open the parcel when
Grandad arrived.

'I've just finished that go-kart,'
he told Dara.
'It's in my van outside.
Come and see.'

Oh no! thought Dara.

He went out.
Grandad opened the van door.
Inside was the pram,
as good as new!

Then Dara opened
Dad's parcel.
It was full of baby things
for his Bouncy Baby doll –

a bib

clothes

a changing bag

a rattle

a plastic bath

a bottle

'Wow! Thanks, Dad and Grandad!' yelled Dara. 'Now I can really practise being a **big brother**!'

The baby arrived
a few weeks later.
It was a little baby girl.

And Dara was the
best big brother ever.